# TOKYO
## PORTRAITS

# TOK

# PORTR

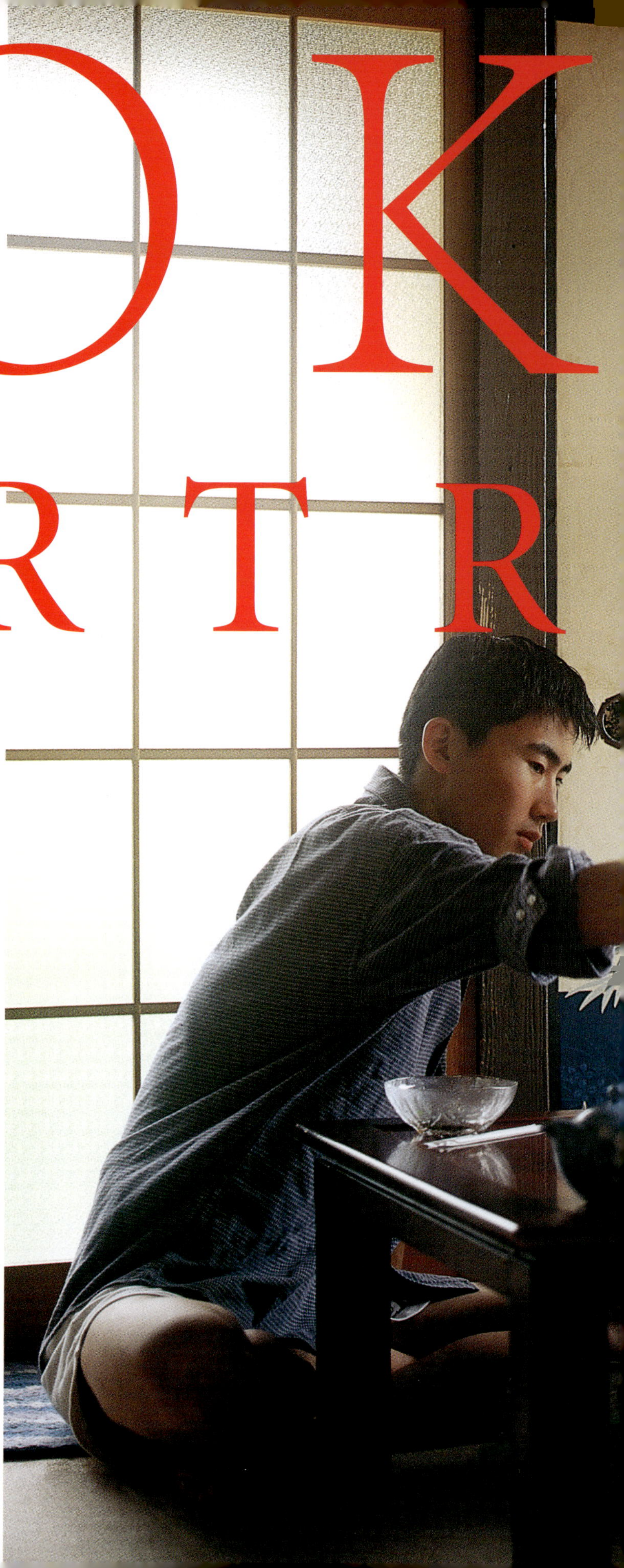

SHUFUNOTOMO CO., LTD
Tokyo Japan

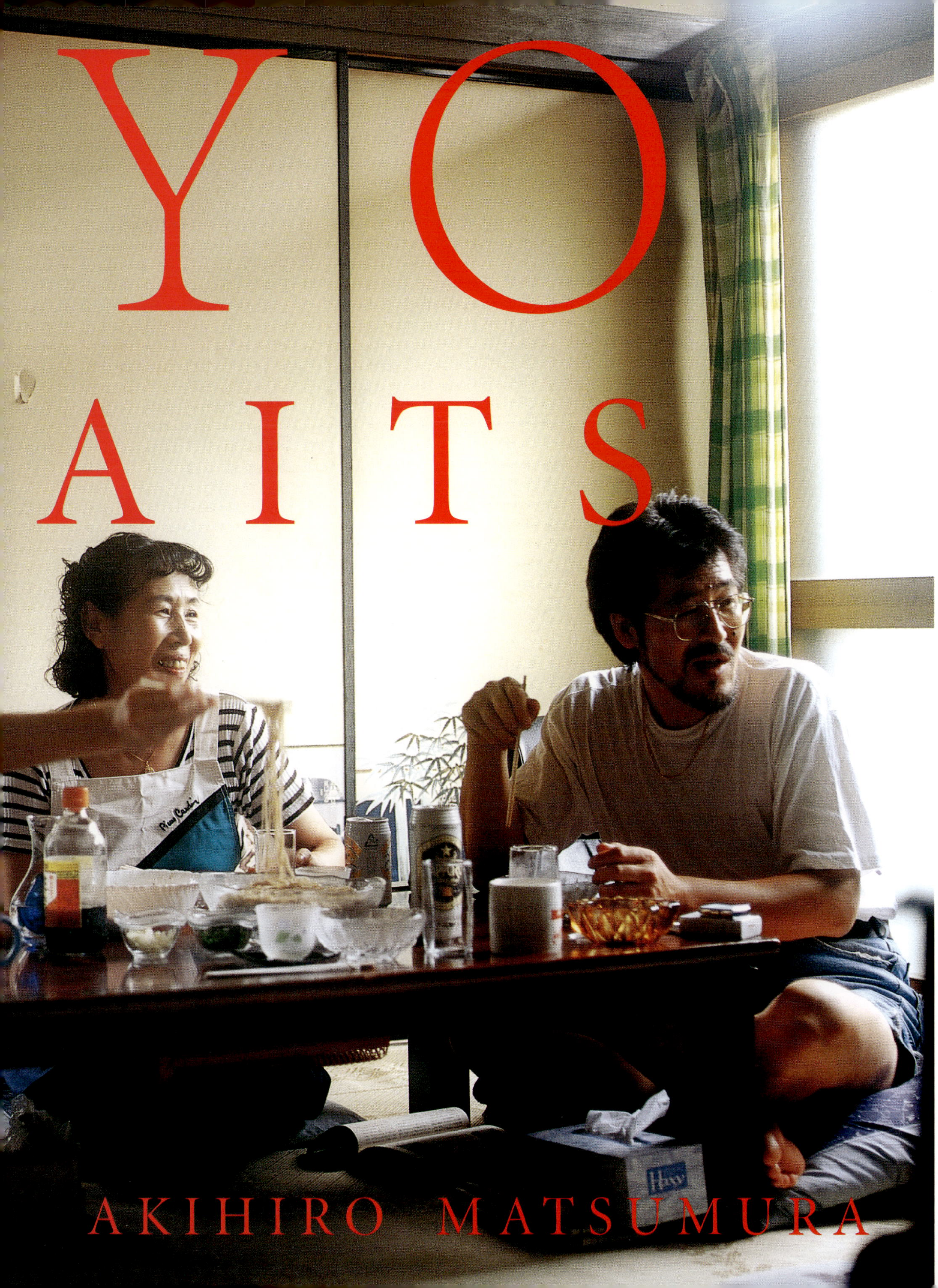

# Y O

# A I T S

AKIHIRO MATSUMURA

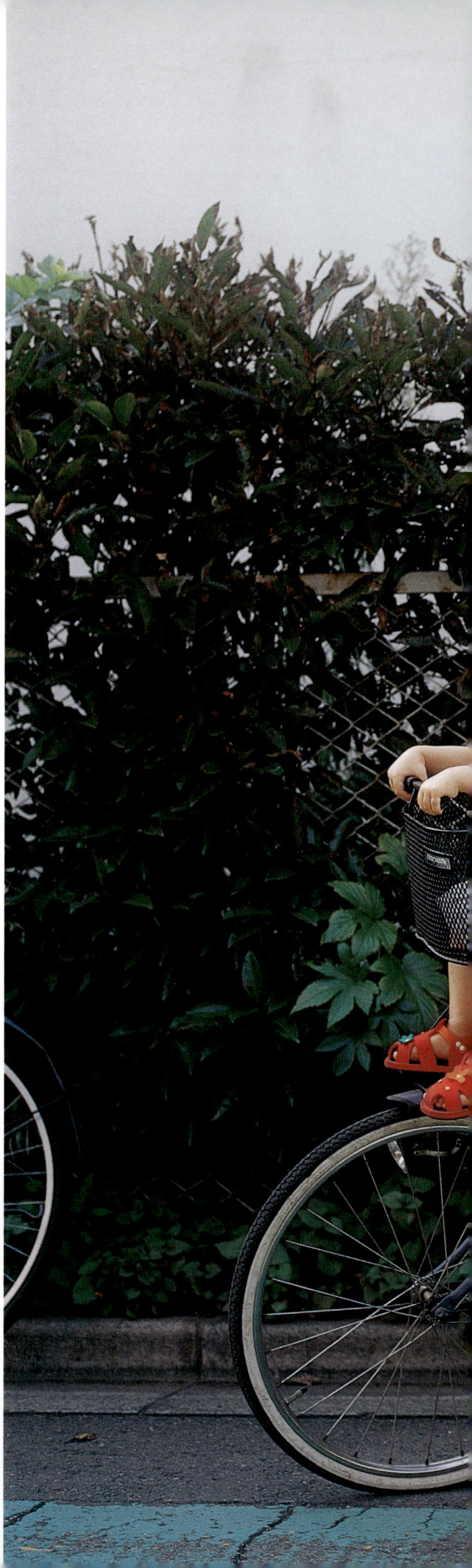

Book design by Isao Suzuki (R&I+Lemon)



First printing, 1997

Published by Shufunotomo Co., Ltd.
2-9, Kanda Surugadai, Chiyoda-ku,
Tokyo, 101 Japan

Printed in Singapore

ISBN4-07-976534-7

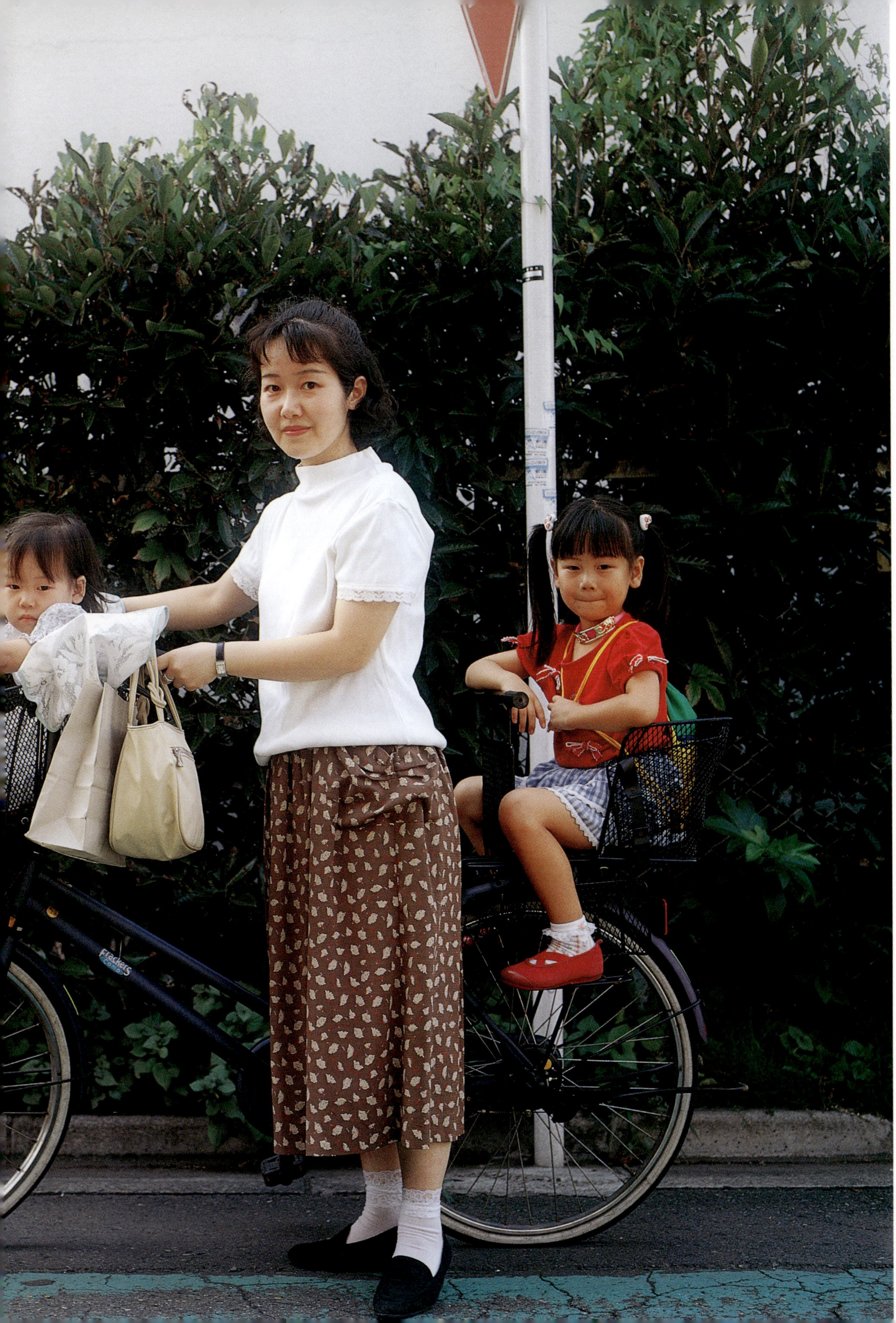

# Introduction

A few years ago, I traveled the world taking photographs. Returning to Japan after a long absence, I found that I had gained a new perspective on my homeland. Scenes and subjects that had previously appeared commonplace took on a whole new aspect. Traveling to different countries, and encountering a variety of people and cultures along the way, gave me a renewed awareness of a place I'd taken for granted. I was particularly struck by Tokyo, Japan's capital and my birthplace. Upon second glance, Tokyo looked to me like no other city I'd ever seen. That was when I began to think I'd like to take a fresh look at Tokyo through the eye of the camera.

As the center of much of Japan's unique culture and history, Tokyo is steeped in tradition. At the same time, though, the city is changing at a pace that accelerates with each passing day. In the process of Japan's modernization, it has absorbed all cultural influences—Eastern and Western alike—with abandon. Tokyo pulsates like a sprawling living organism that is impossible to confine. I began to look for the source of the city's vibrant energy, and as I searched, my attention was invariably drawn toward the people who live here.

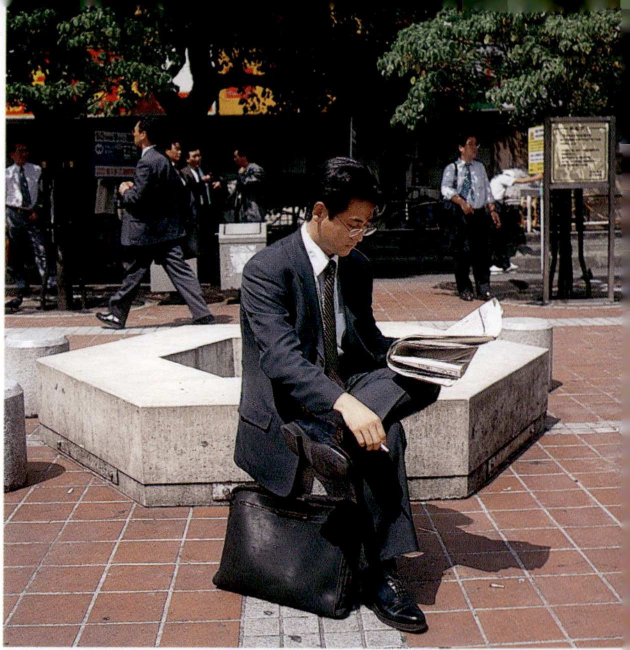

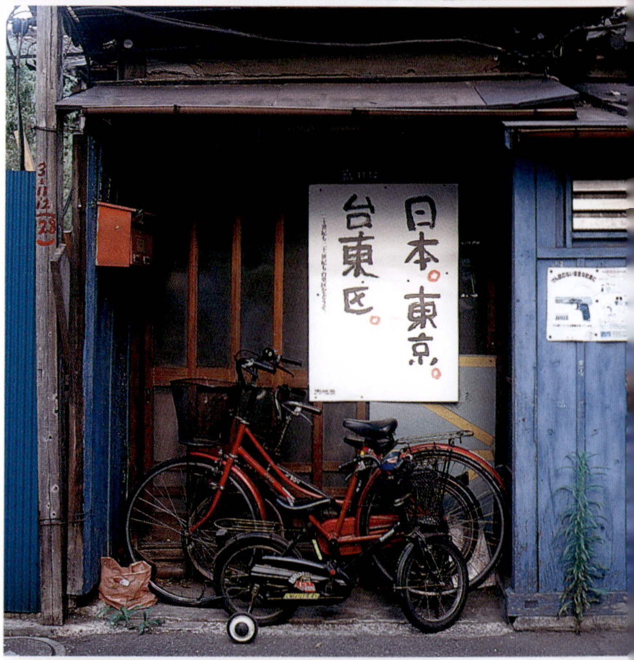


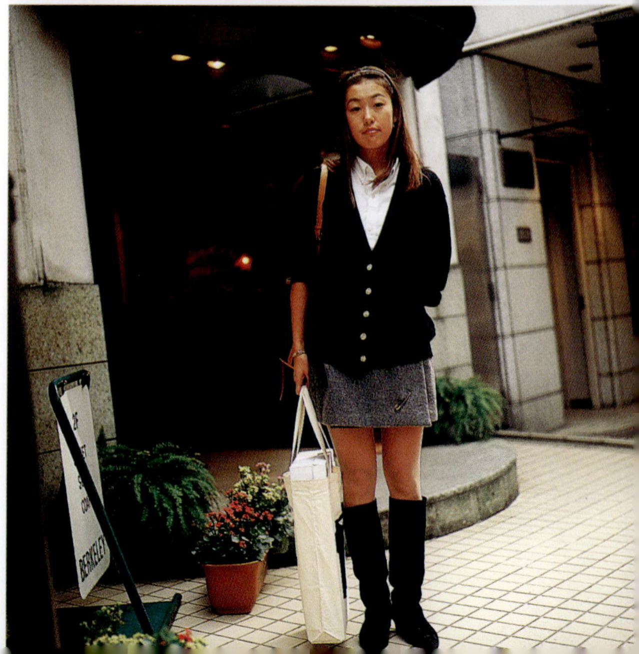

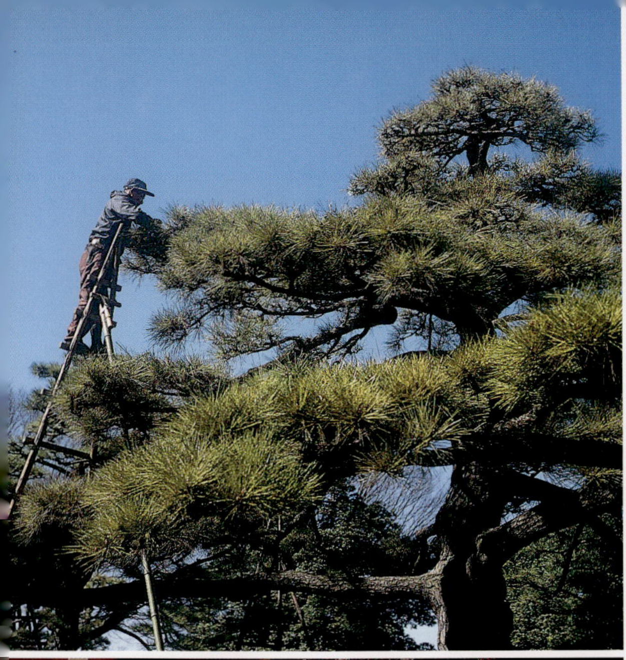

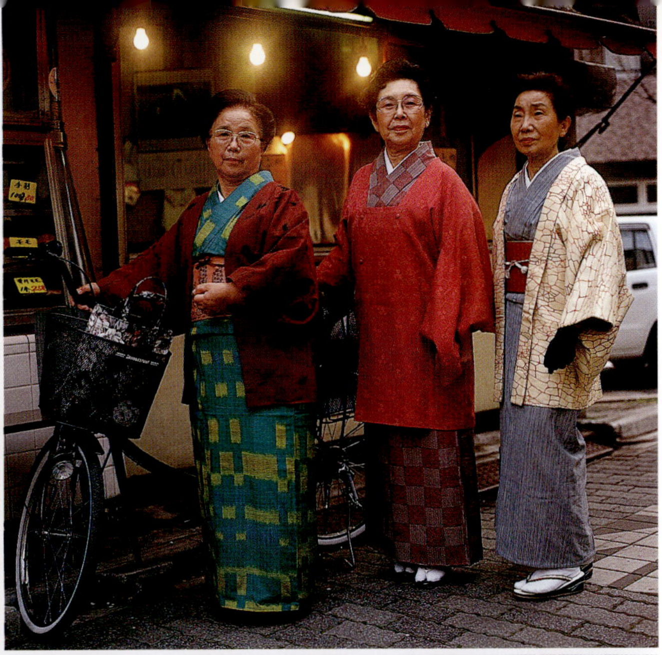

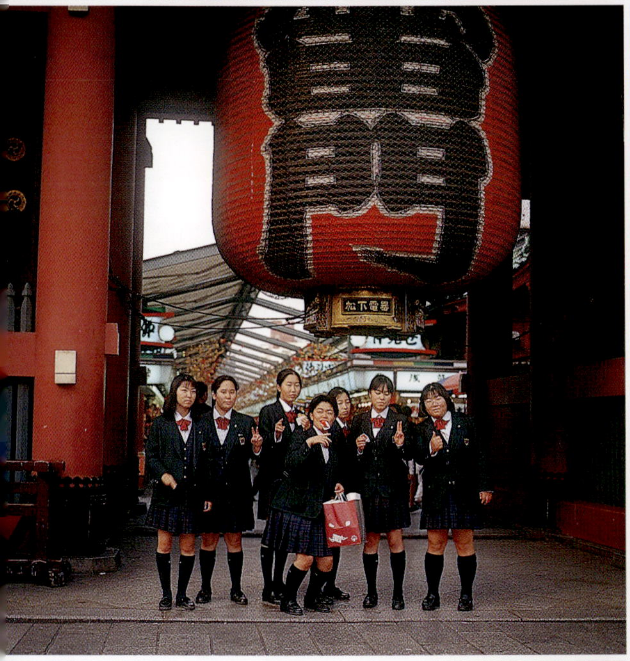

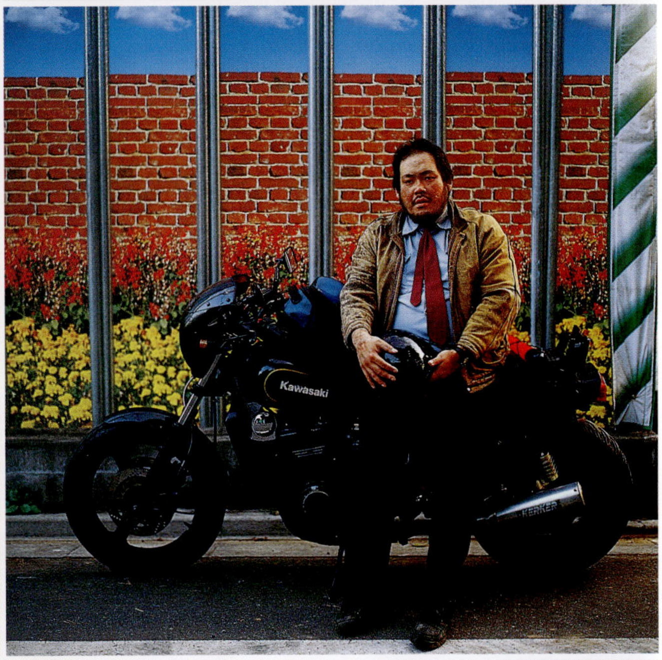
Kawasaki

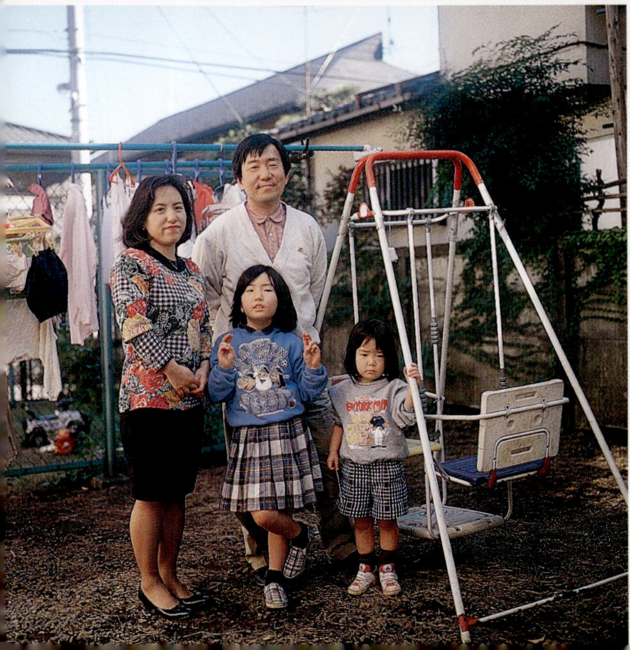

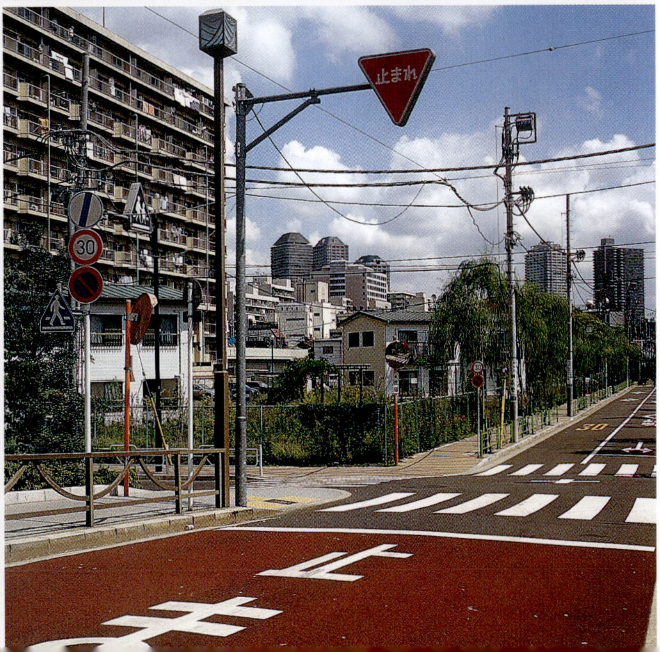
止まれ
30

In Tokyo, I see people trying to survive in an environment where many elements—the old and the new, the beautiful and the ugly, the human and the inhuman—exist side by side in a jumble that somehow constitutes a harmonious whole. As I walk through the streets of Tokyo, meeting people, coming into contact with people, I physically sense the energy emanating from each and every individual, and I realize that the city's energy arises from the combined presence of its people. And as I look at these people—candid and unselfconscious amid the context of their everyday surroundings—a picture of the real Tokyo comes into focus.

As I see it, other countries hold two distinct yet opposing images of Japan. First, there is the classical Japan: the traditional culture and the uniquely Japanese scenery that are literally vanishing before our eyes. And then there is "Japan, Inc.": the manufacturing industries with their sophisticated technology that have made this country into the economic superpower it is today. But neither of these views is particularly relevant to everyday Japanese life. As yet, people in other countries haven't had sufficient opportunity to glimpse ordinary Japanese people and the world they inhabit today.

That is why I have put together this collection of photographs. I want to show the rest of the world something that is still relatively unknown: the true face of Tokyo—which can rightfully be considered the face of Japan—and the humanity that lives and breathes behind that face.

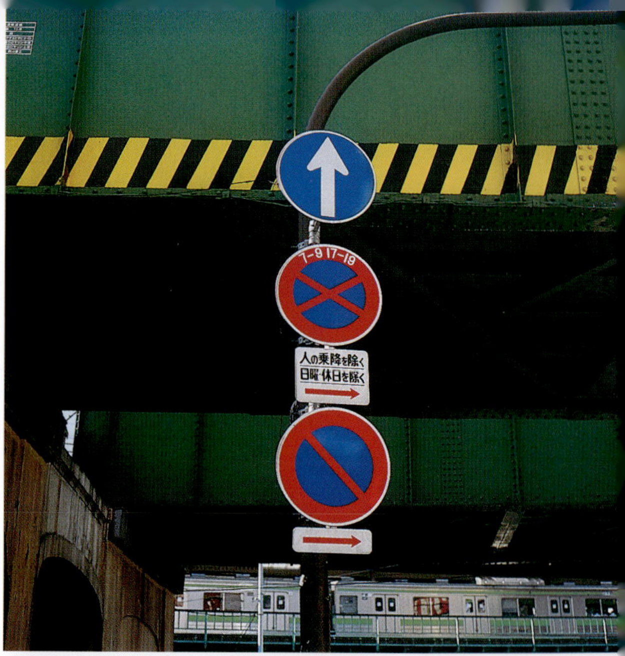


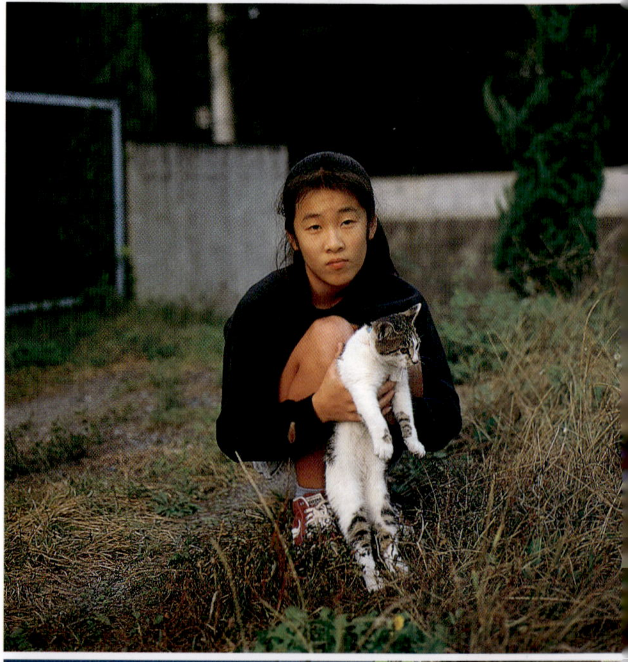

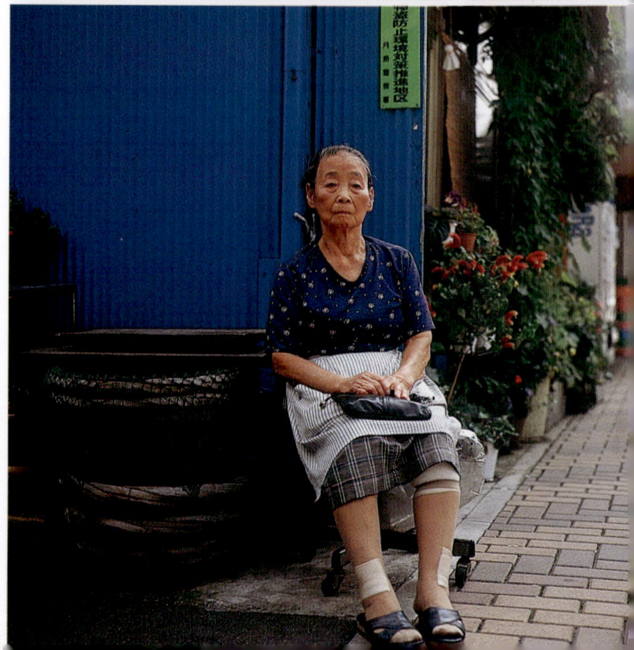

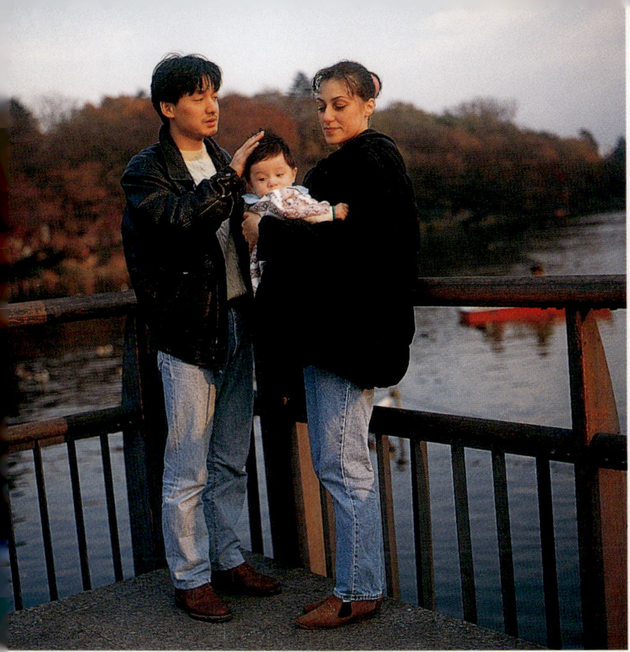

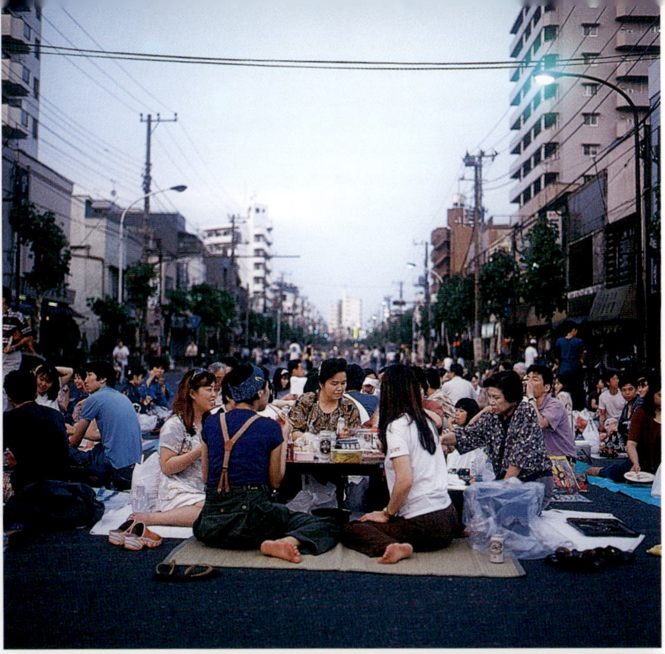

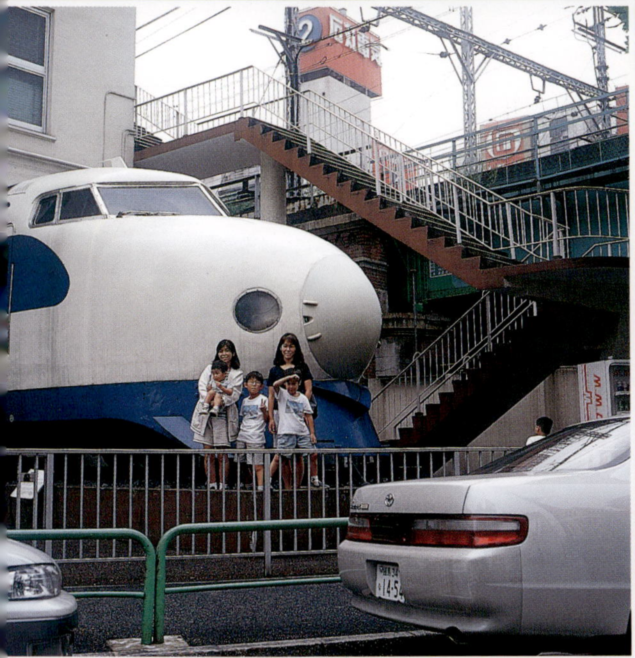

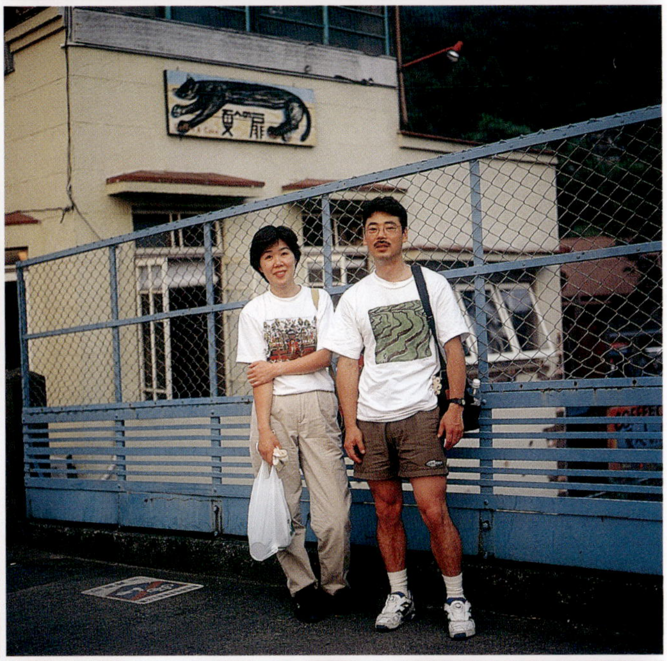

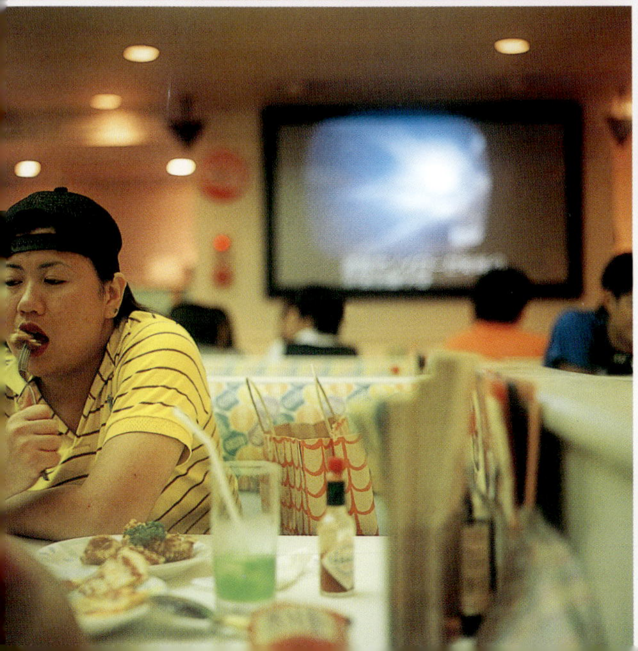

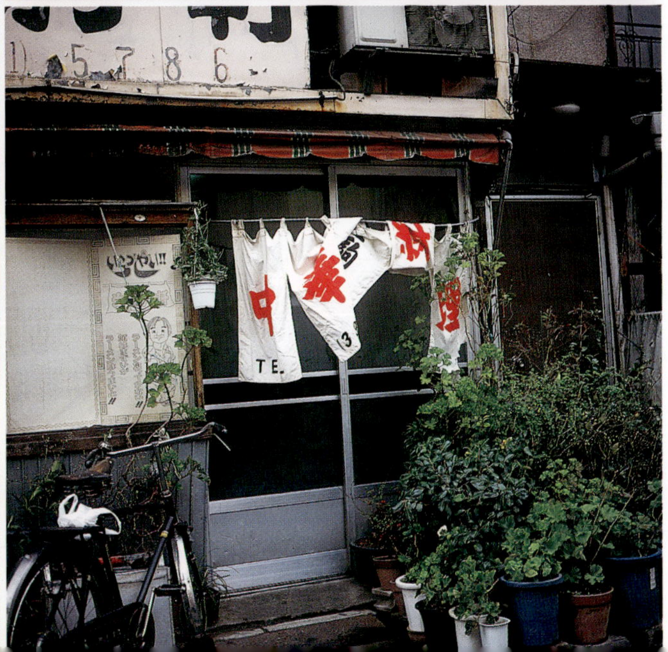

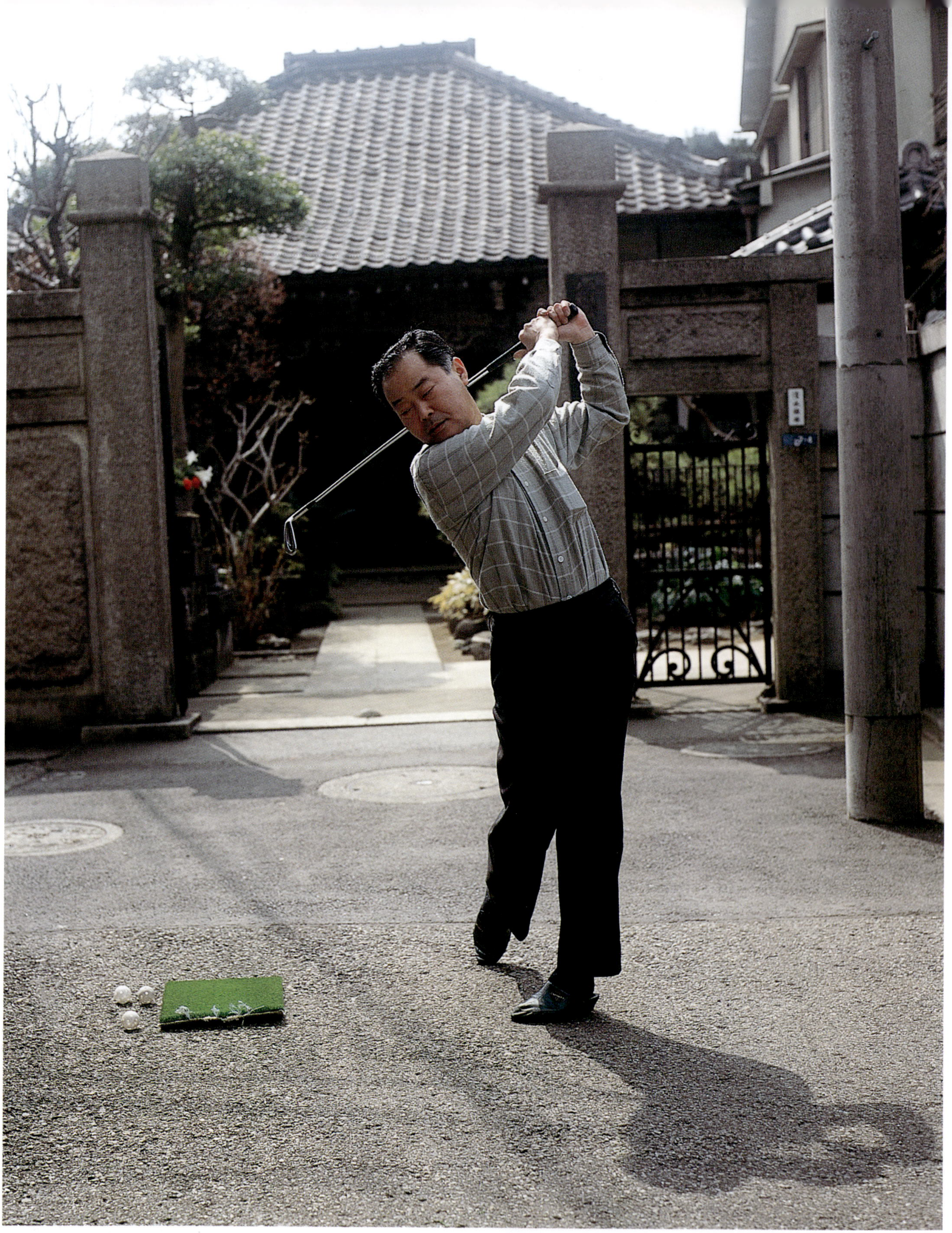

Among Japanese businessmen, golf is the favored sport. Why is this man practicing in the street? Because of skyrocketing land prices most residents can only dream of having a yard big enough to practice in.

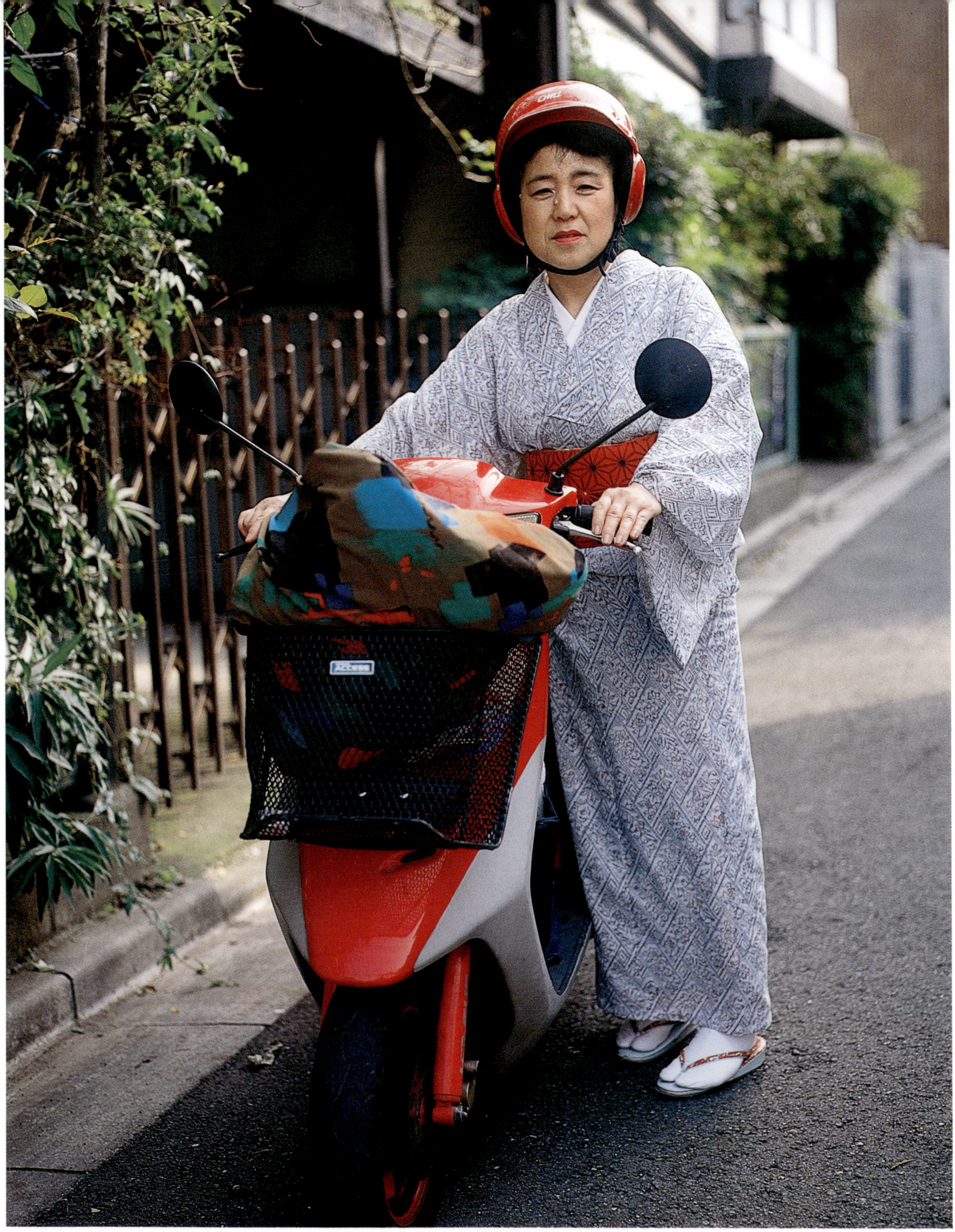

Kimono on a motor scooter. This woman, a teacher of Japanese dance, is on her way to the local community center to teach a class. These days, it is unusual to see a woman in traditional Japanese dress in an everyday setting.

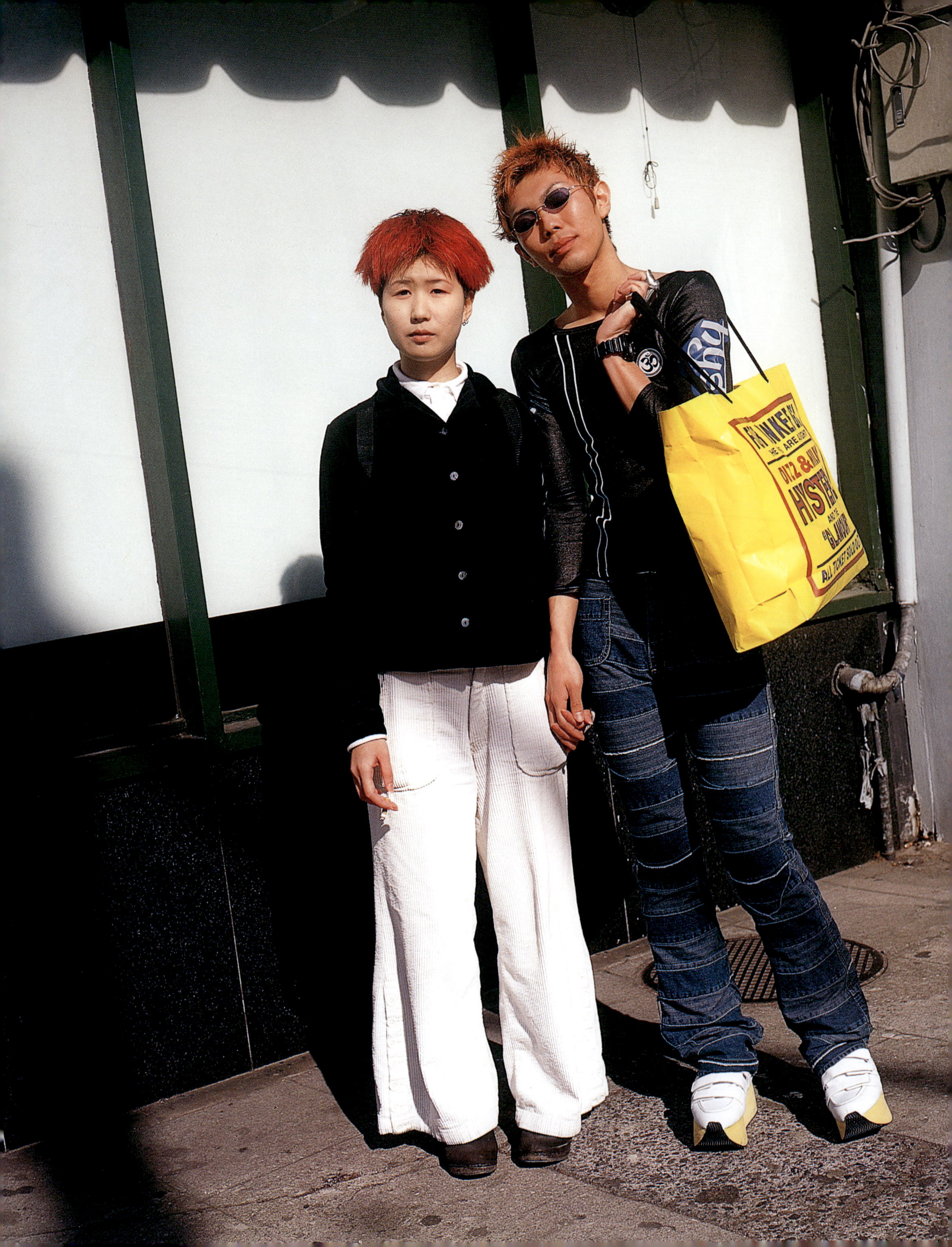
ARE
ALL TICKET SOLD

The setting is Harajuku, a trendy Tokyo district which sets the pace for teenage fashion. On weekends, crowds of young people come from other parts of the city or from surrounding prefectures to throng the streets of this neighborhood.

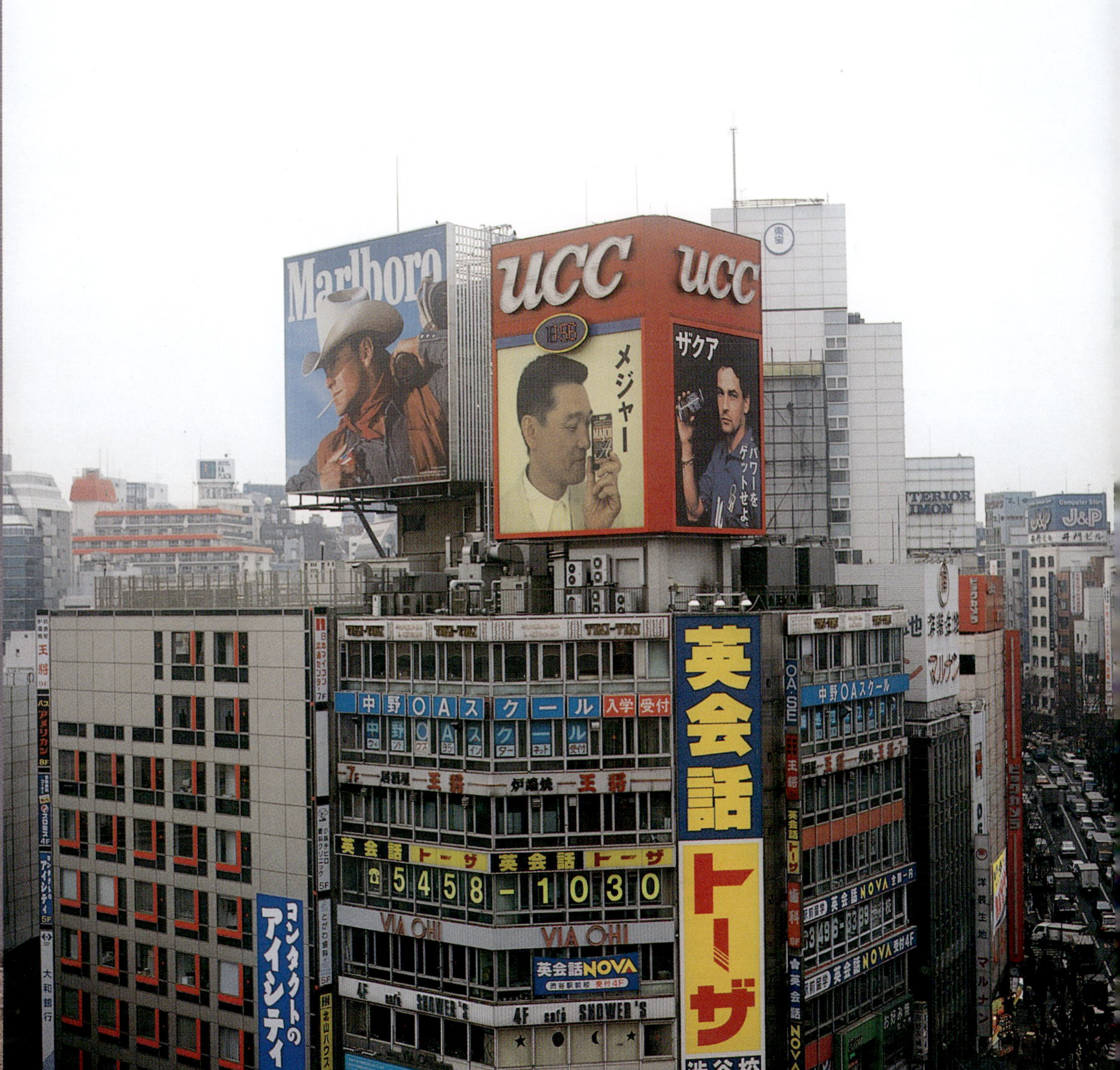


The area in front of Shibuya station is prime real estate. Buildings are transformed into three-dimensional billboards, with advertisements covering every available surface: the walls, the windows—even the roofs.

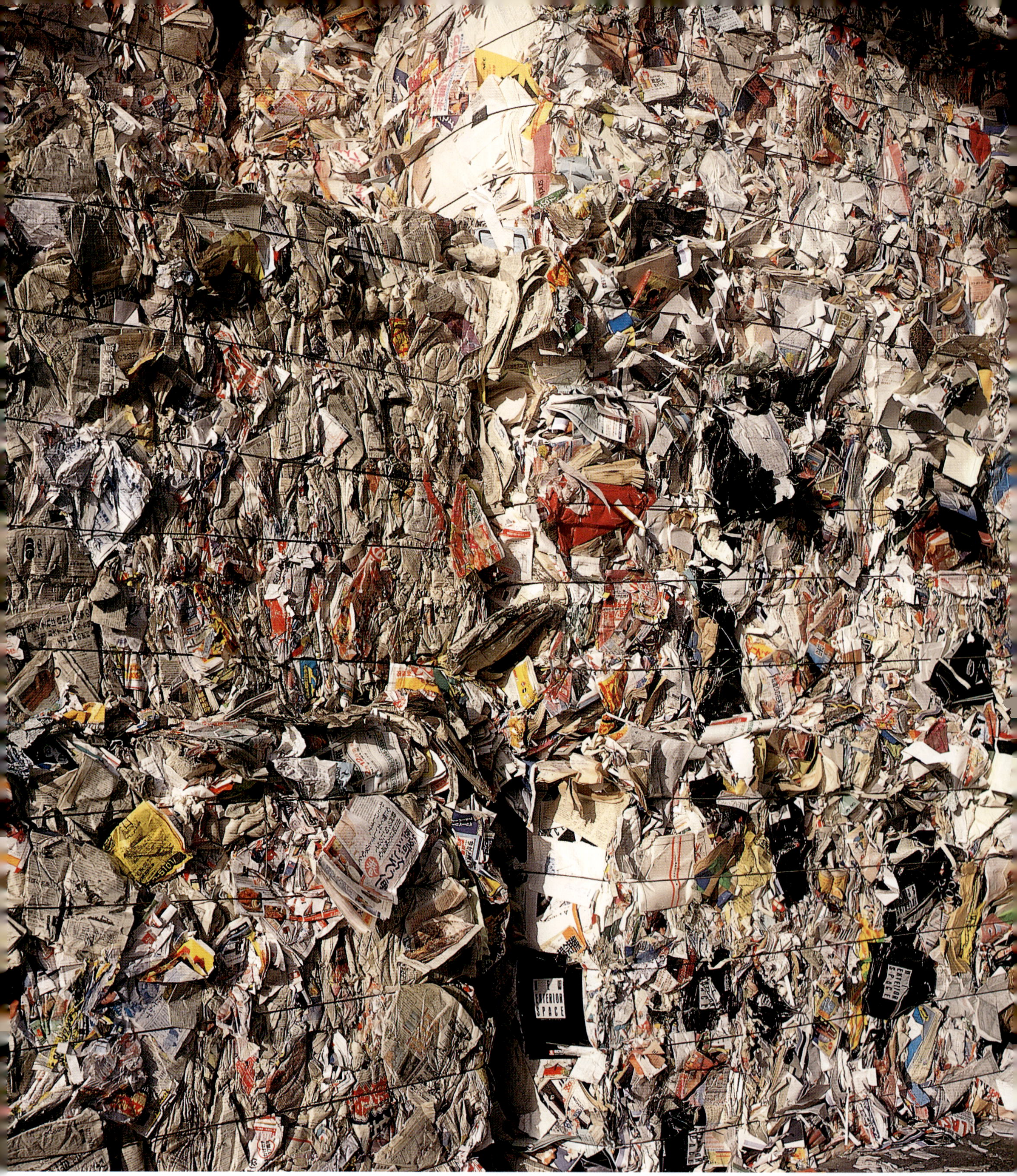

A mound of compressed trash. Each day, Tokyo generates about 15,000 tons of garbage.

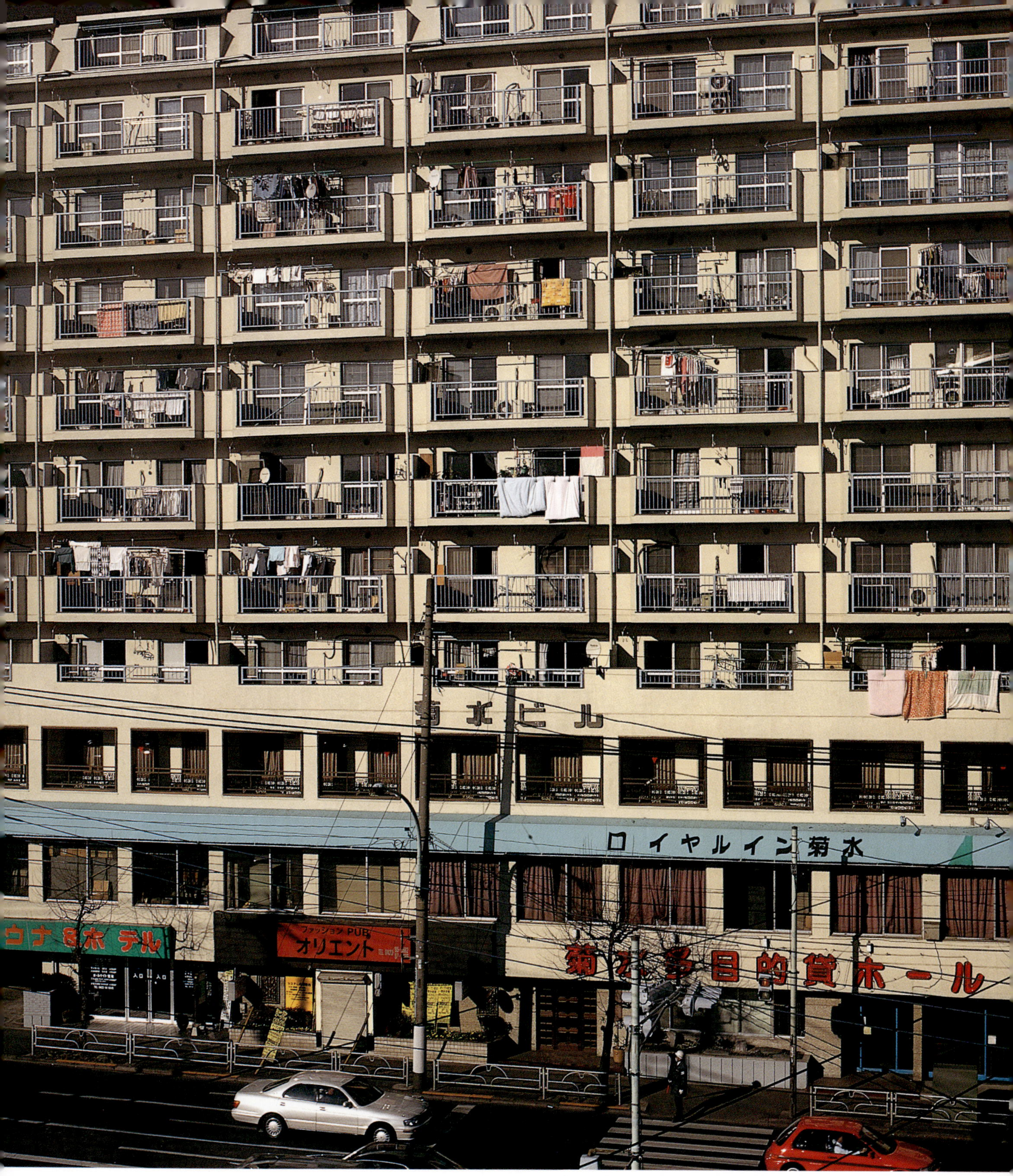


Behind each set of windows, a different household goes about the daily business of living. On sunny days, the balconies are festooned with drying laundry, and the railings draped with bedding that has been set out to air.

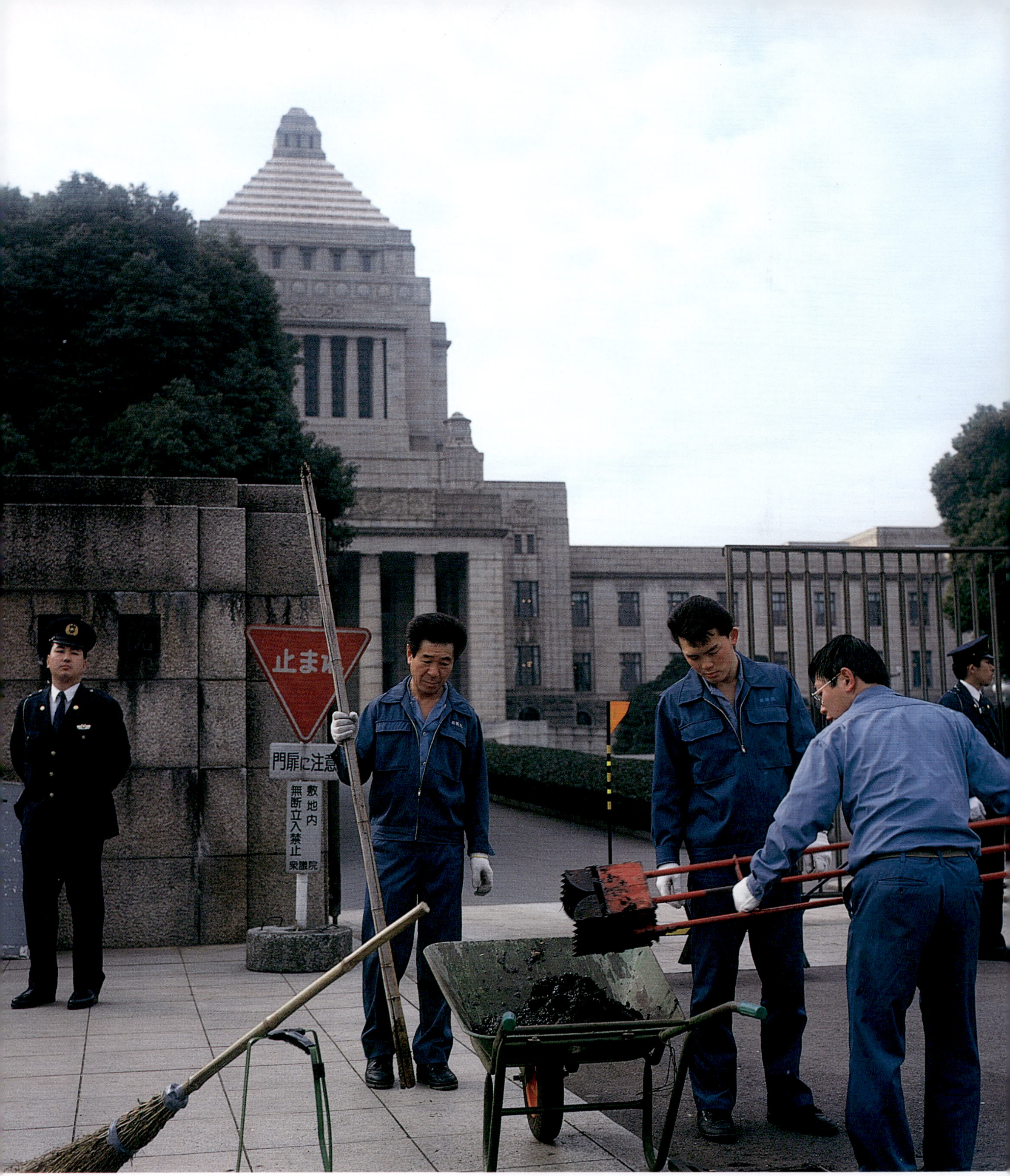


The edifice pictured here is the Diet Building, which houses the legislative branch of Japan's government. In recent years, the media and the public have been calling for cleaner politics. Ironically, these workers have been sent here to remove sludge.

Yanaka, in northeastern Tokyo, is a city with a high concentration of temples and cemeteries. Rounding an ordinary street corner, one unexpectedly comes upon this wondrous sight: a gold statue of the bodhisattva Kannon.

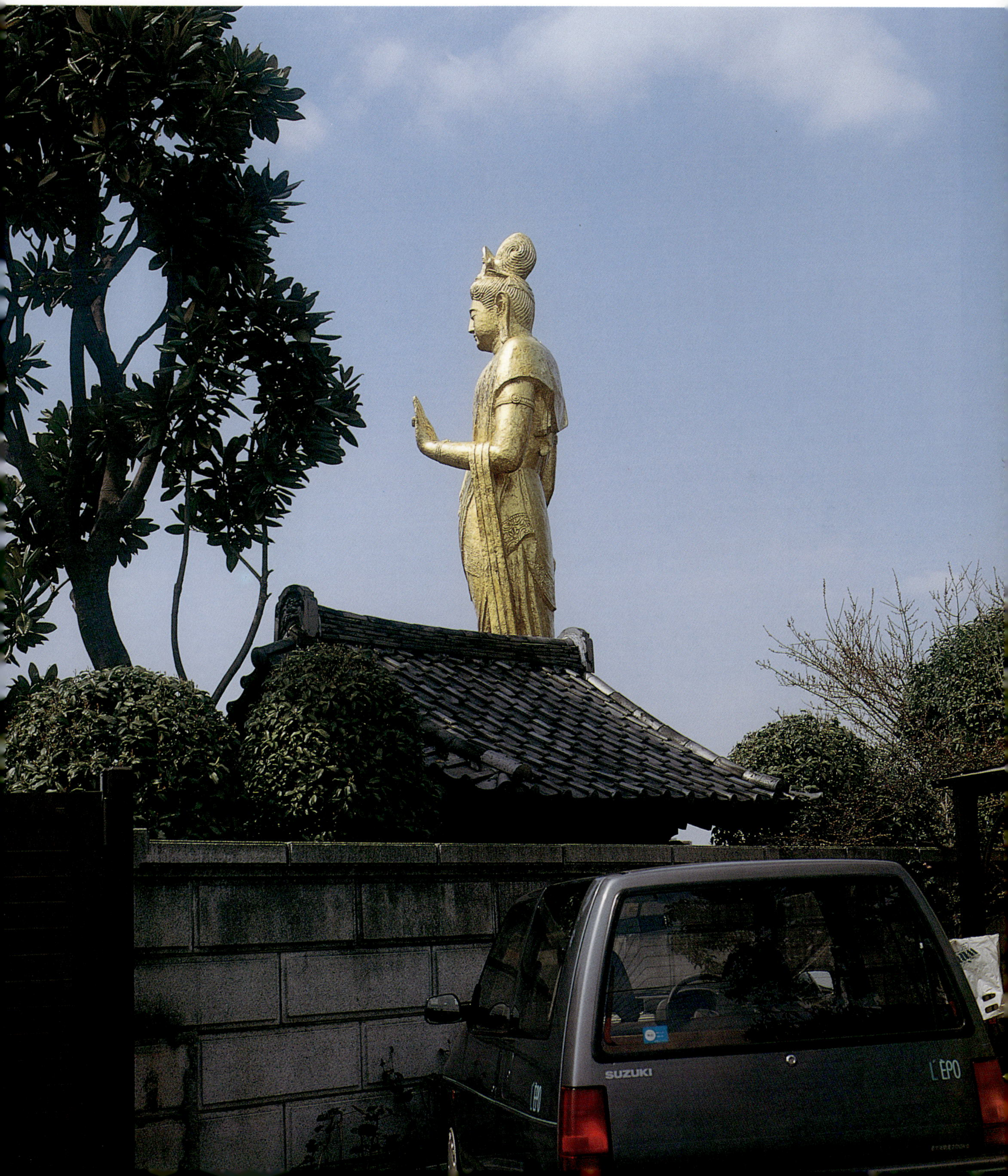

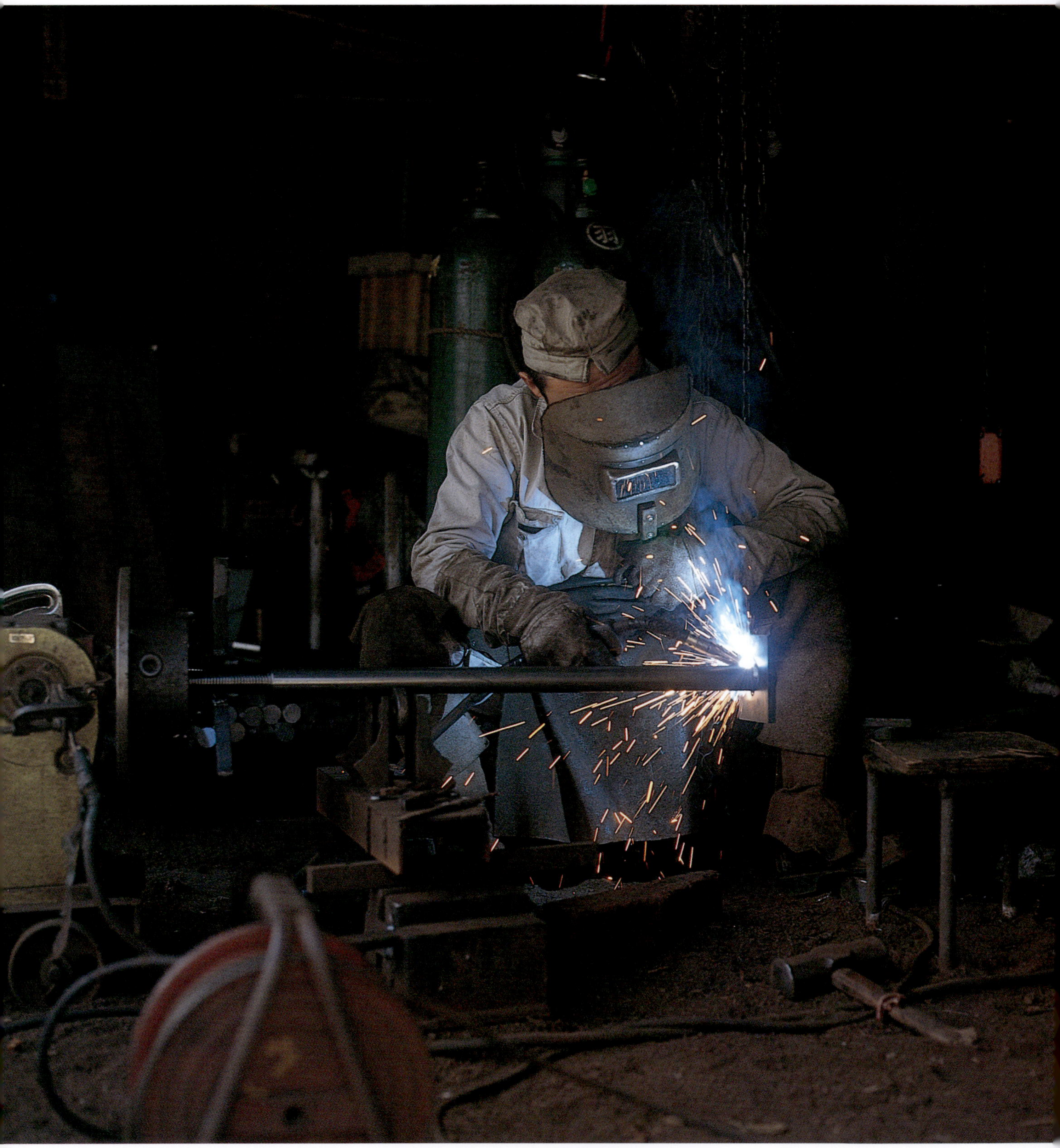

Small and medium-sized manufacturing shops, like this ironworks in Tokyo's Ota Ward, support Japan's growth and development from behind the scenes. In Ota Ward alone, there are over 7,000 of these garage factories.

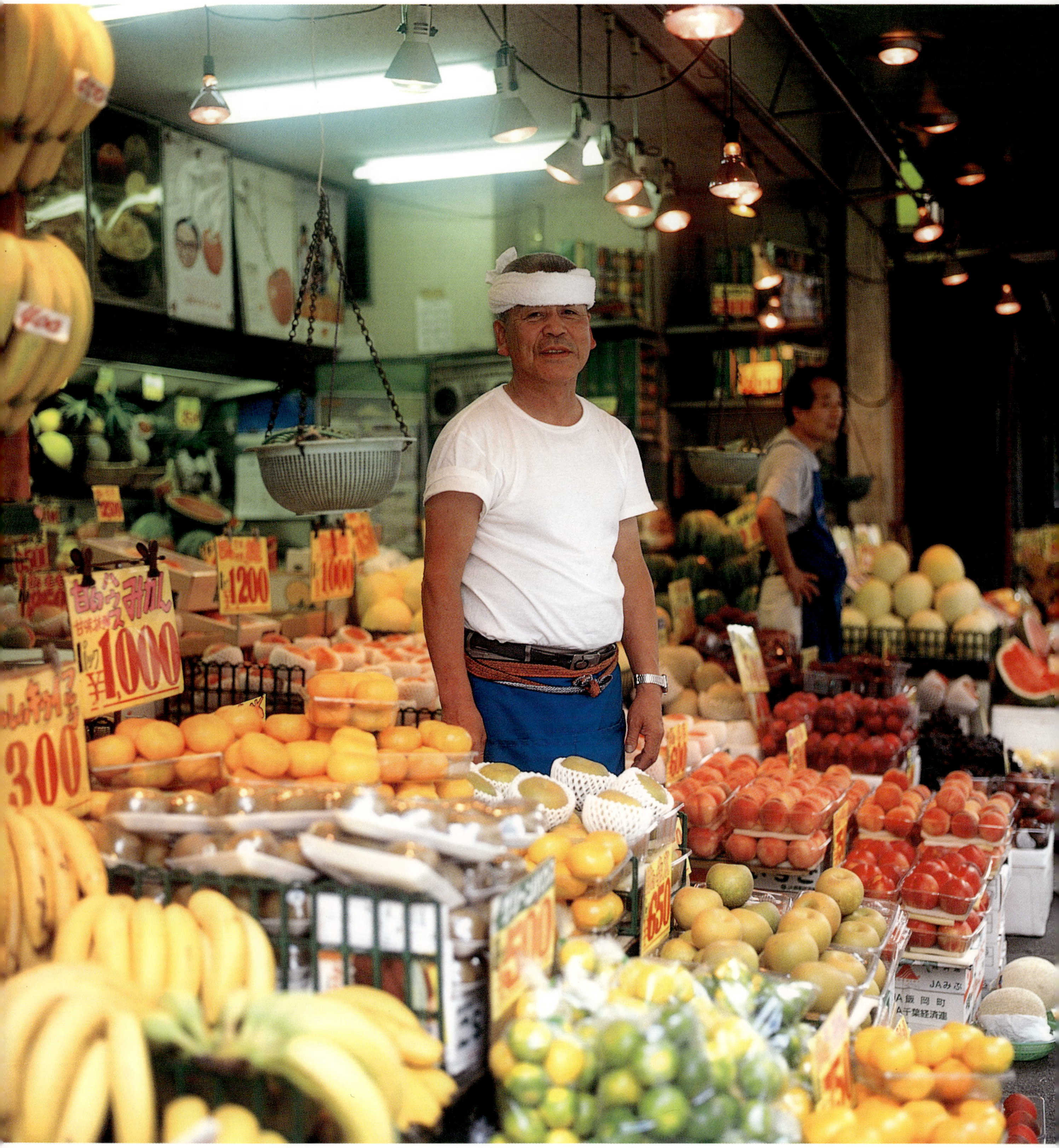


This fruit vendor brings his customers not only the domestic offerings of the season but imported varieties as well. "Even though I've been doing this for over 30 years, setting prices is still a difficult job."

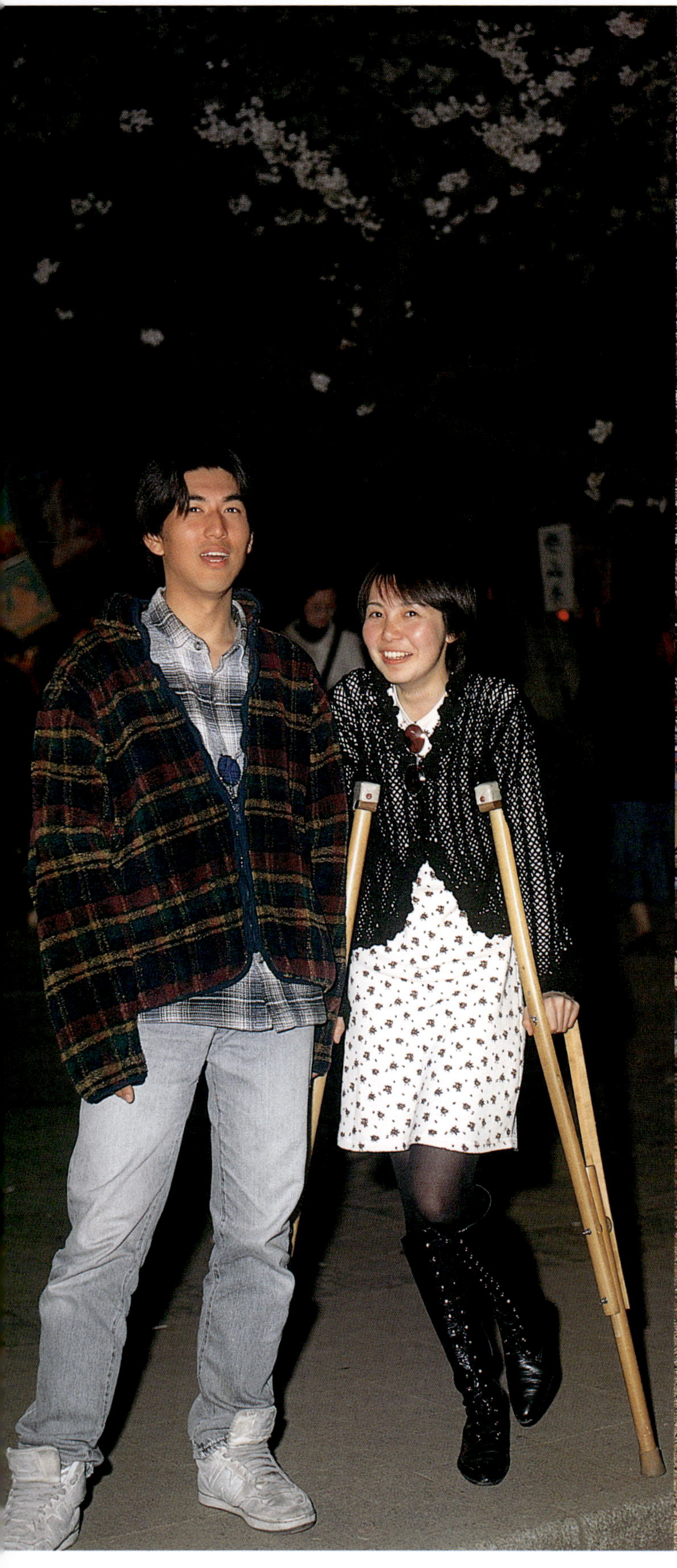

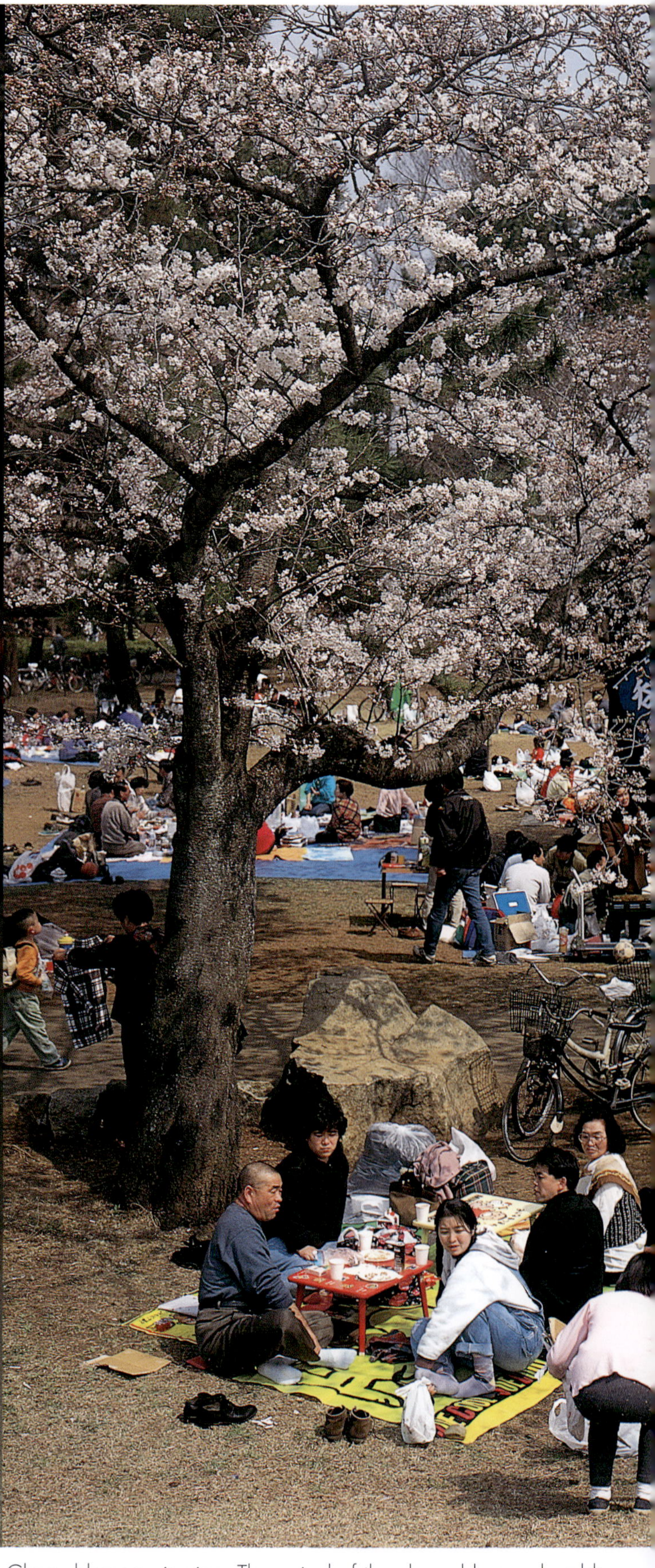

Cherry-blossom viewing. The arrival of the cherry blossom heralds the long-awaited spring, an event which the Japanese people have been celebrating since Edo times by holding blossom-viewing

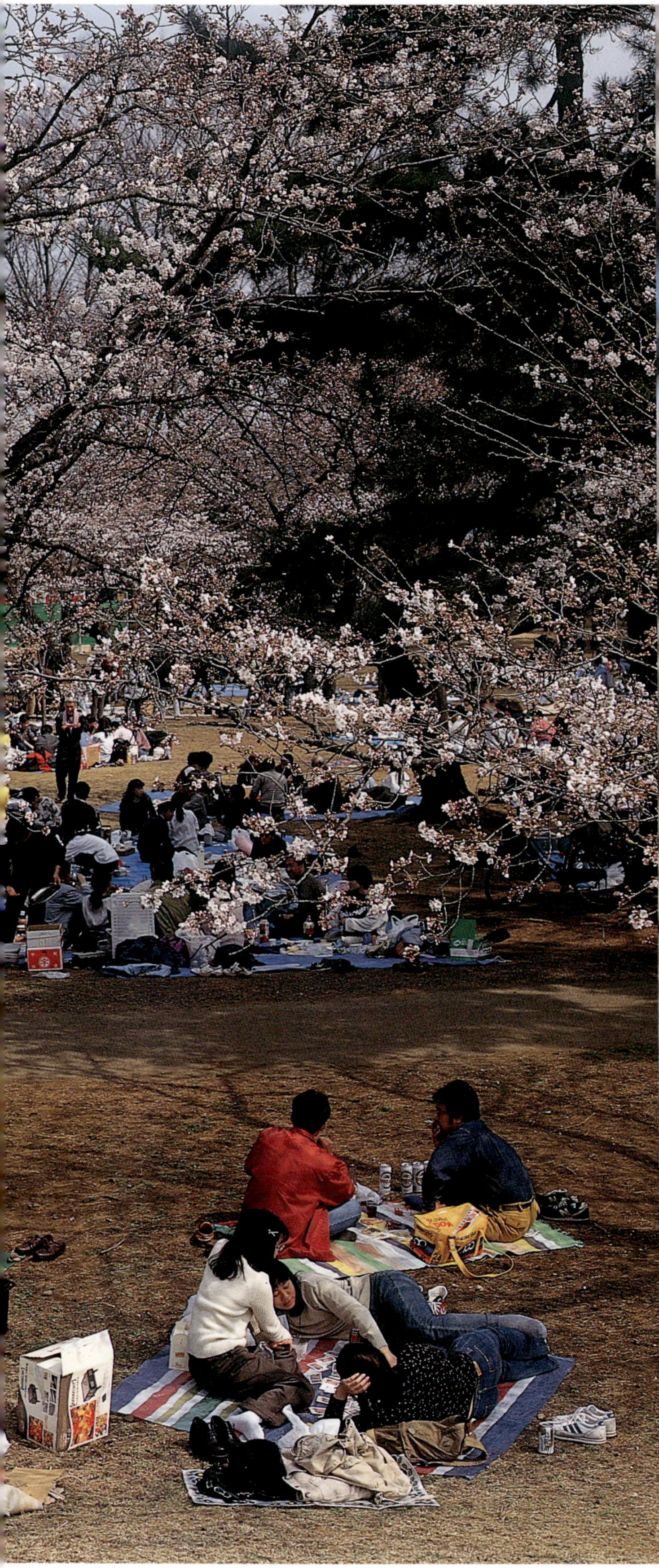

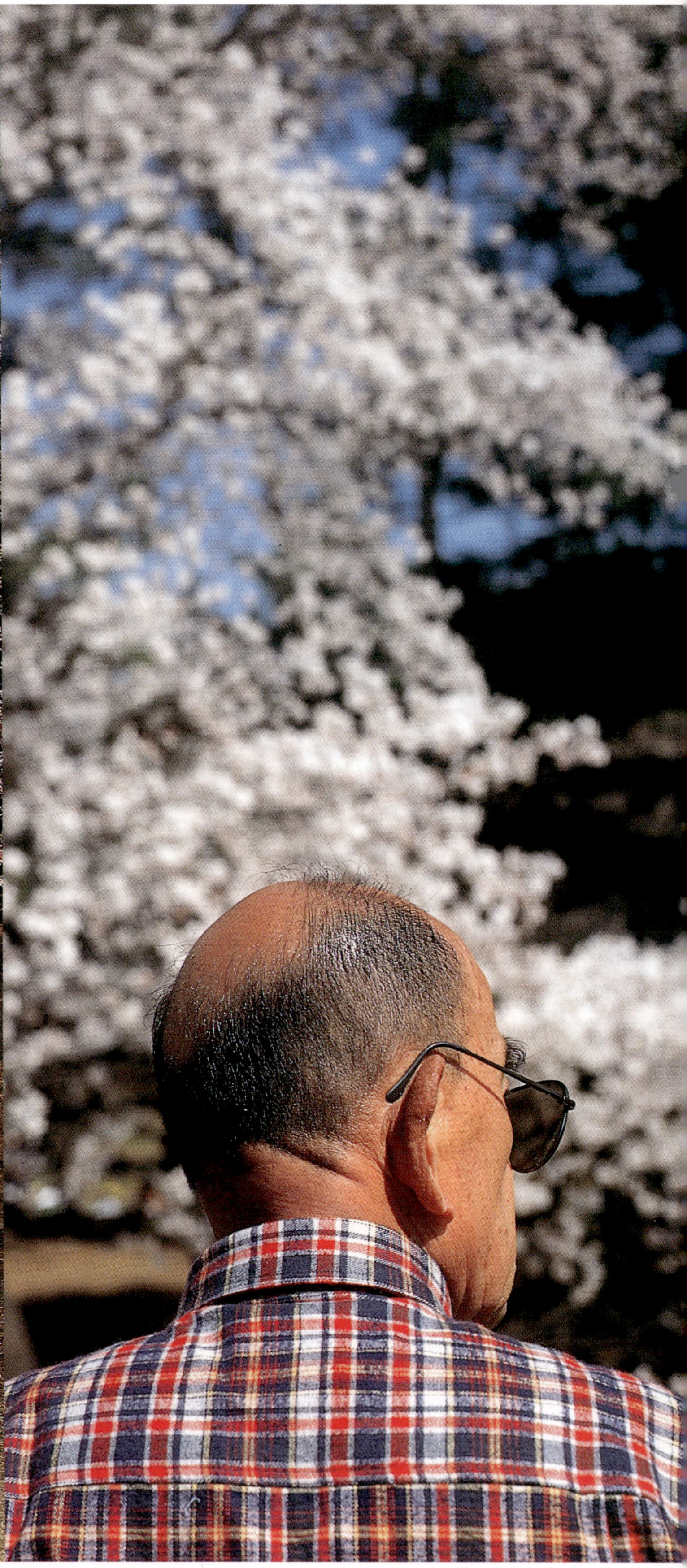

parties under the trees. The custom of eating, drinking, and singing one's worries away amid the falling petals has been preserved faithfully over the years. *O-hanami* is a major spring event in Japan.

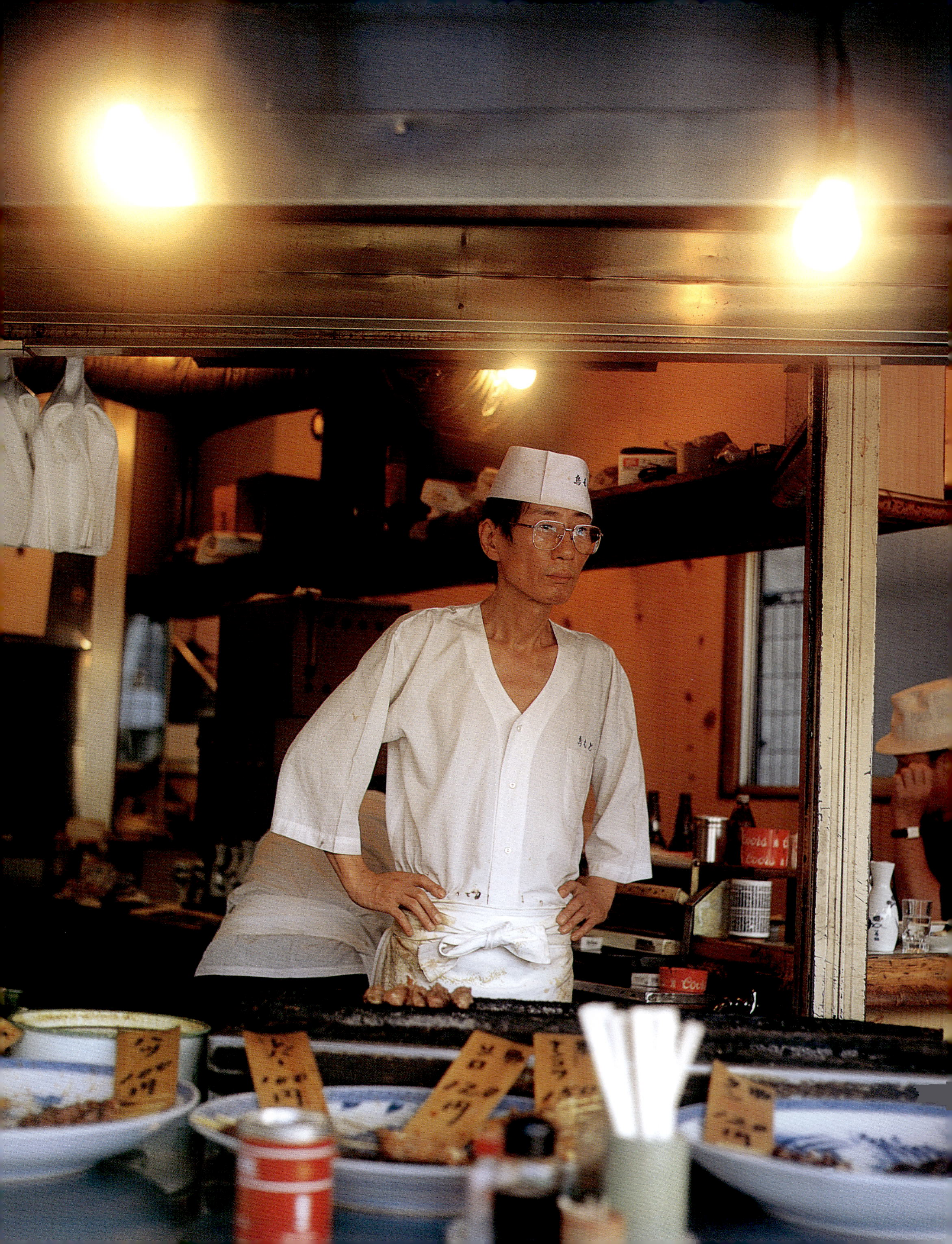

The tantalizing aroma of grilled chicken from this *yakitori* restaurant wafts into the street, beckoning passersby to stop in for a quick drink and a bite to eat.

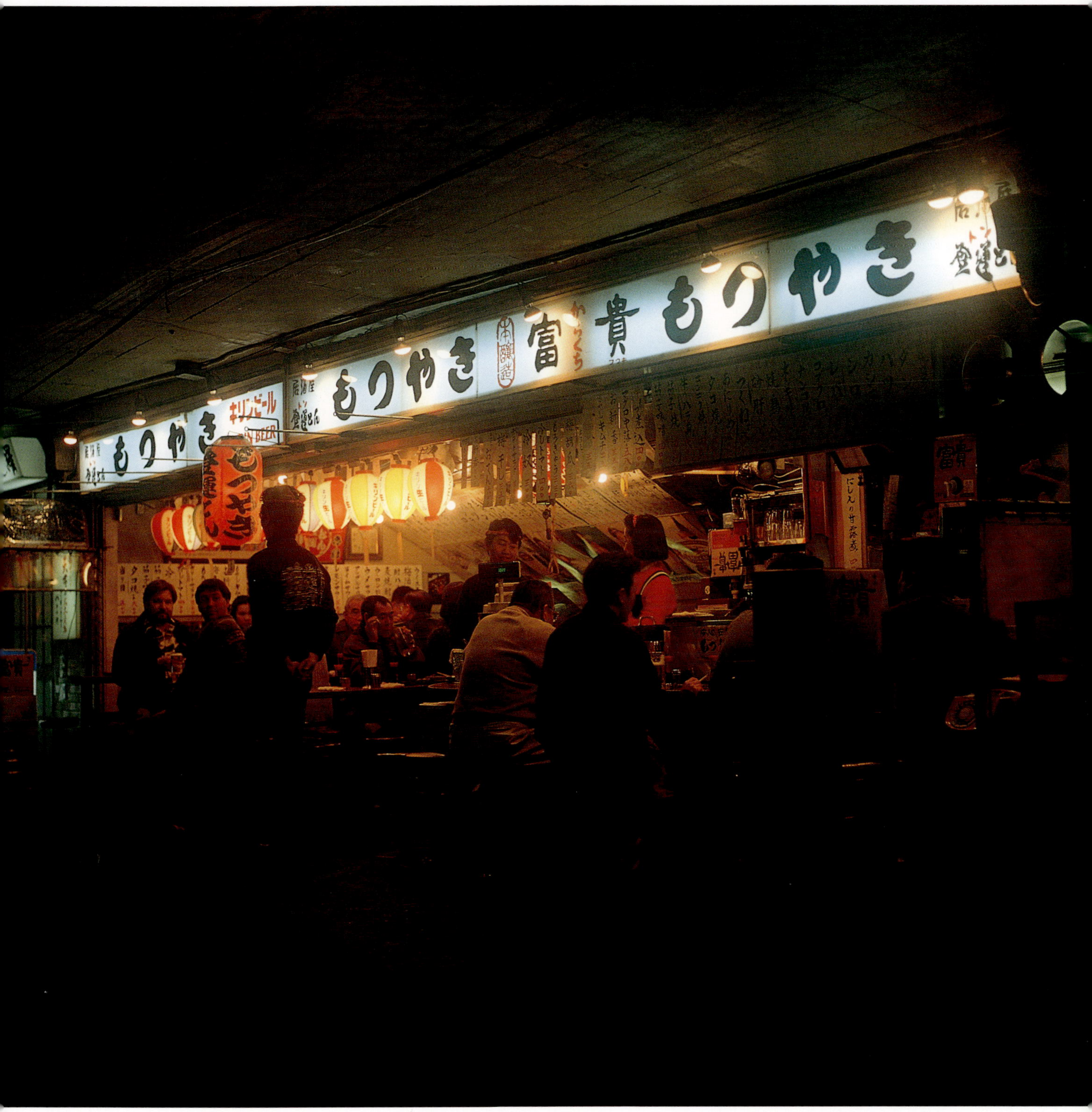


Located under the train tracks around Shimbashi station, this strip of small drinking establishments is abuzz with office workers (mostly men) who stop in to drown their workday sorrows before heading home. Amid the sleek modernity of high-tech Japan, this neighborhood is a pocket of traditional Asia.

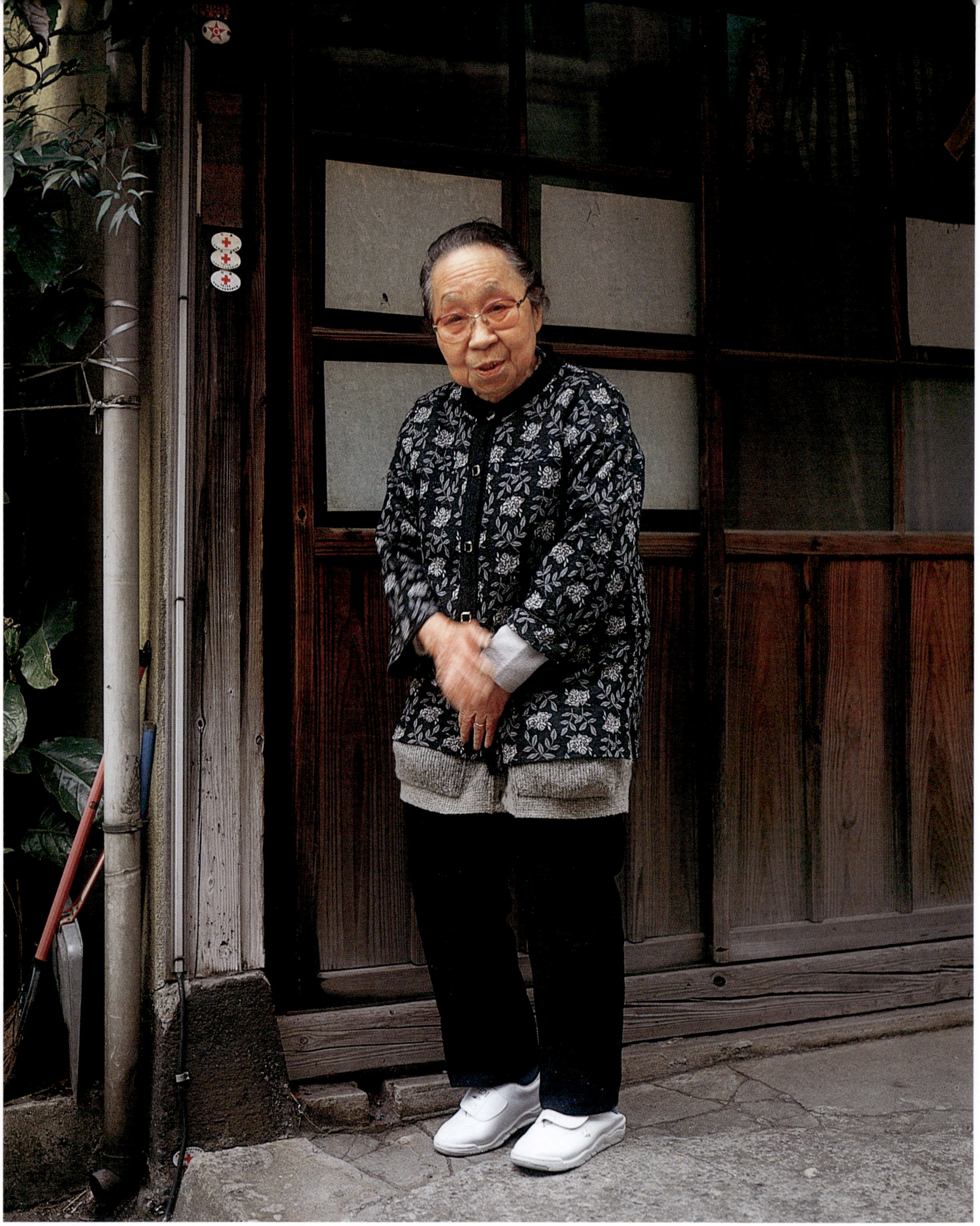

Here and there in patches throughout Tokyo, one can find pre-World War II houses still standing. The flavor of a bygone era lives on in these rows of wooden houses, which are often inhabited by elderly people.

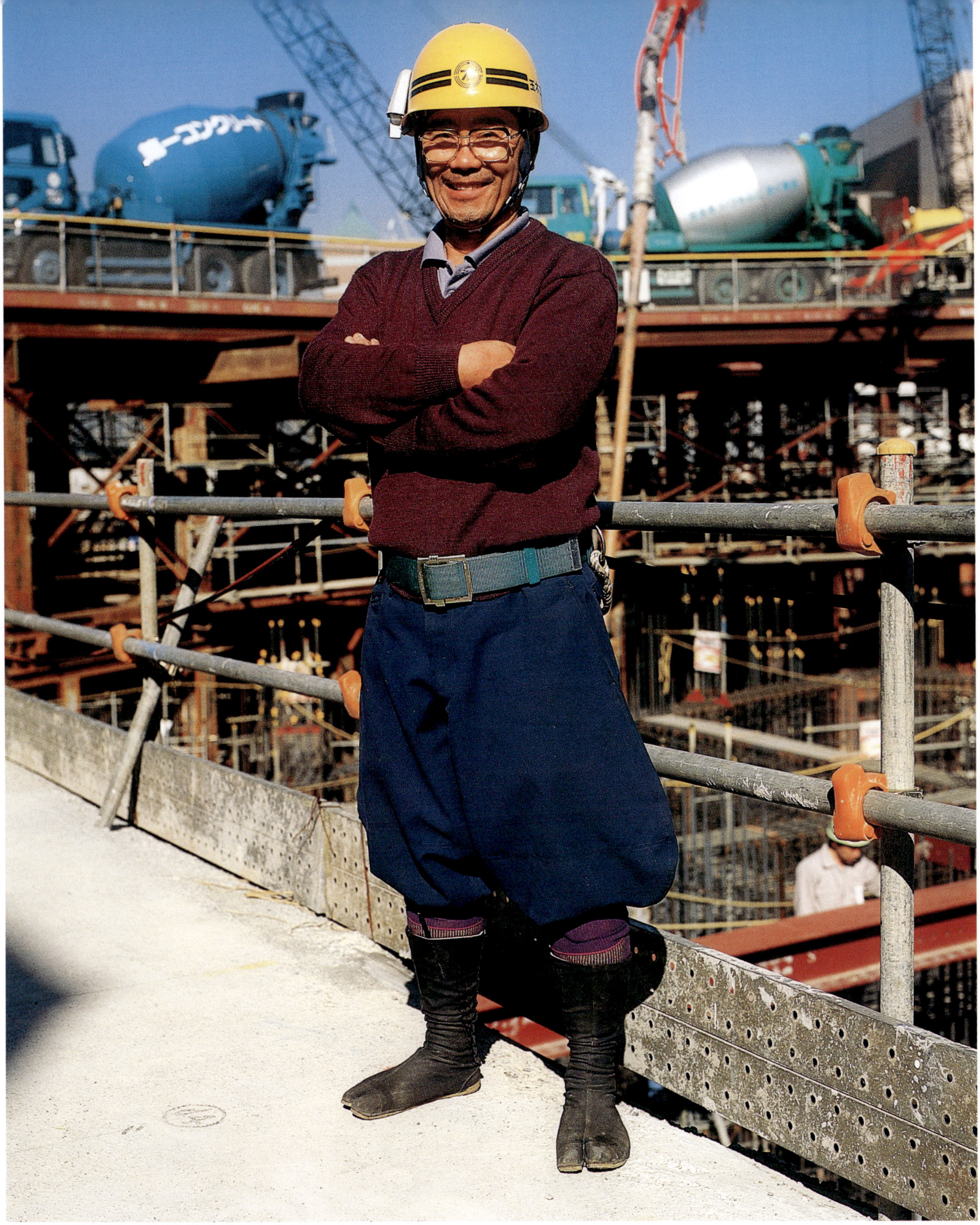

The rigors of manual labor, together with the ever-present risk of bodily harm, make construction a demanding job that requires constant vigilance. Nowadays, younger laborers don't stay with this kind of work for very long. Well-trained workers, such as this man, are decreasing in number year by year.

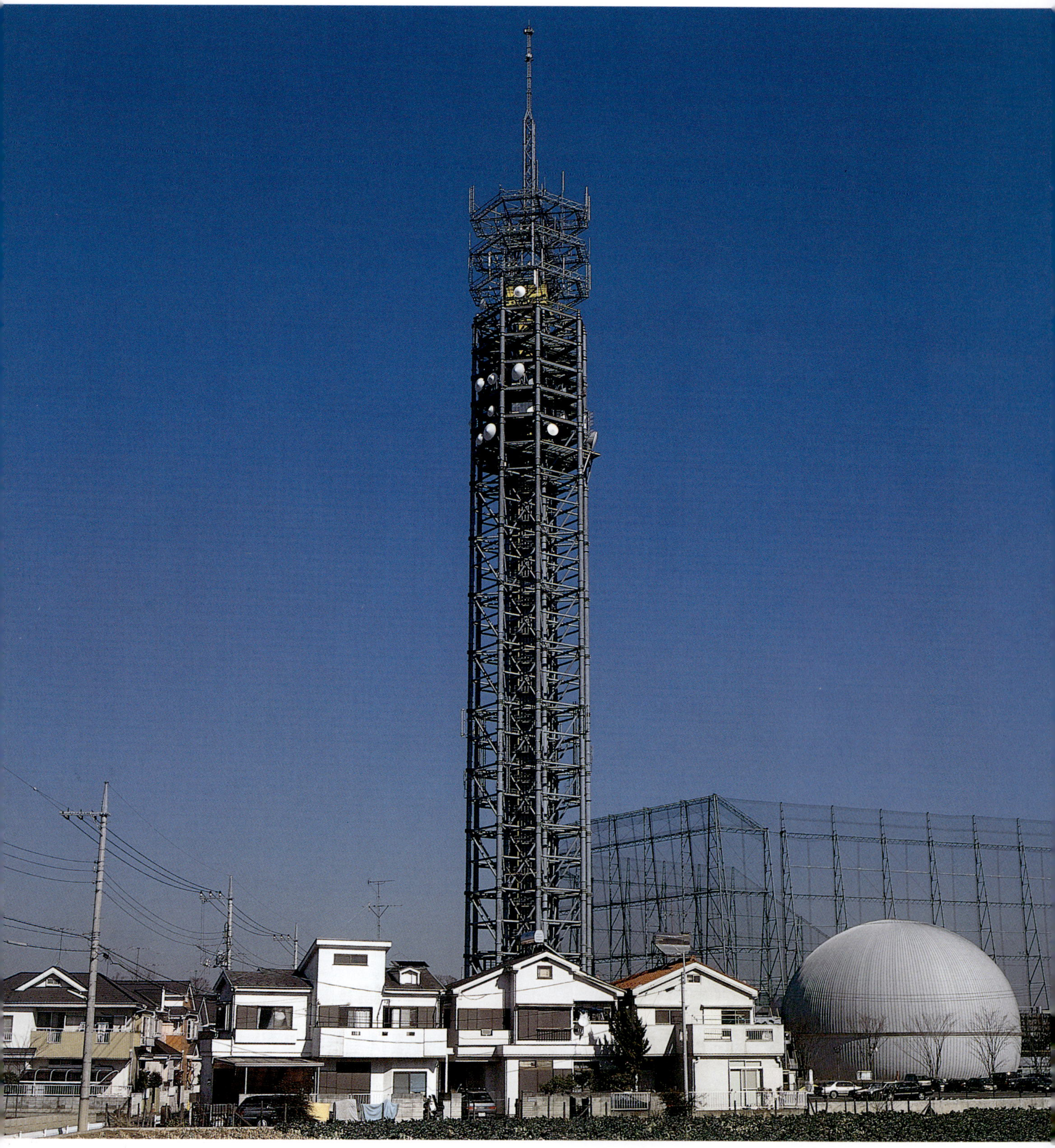

A planetarium dome, a net-enclosed driving range, and a high-reaching radio tower together create a futuristic scene.

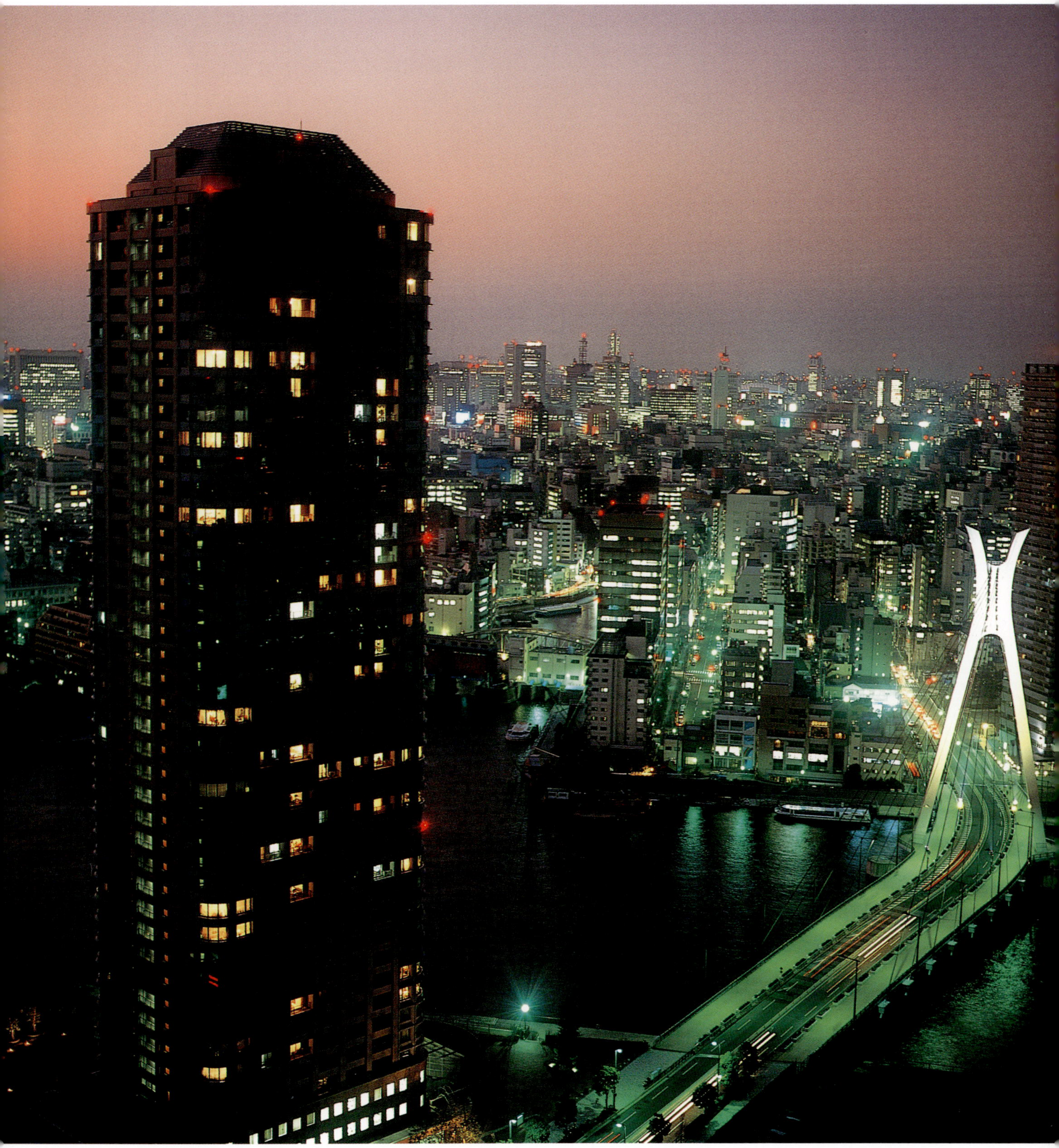

Beneath the balcony of a Tokyo high-rise apartment, the evening cityscape unfolds. Until just over 10 years ago, this was a traditional *shitamachi* neighborhood; now the past and the present coexist side-by-side.

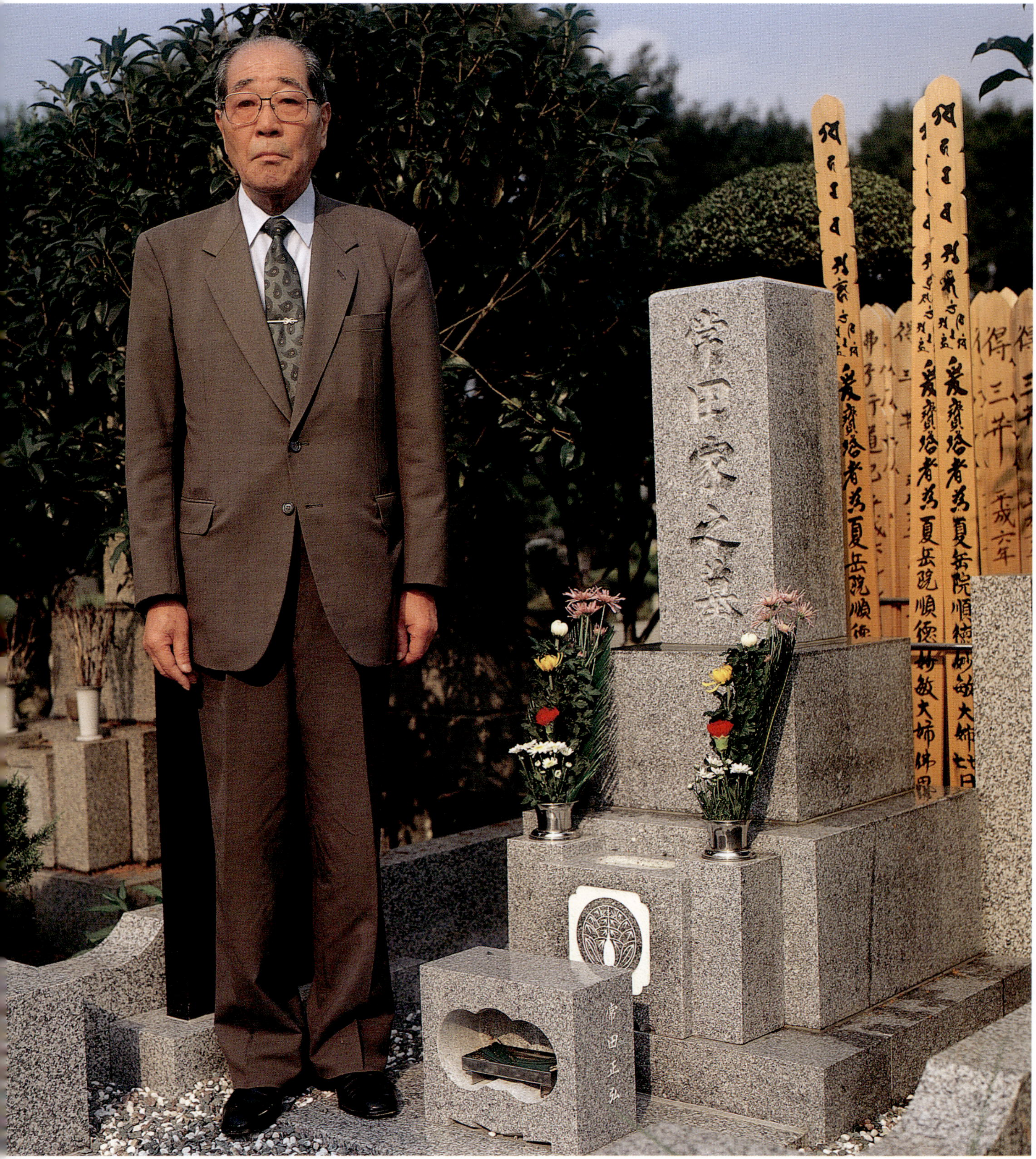


Most of the time, cemeteries are deserted places. But on the spring and autumn equinoxes, they are filled with people who come to pay their respects to deceased relatives and friends, in keeping with Buddhist practice. The man in this picture is visiting his wife's grave. "In my heart," he says, "my wife lives on."

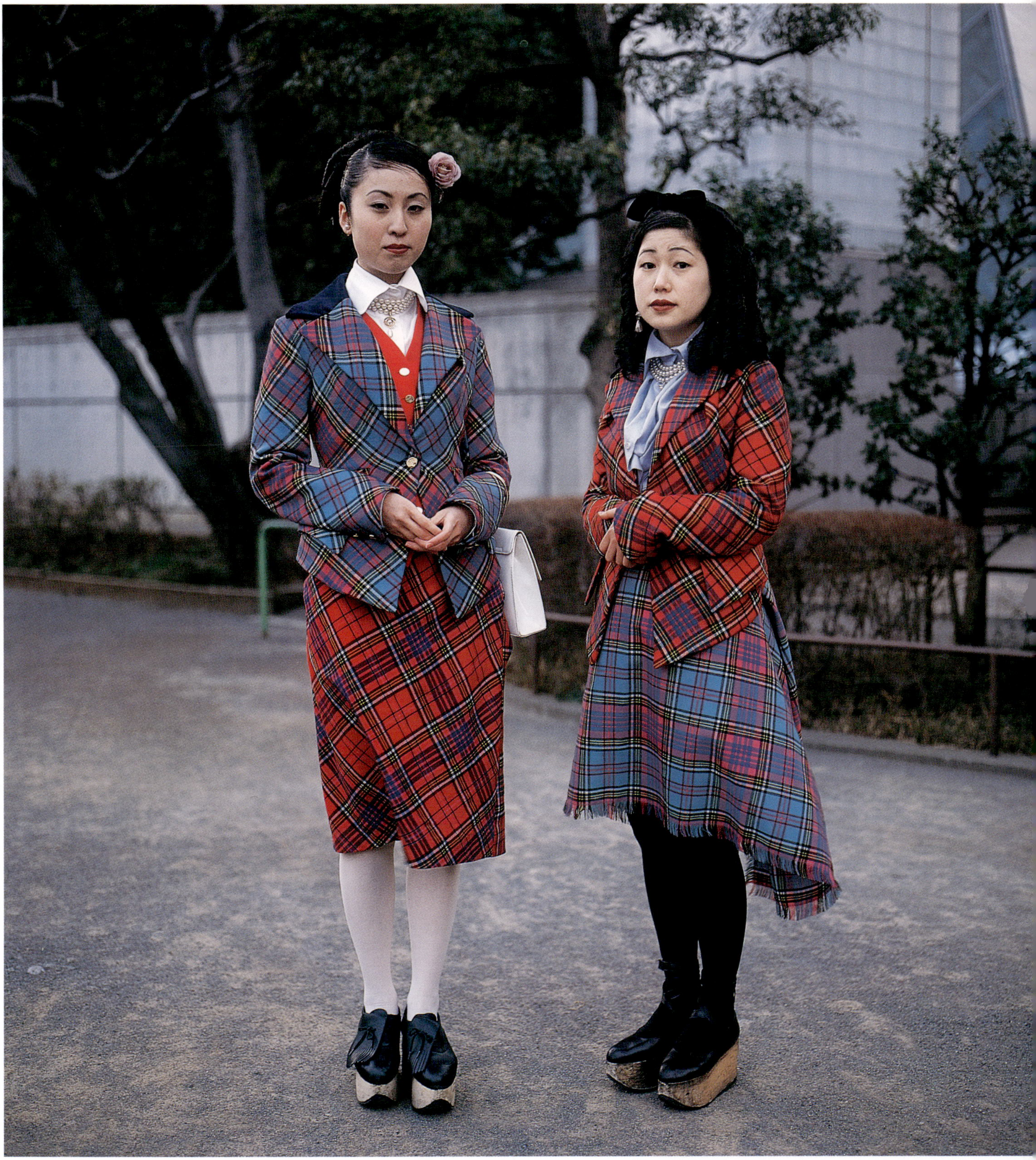

Fashion-design students on graduation day: "We planned our outfits to match. What do you think?" The total cost of these ensembles — clothing and shoes combined — comes to about $5,000.

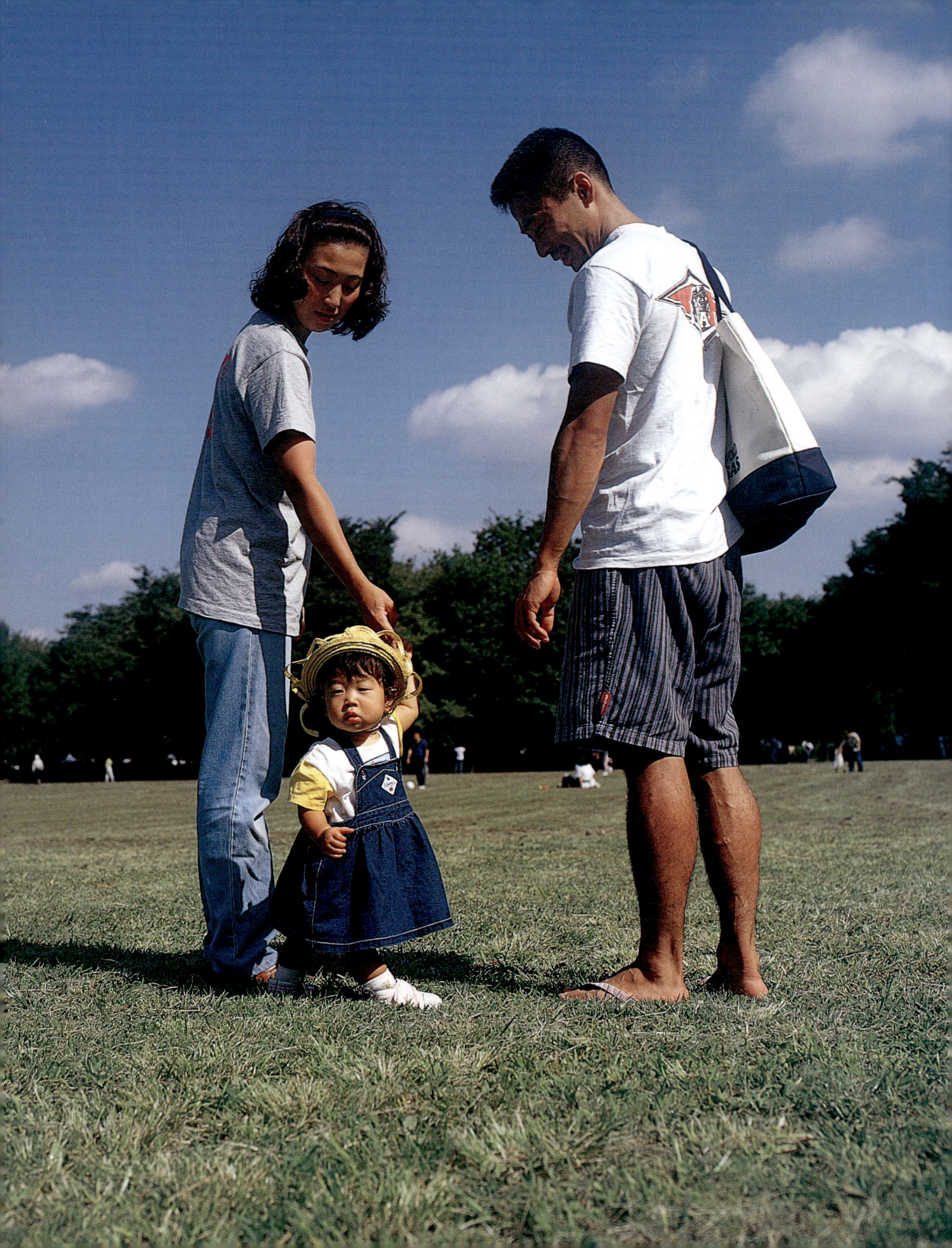

On weekends and holidays, parks are filled with parents and their children. This family scene, though ordinary, imparts a feeling of extraordinary peace.

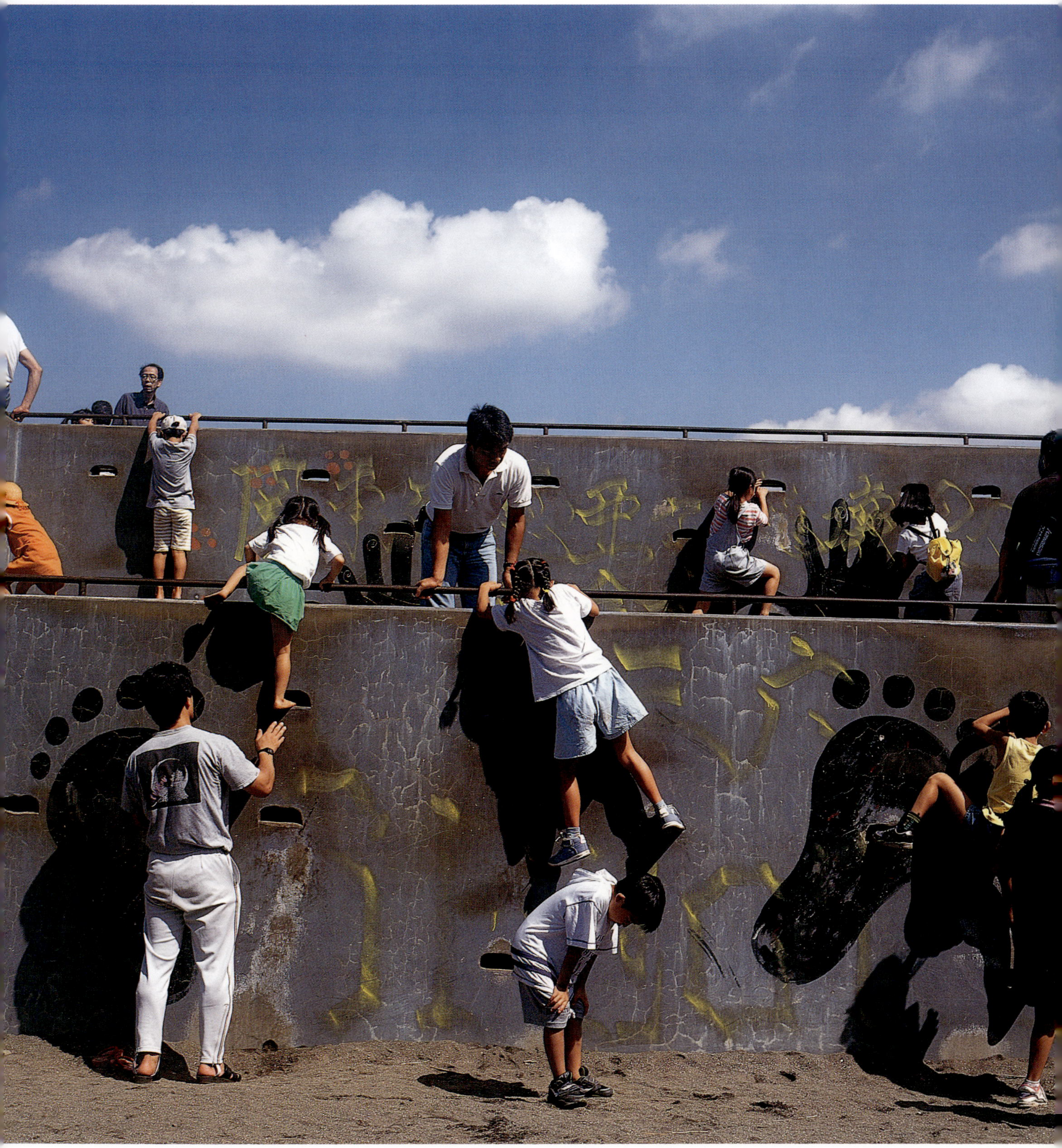

Children, full of life, play under an azure sky that seems within arm's reach.

This fishing moat, located in the heart of the city, offers an escape to a more tranquil world.
Some of the anglers here are businessmen in neckties.

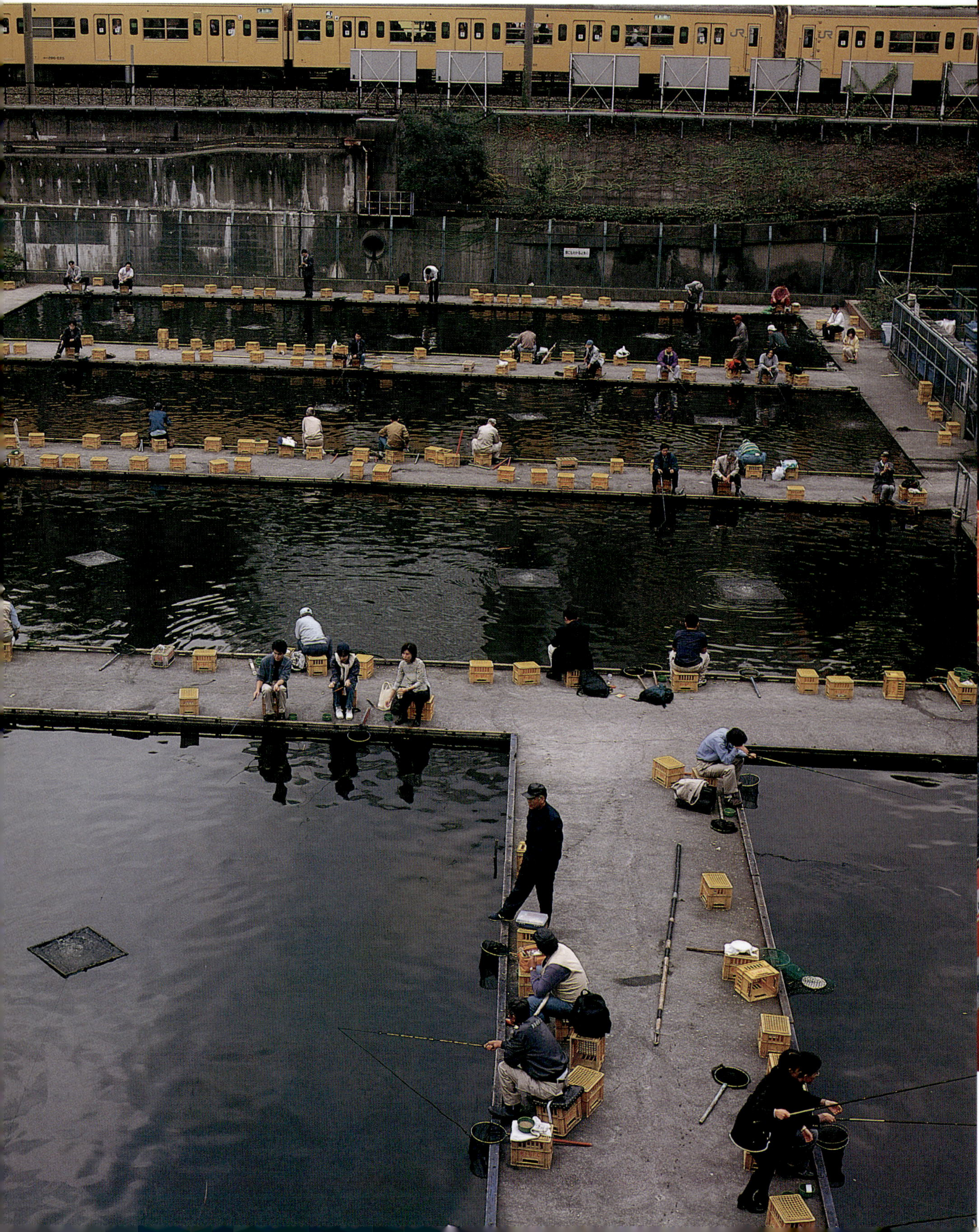

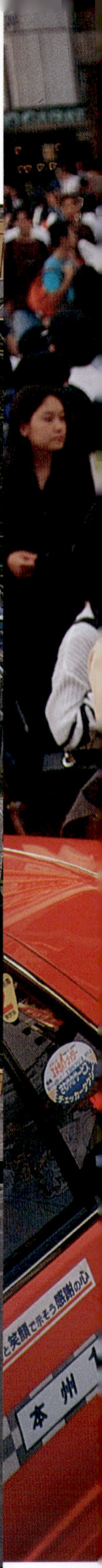

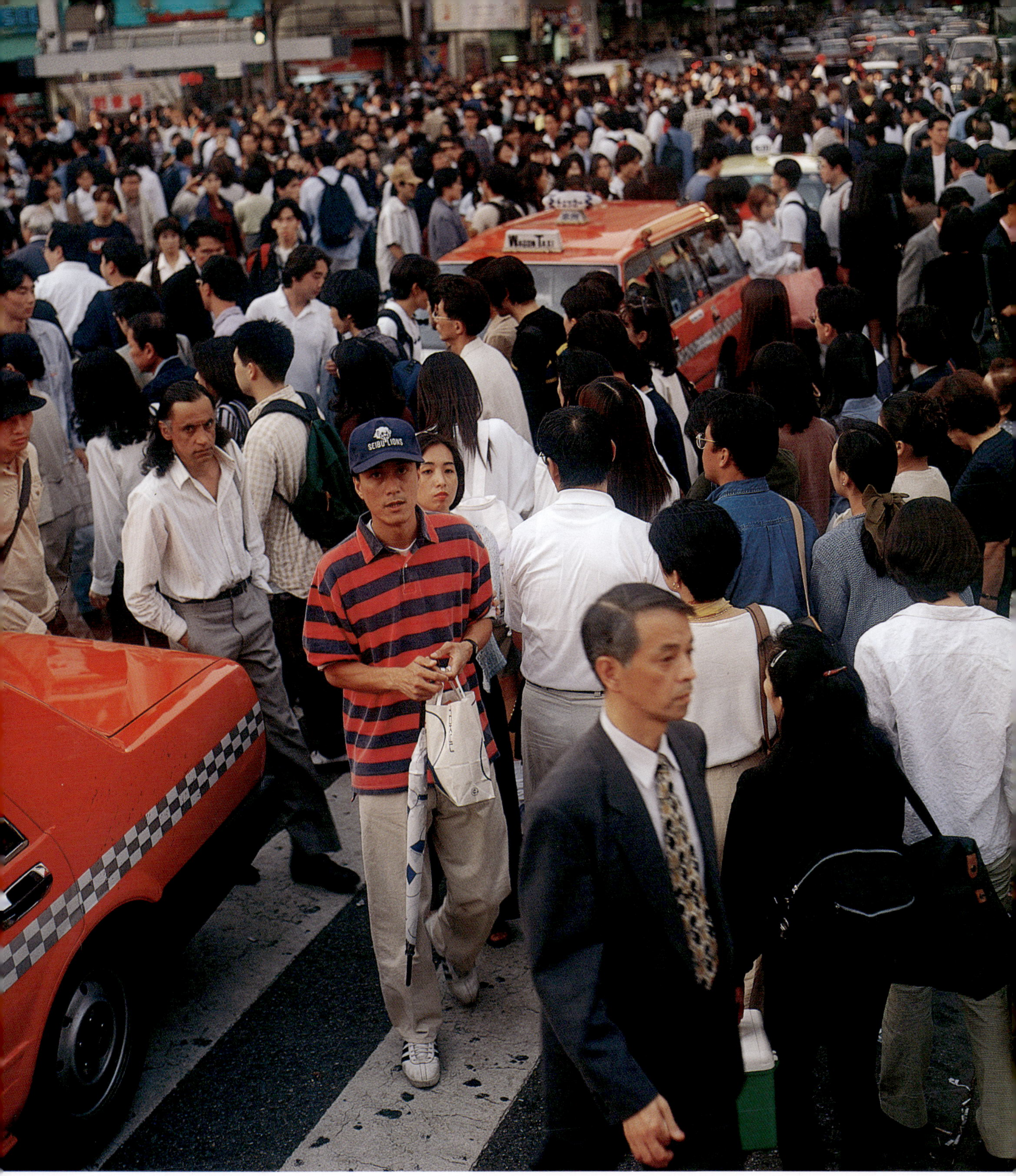


Here at the intersection in front of Shibuya station, every change of the traffic signal sends a vast wave of humanity surging into the street.

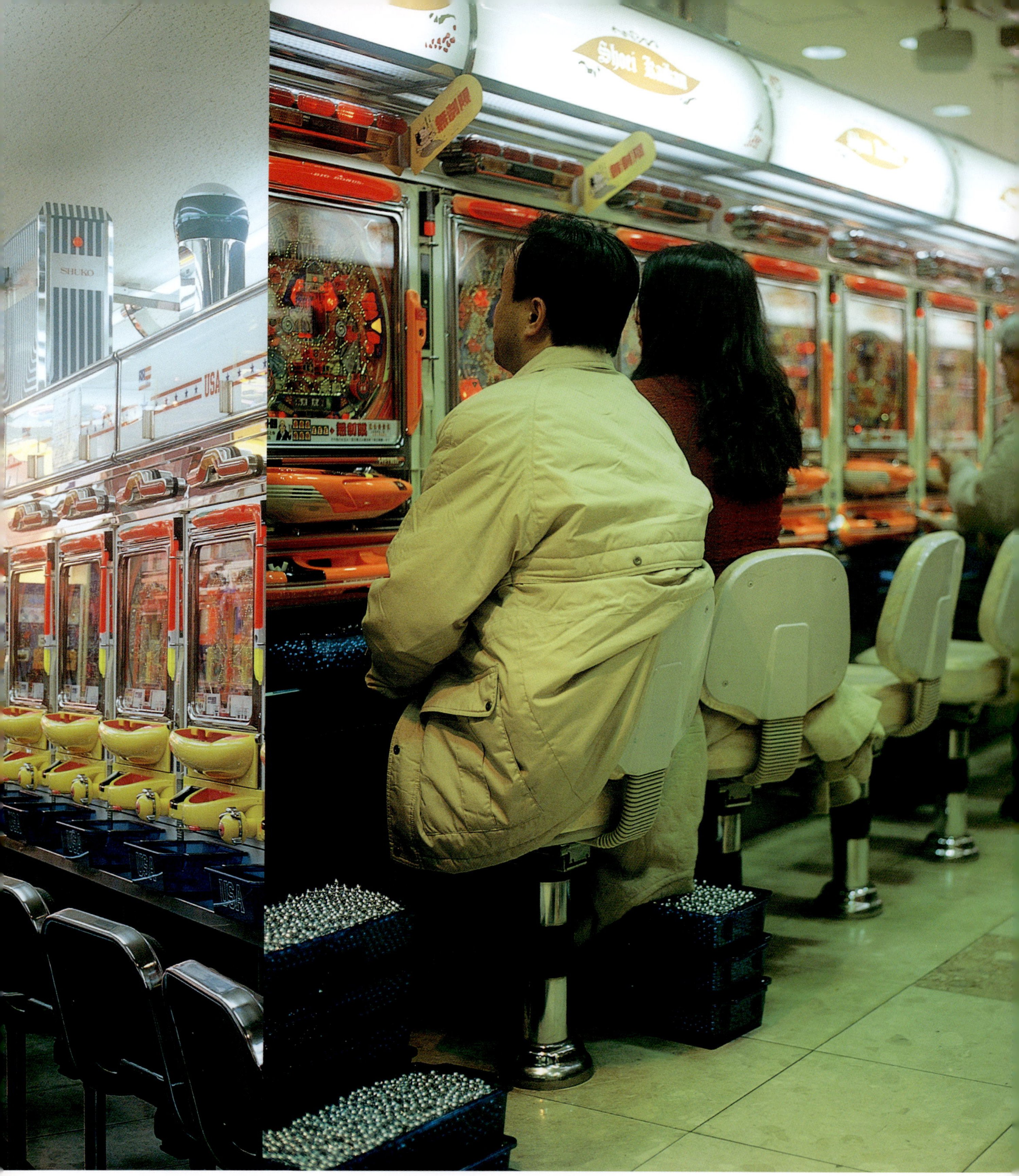


Pachinko, a variety of pinball, is a readily accessible form of gambling. You can find a pachinko hall on any busy street. Each year, the pachinko industry rakes in nearly ¥3 trillion (about $28 billion) in Tokyo alone.

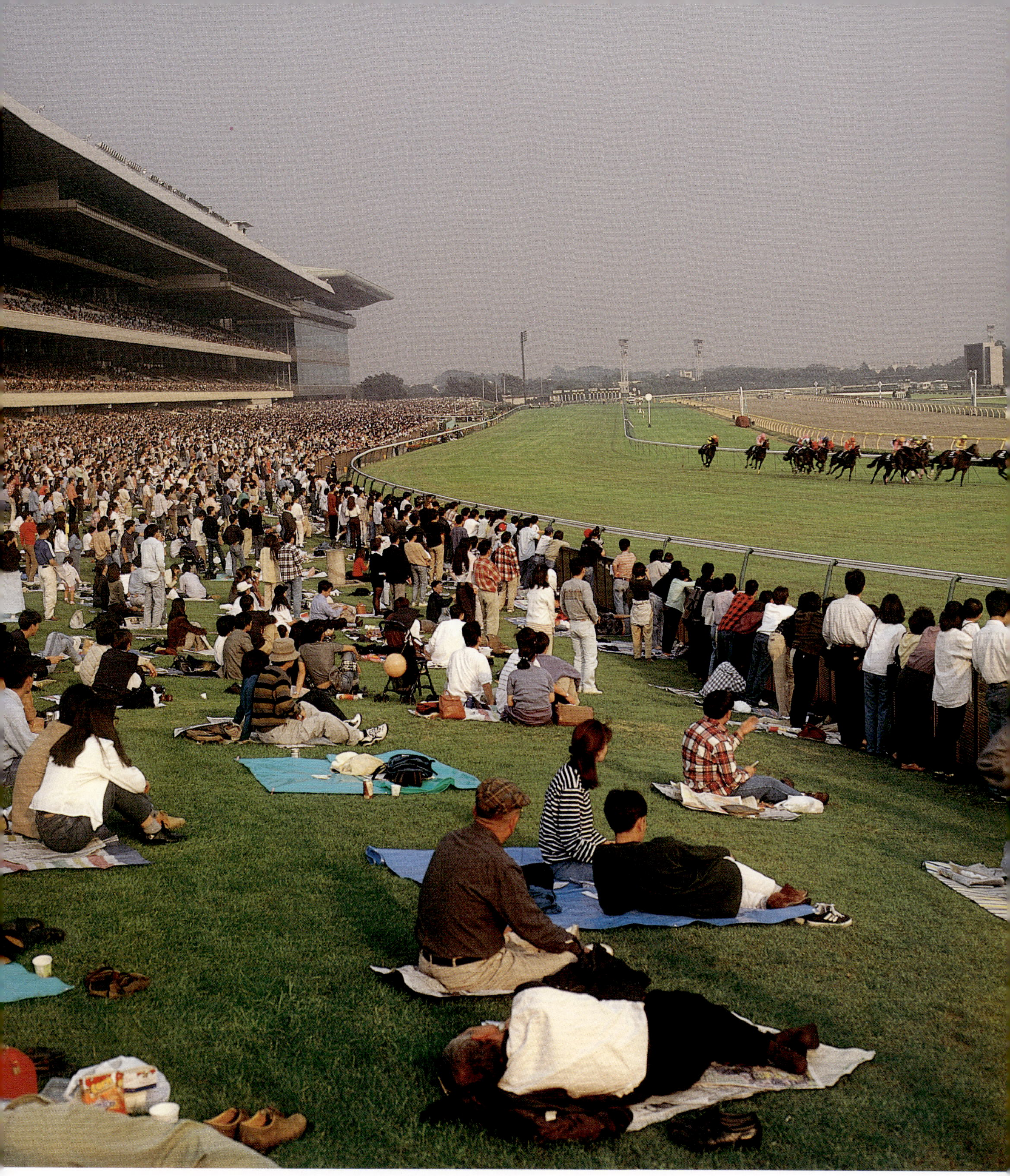

The Tokyo Racecourse can accommodate 200,000 spectators. On weekends and holidays, the crowd includes many couples and families. Gambling has become a common pastime in Japan.

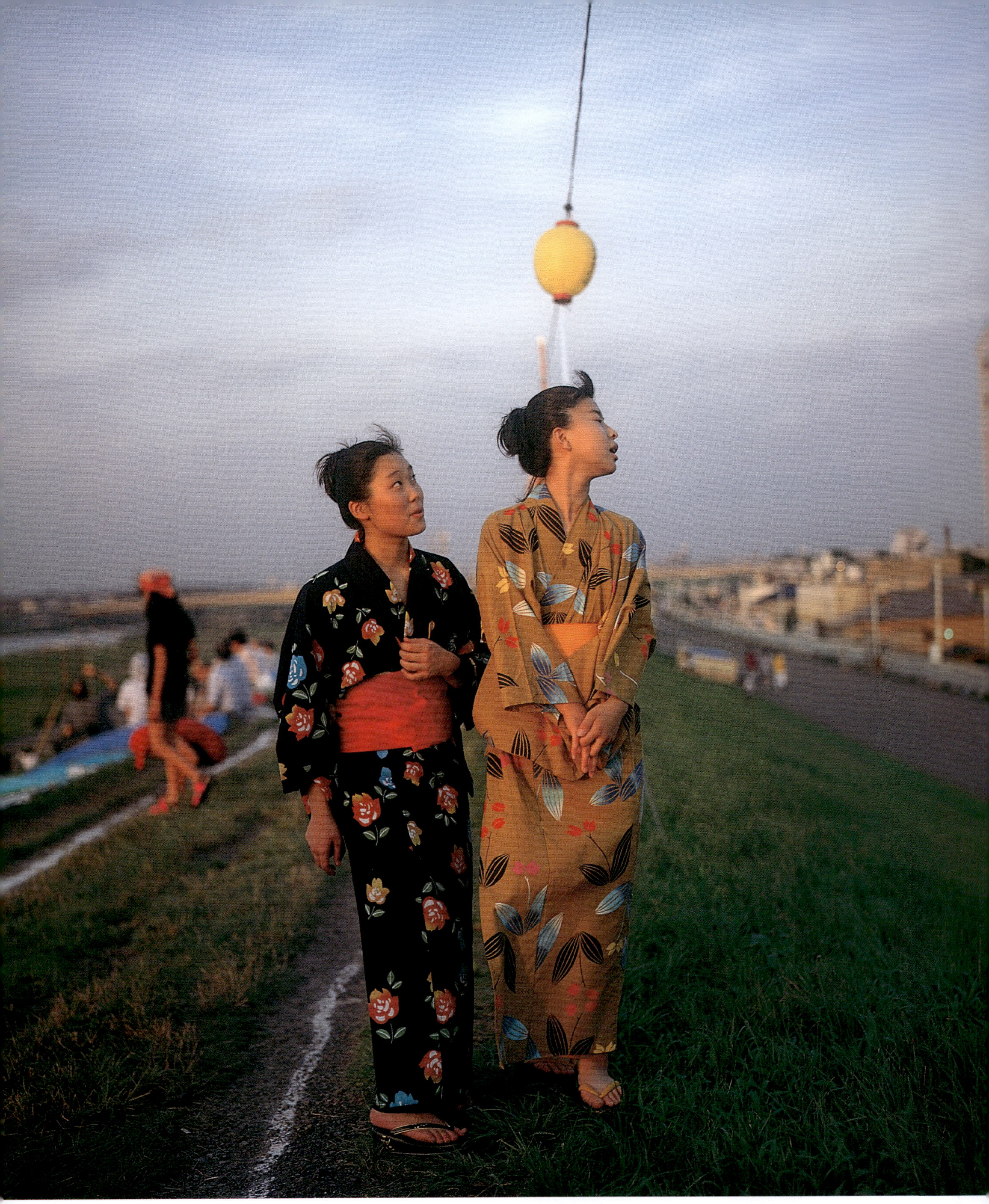

In summer, the Japanese landscape is dotted with groups of people who gather to view fireworks and to light sparklers. Women often don lightweight cotton kimonos (*yukata*) for the occasion.

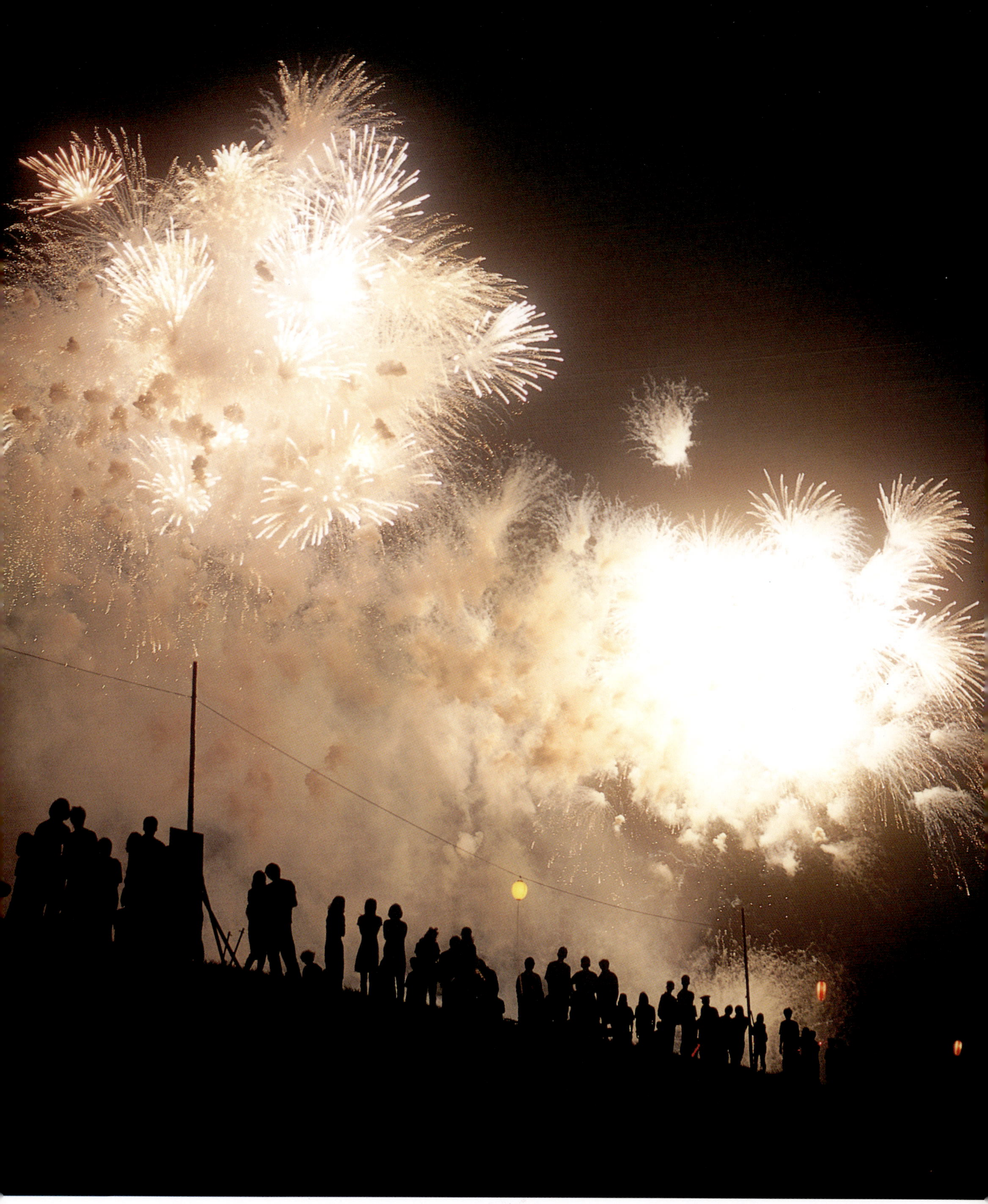

The silhouettes of spectators stand out against a night sky ablaze with fireworks that are made all the more beautiful by their transience. This photograph was taken along the Arakawa river.

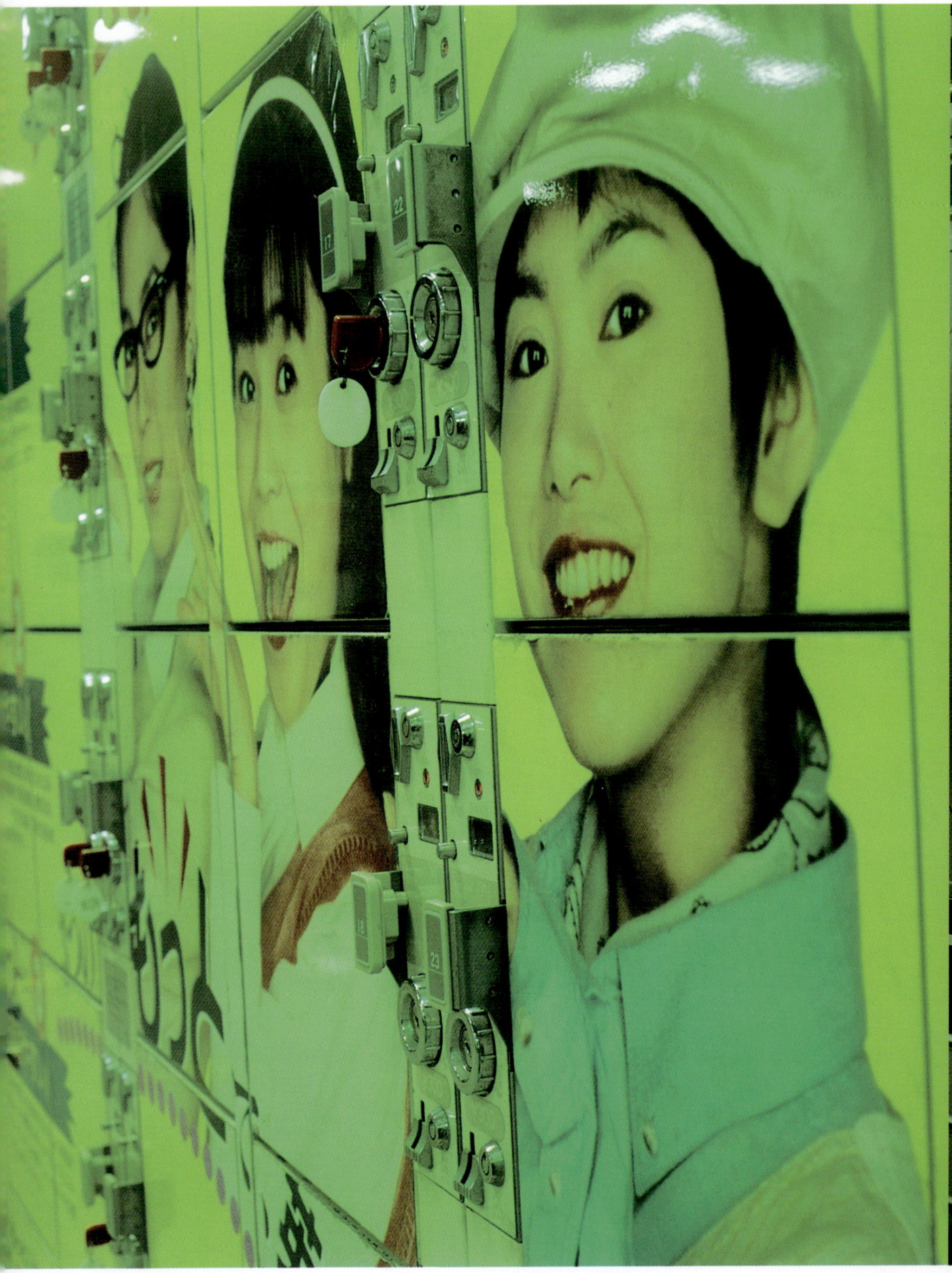

Coin-operated lockers at a train station. Serving a two-fold purpose, the smiling faces in this advertisement boast, "You, too, can learn to speak English like us!"

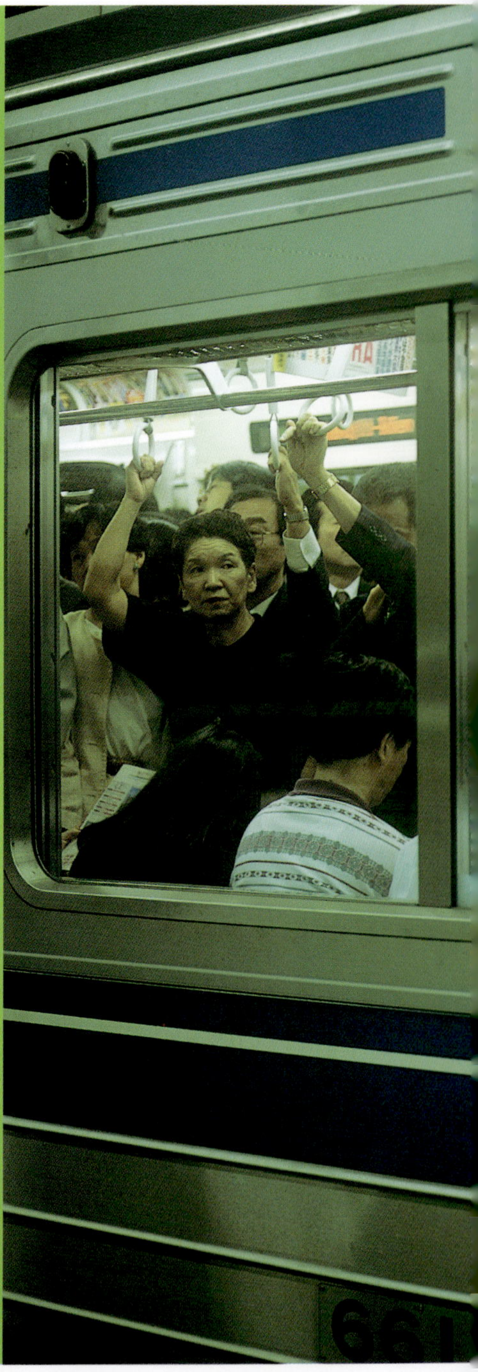

A train packed with commuters. The morning and evening rush hours find passengers on every train line jammed in like sardines. It's not unusual to have to endure an hour-long commute under these conditions.

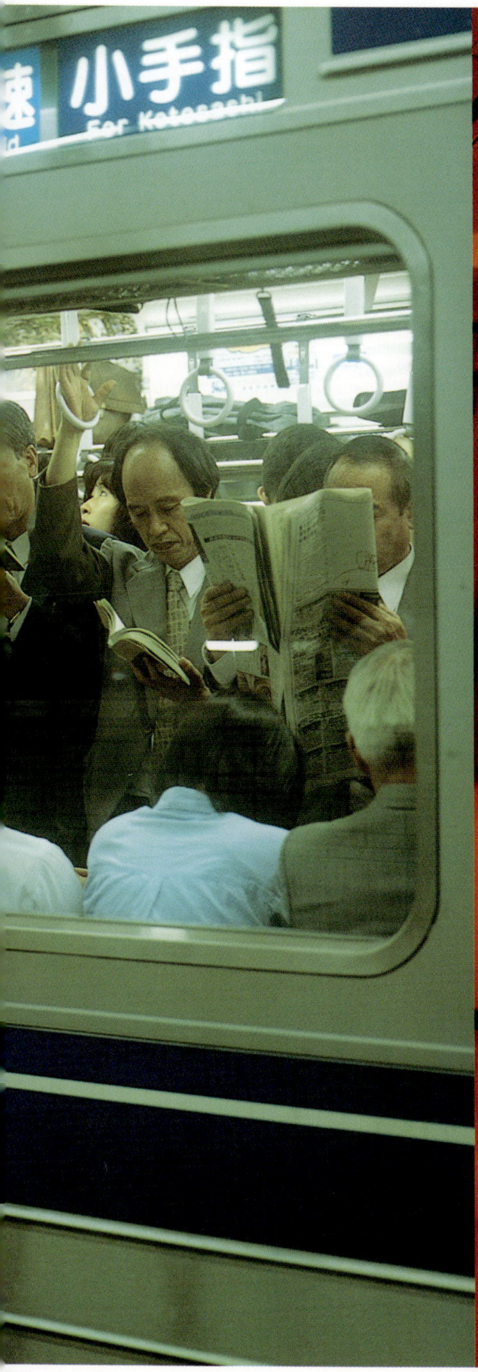


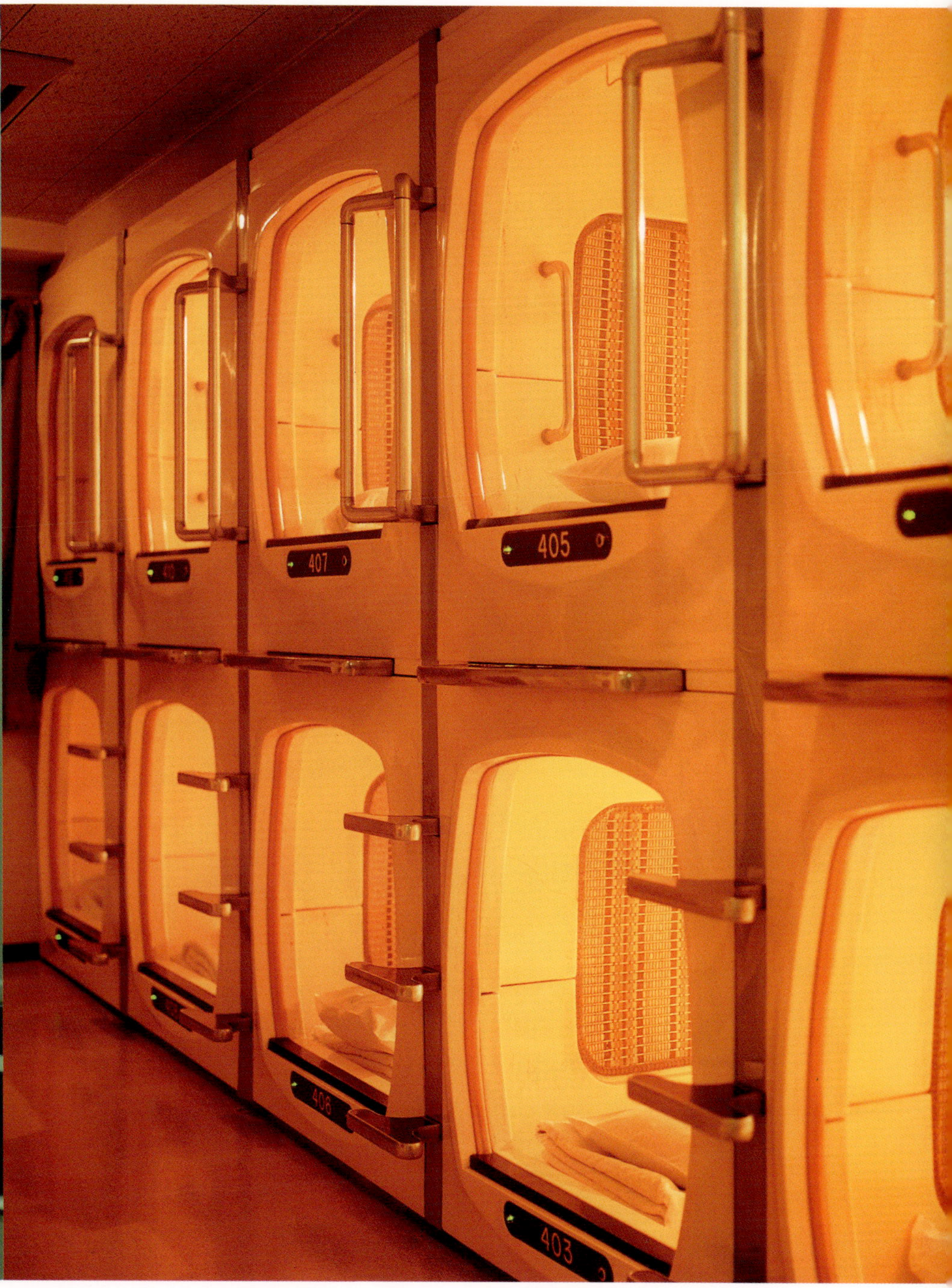


A capsule hotel. Here, a space just big enough for one person to lie down in also contains a TV and a radio. For late-working (or late-drinking) businessmen who have missed the final train of the evening, this is the last stop.

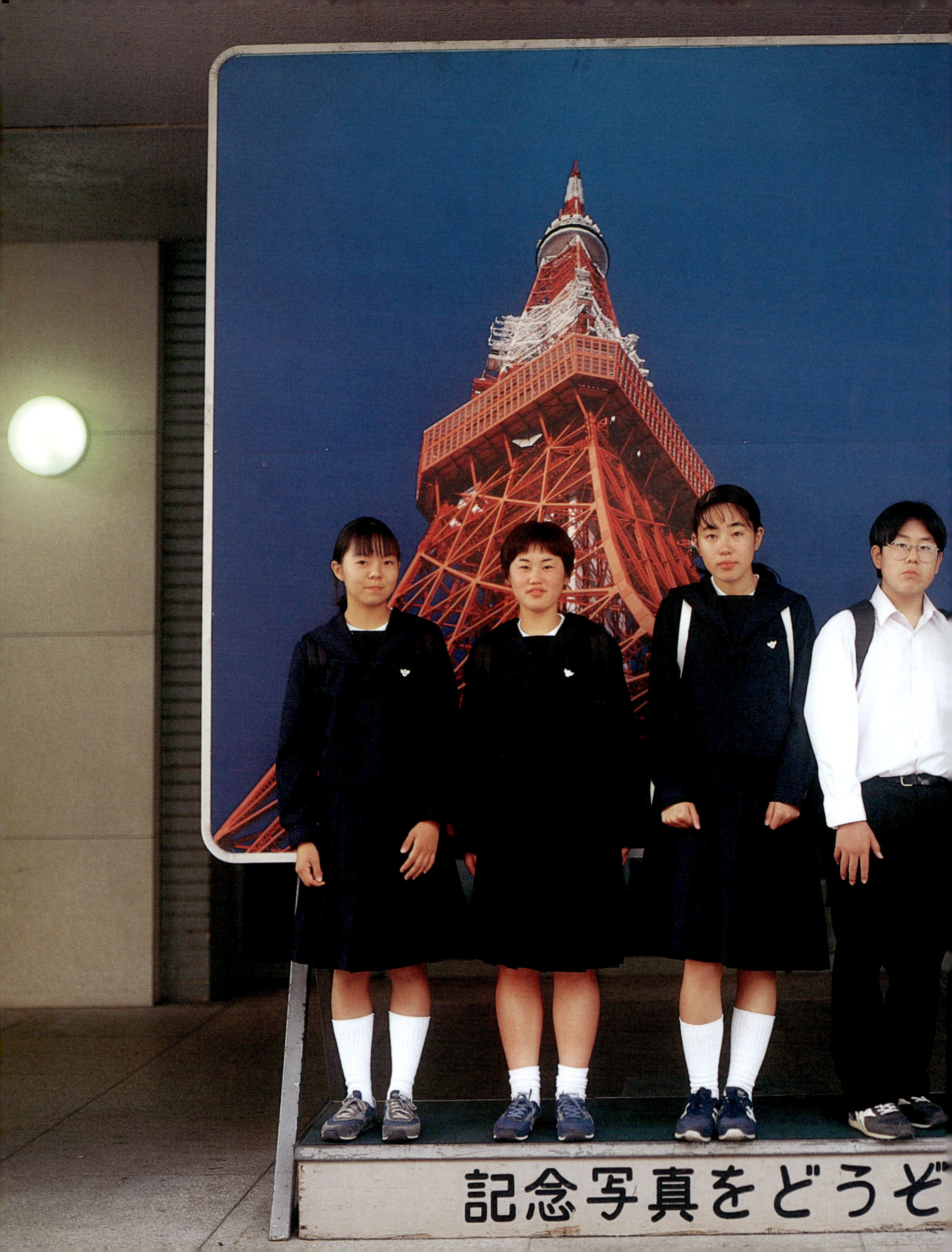
記念写真をどうぞ

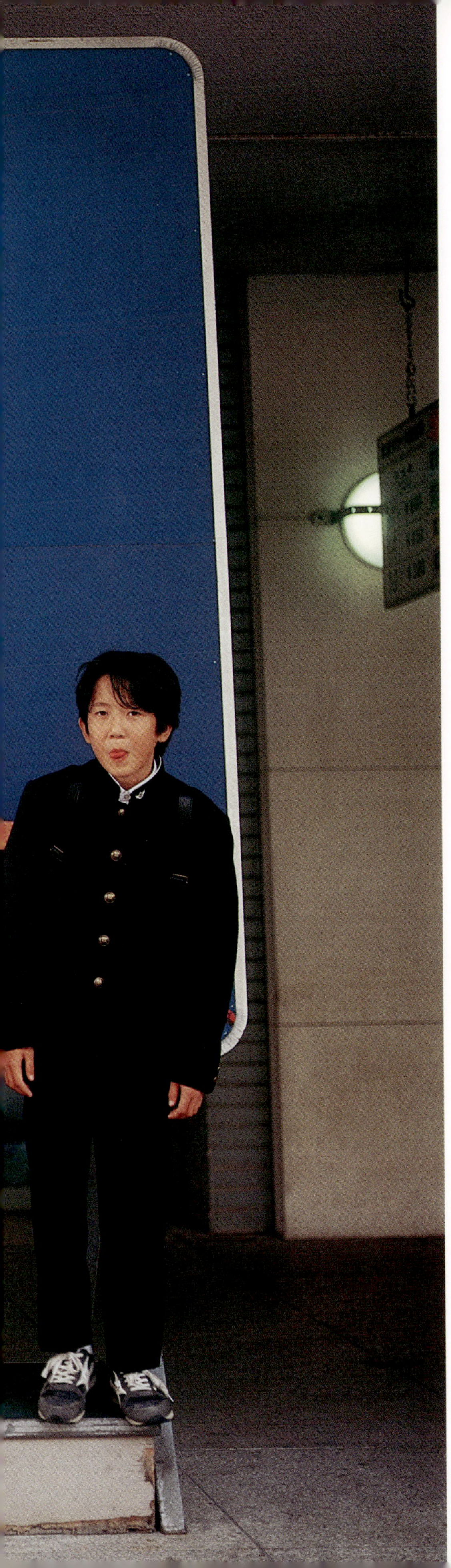

Standing 333 meters high, Tokyo Tower is a city landmark. Built in 1958, the tower has been overshadowed to some degree by the profusion of high-rise buildings that have sprung up throughout the city. But even now, a visit to the tower symbolizes the grand tour of Tokyo for people like these students, who have traveled from the provinces to sightsee.

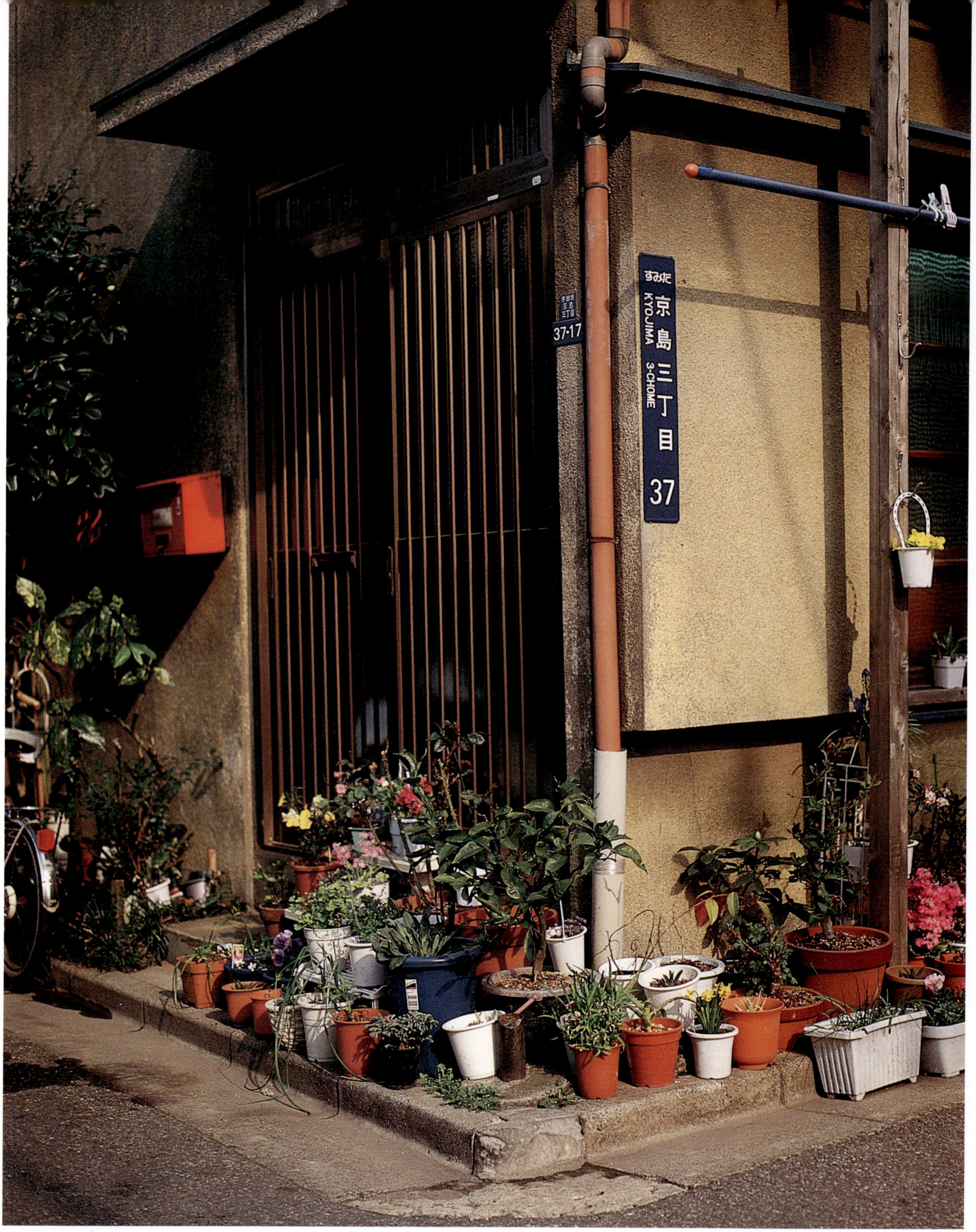


There is something about the alleys of *shitamachi*, the traditional commercial districts in the eastern part of Tokyo, that soothe the spirit. By covering their tiny lots with potted plants, residents of houses like this one valiantly transform even the most minute spaces into gardens.

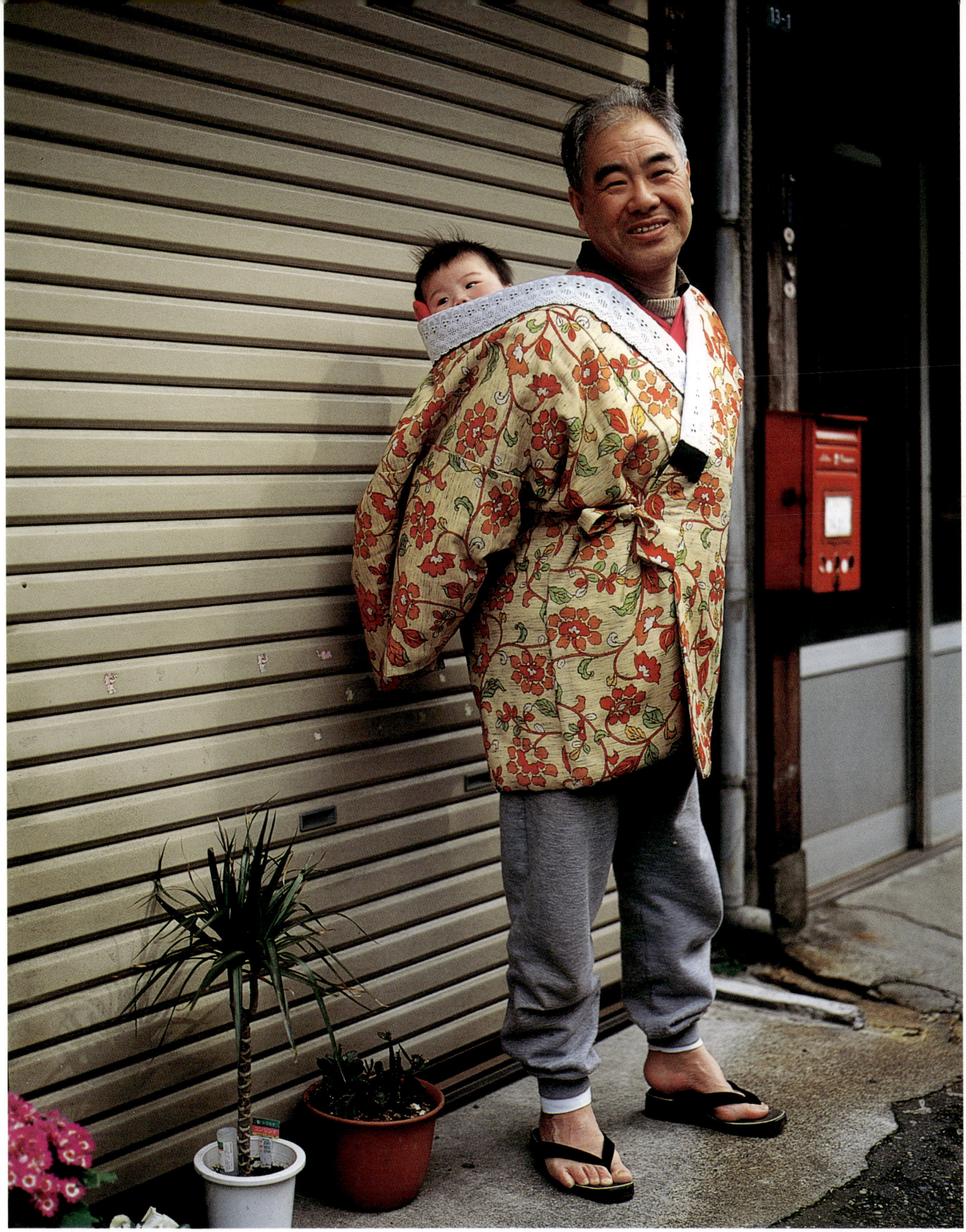

For this child, Grandpa's back is the ultimate cradle. The man in this photograph is wearing a *nenneko*, a short coat designed with extra room in the back for carrying children. In the past, *nenneko* were often worn by people taking care of young children, but these coats are rarely seen anymore.

Kabukicho, the famous tenderloin district located in eastern Shinjuku, is a place that never sleeps.
Signs for clubs and restaurants tower overhead like neon pagodas.

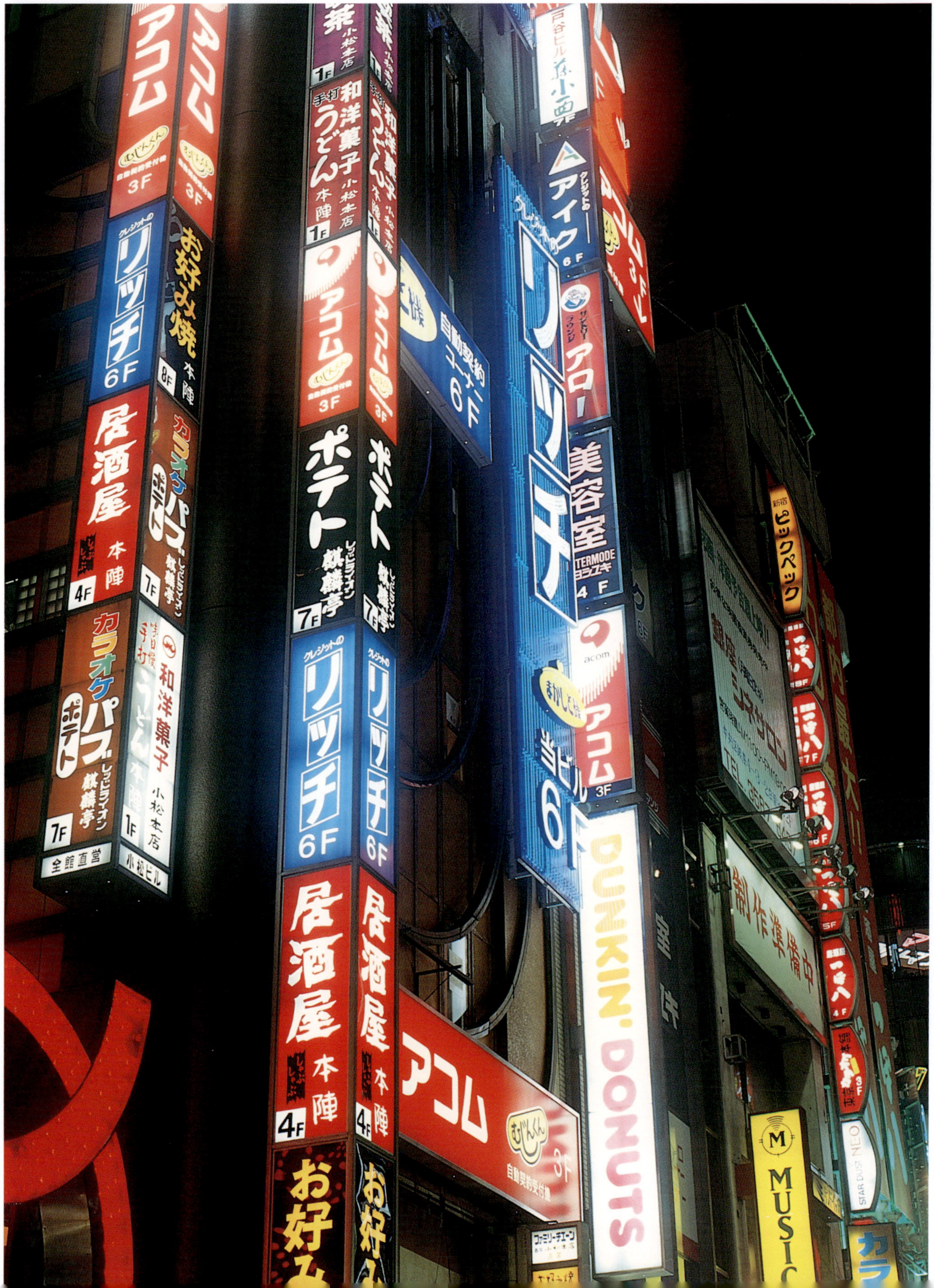

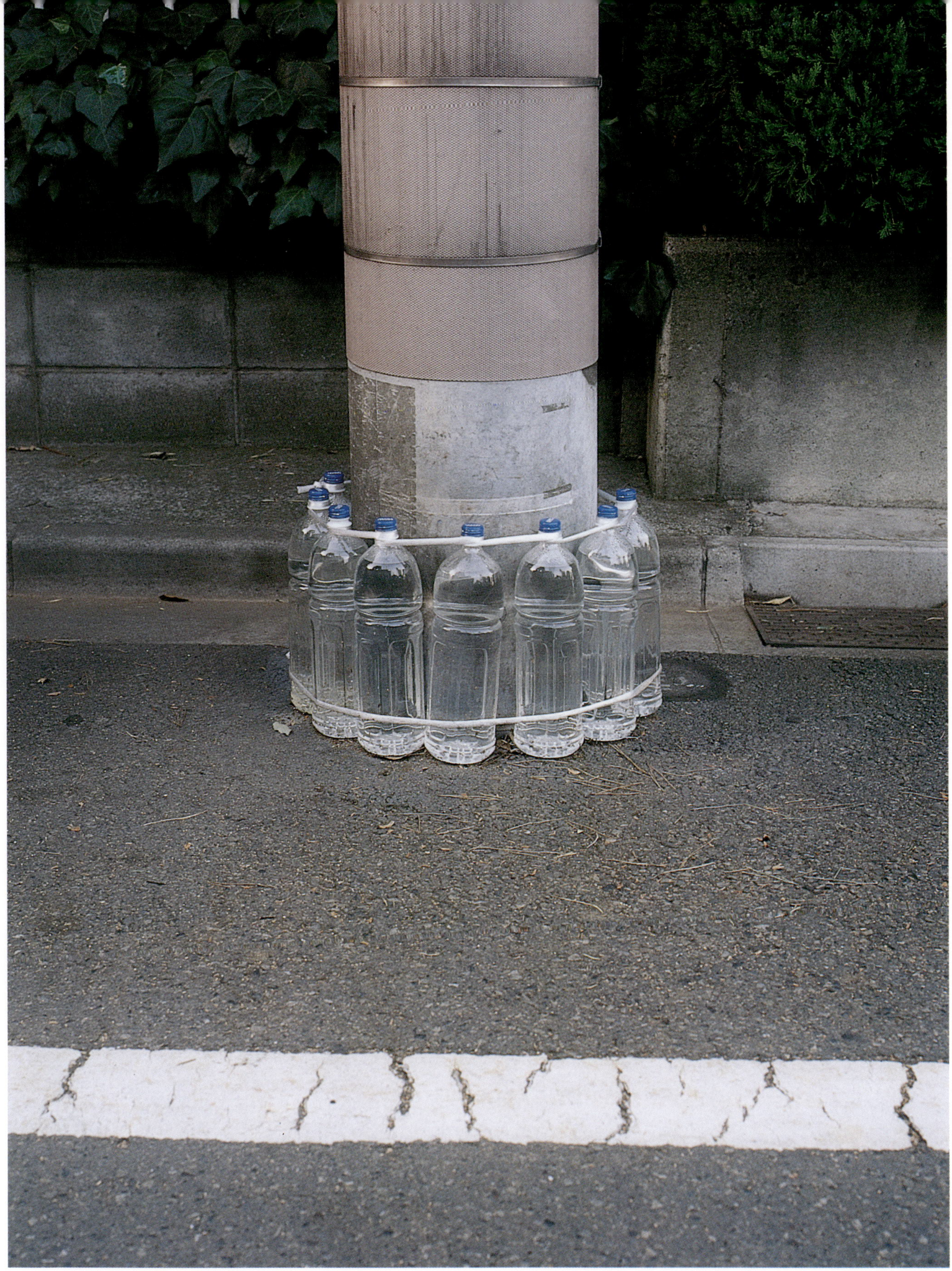

The water-filled plastic bottles encircling this utility pole are intended to frighten away dogs or cats who might otherwise urinate or defecate there. Somewhere along the line, this use of bottles to repel animals became widespread—though no one knows how effective it really is.

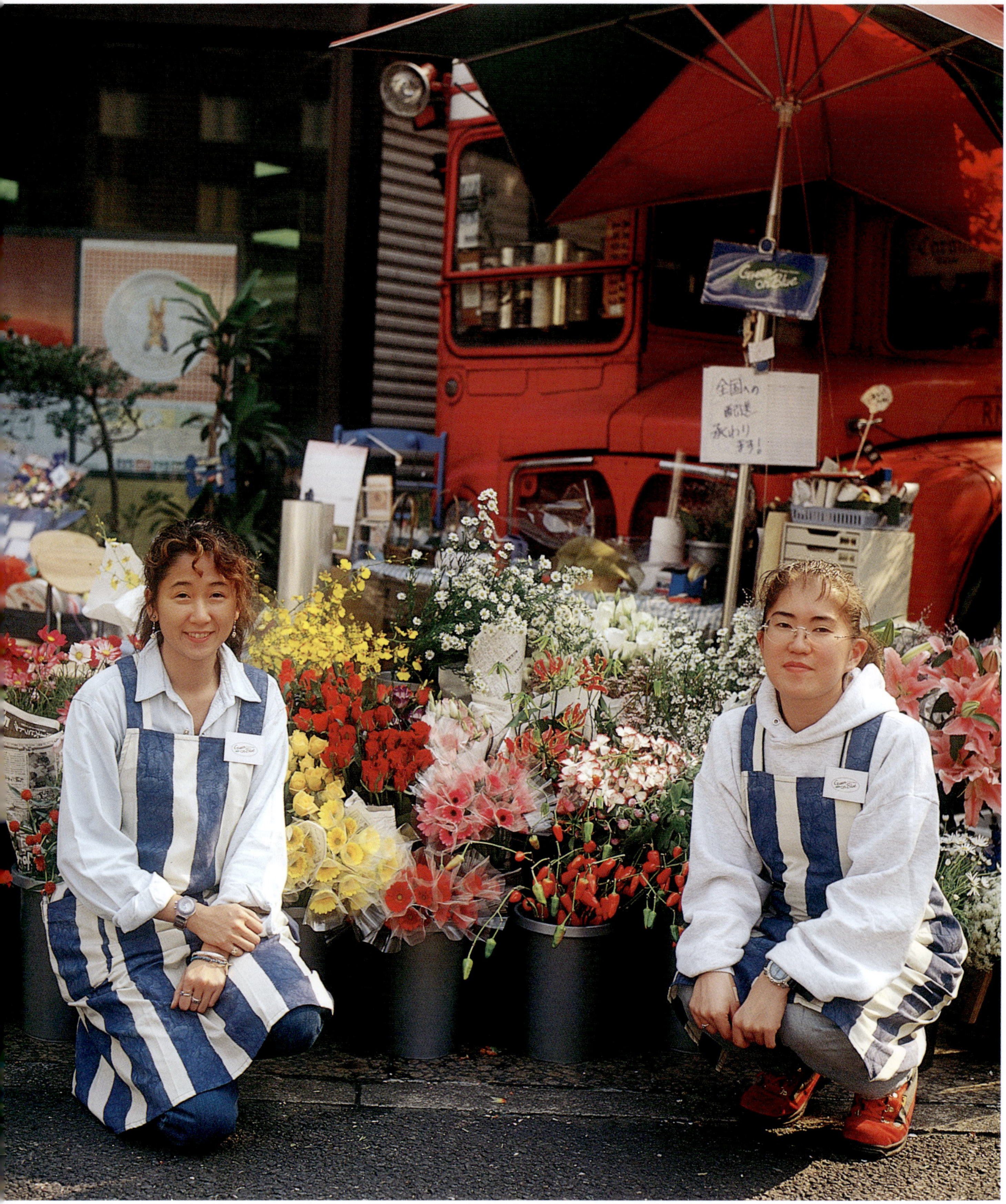

This florist shop is located in the heart of a business district. As often as not, the customers are businessmen buying flowers for a co-worker's farewell party.

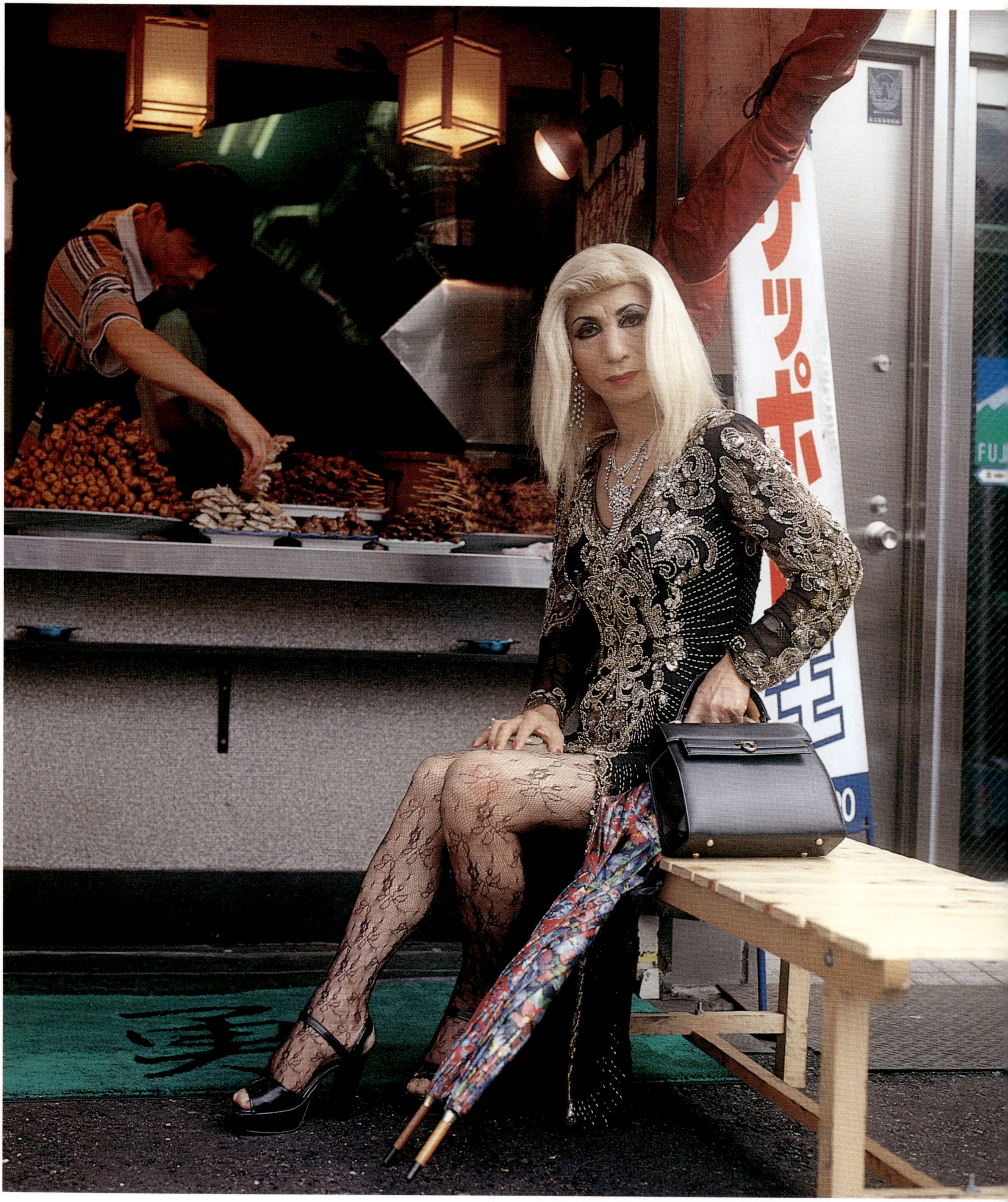

Even Tokyo has its drag queens.

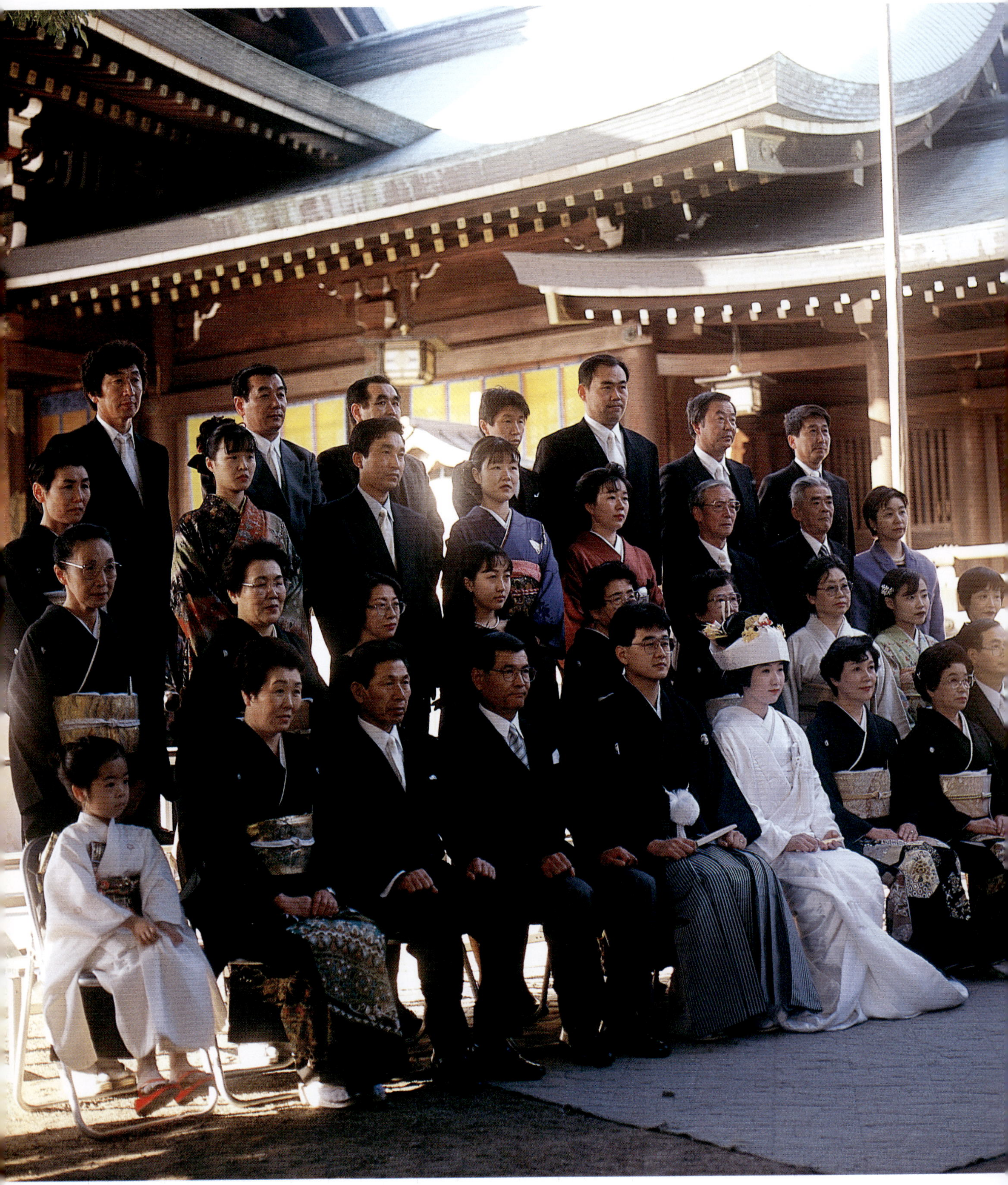

This wedding ceremony is taking place at a shrine—a solemn setting for a couple starting out their married life. Here, relatives of the bride and groom have assembled for the customary family photograph.

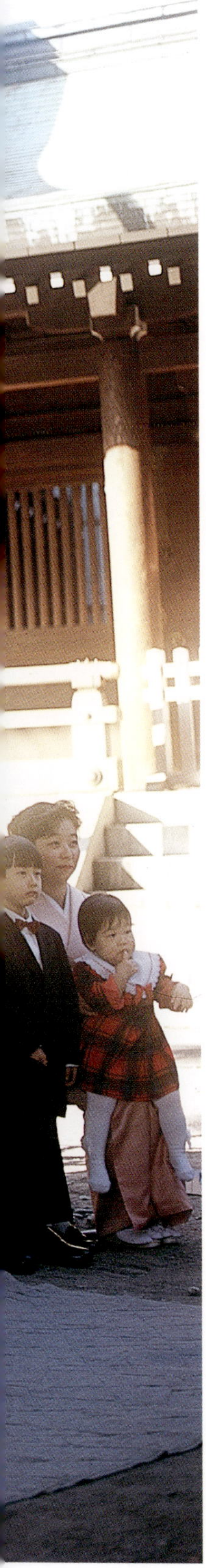

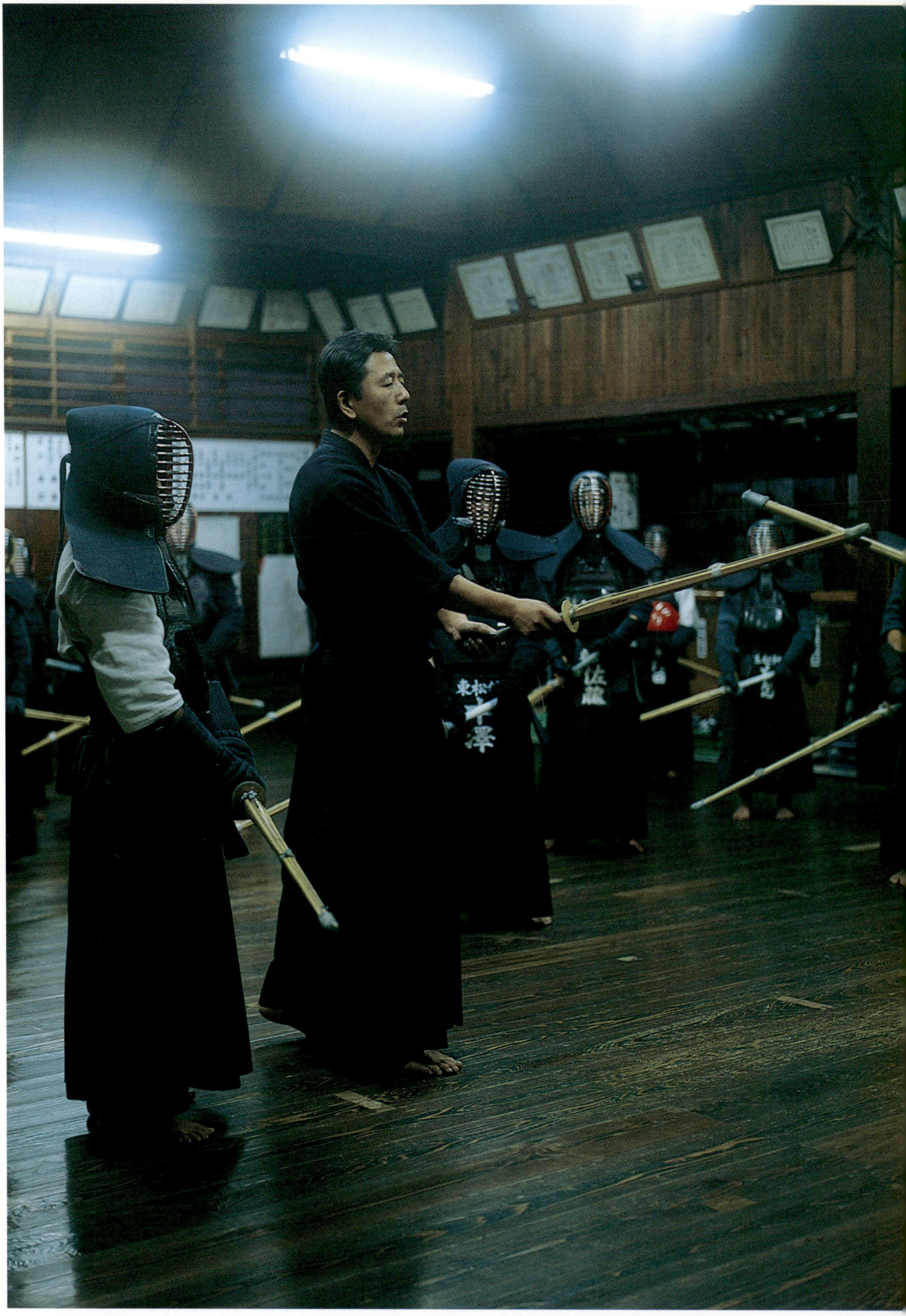

Practicing Japanese fencing, known as *kendō*. *Kendō* and other traditional Japanese martial arts live on today as popular sports.

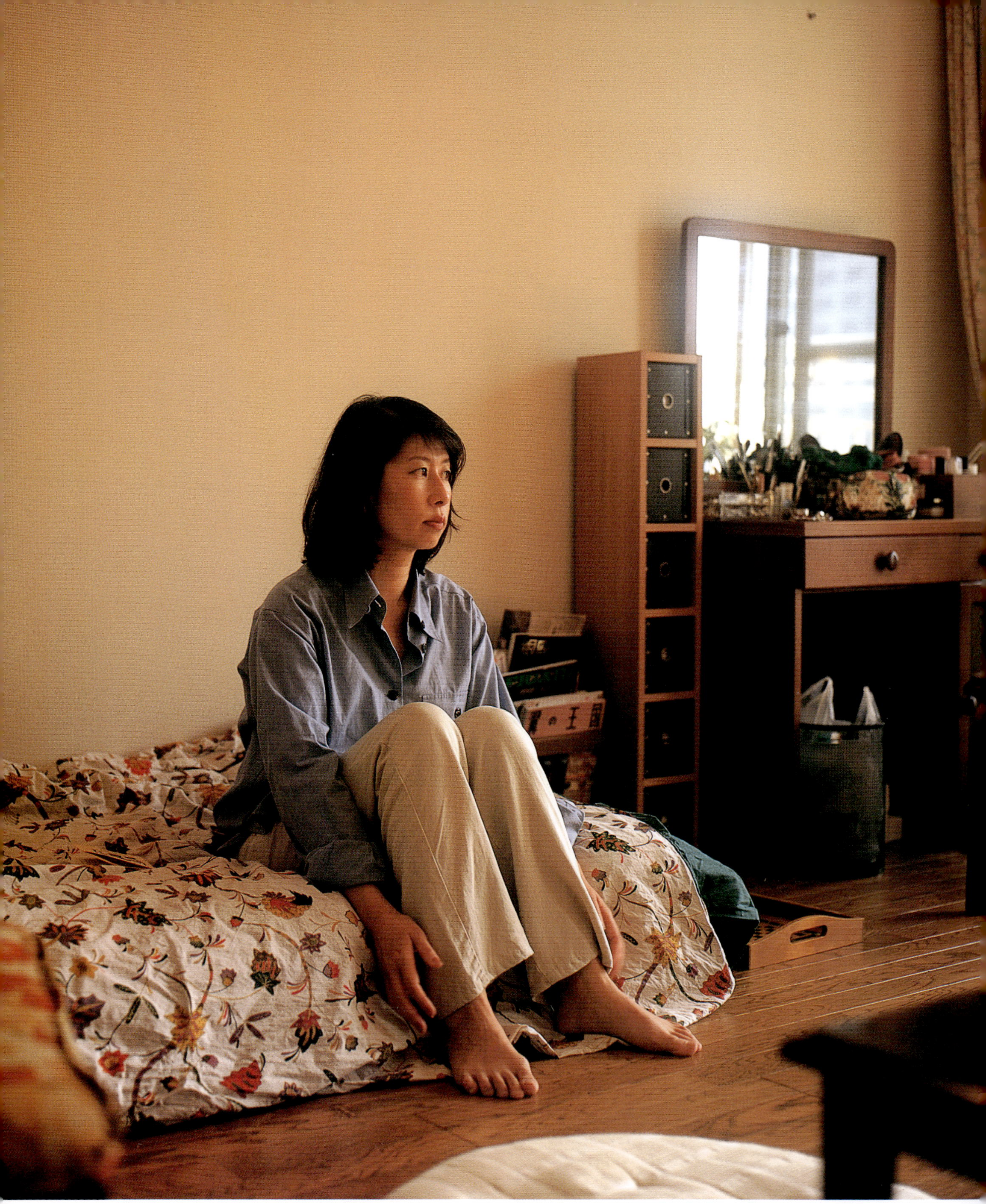

Human beings are building solitary nests in high places these days. This woman lives alone in an apartment on the 16th floor. She is one of the estimated 1.7 million Tokyoites who live alone.

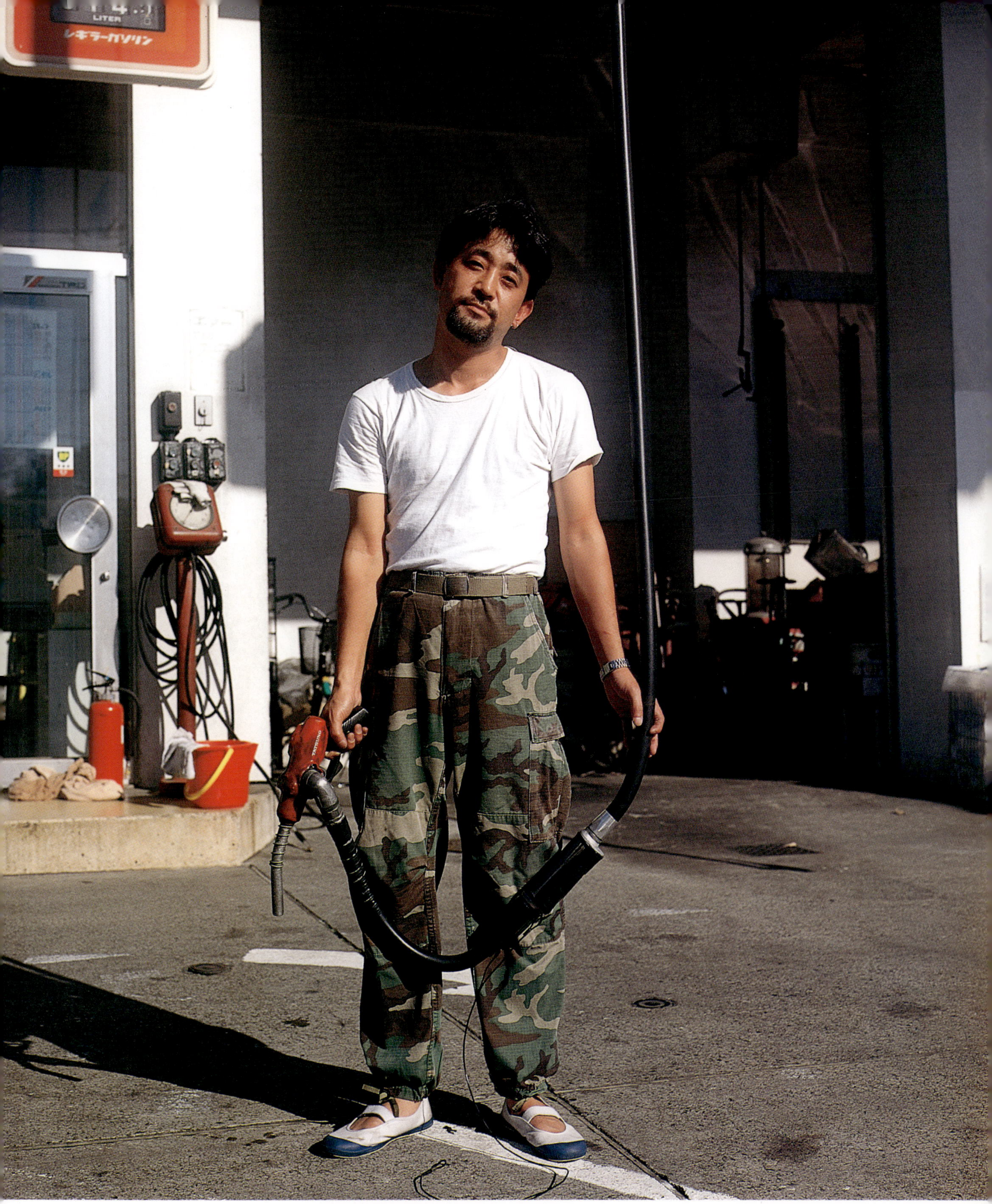


Gas-station attendant is but a temporary guise for this young man, who is a musician by trade. "Three hours ago," he quips, "I started to think about living a serious life."

This street vendor sells used appliances and other goods. In Japan's consumerist society, the offerings inevitably include many items that are nearly new. Thanks to this throwaway mentality, "recycle shops" like the one you see here will probably never have any trouble replenishing stock.

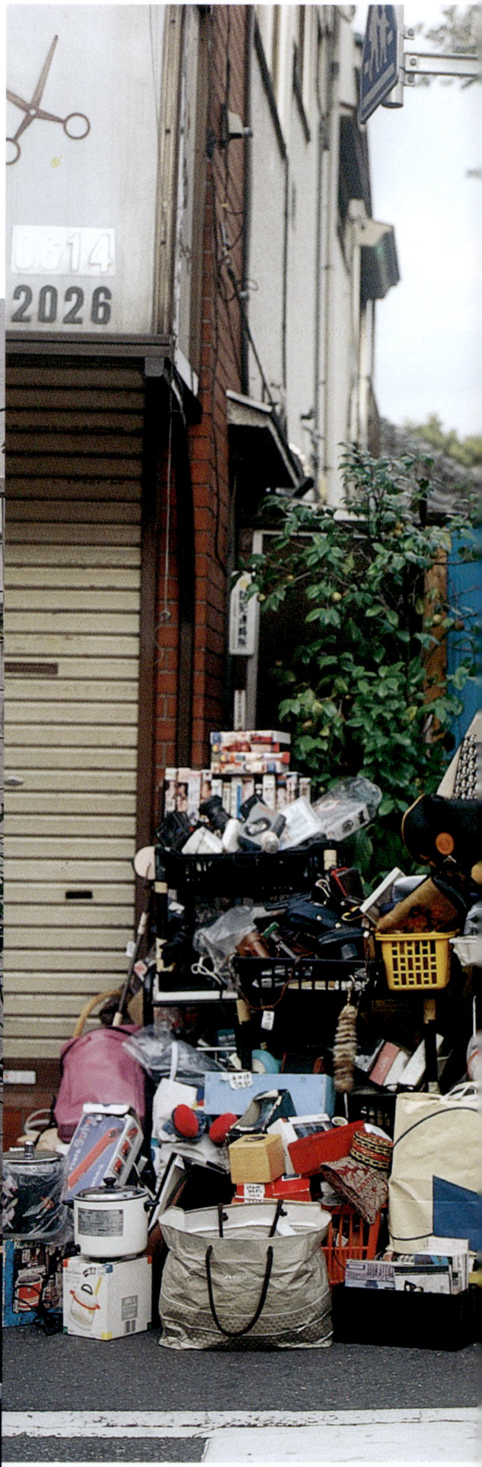


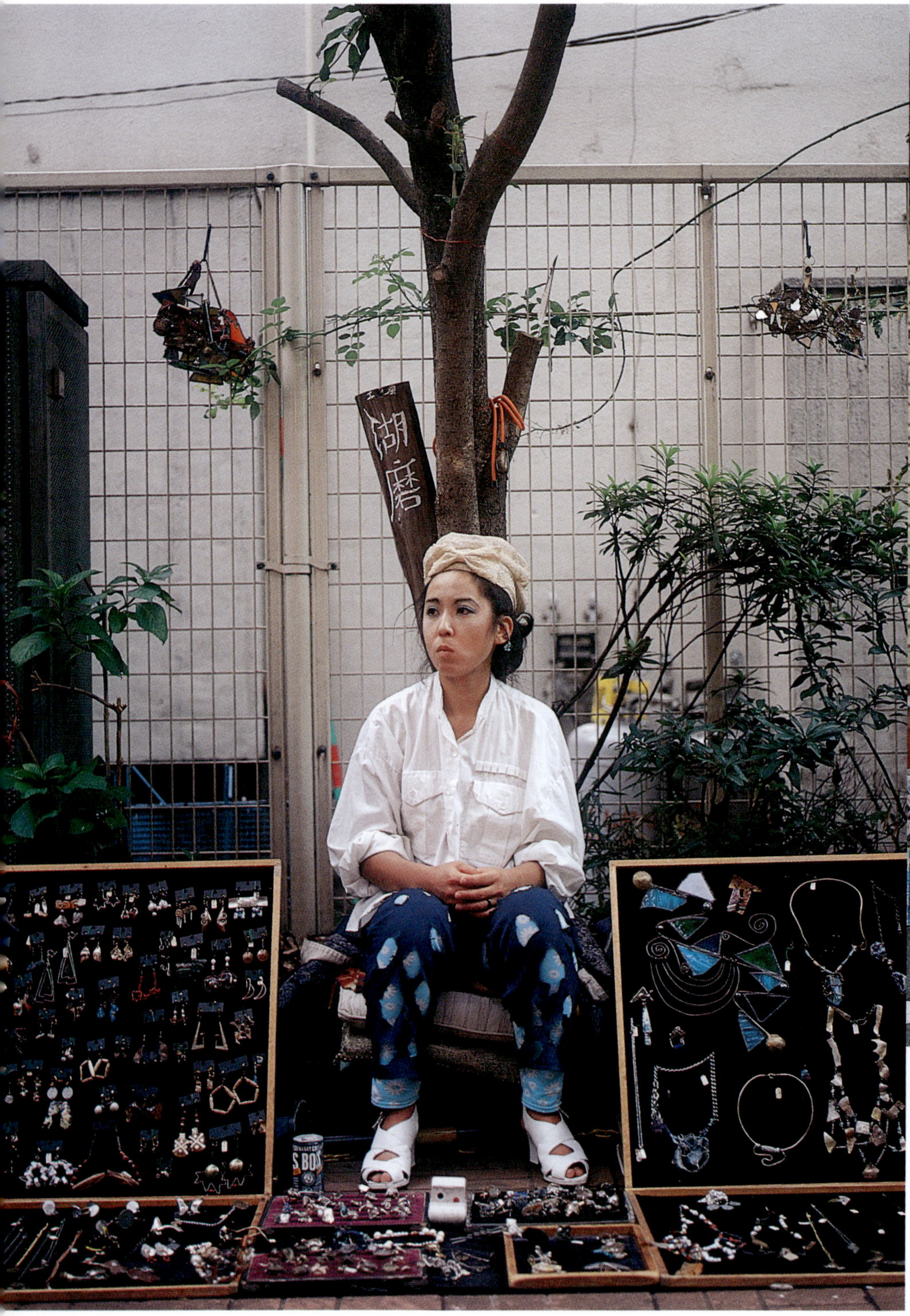


"I started out in this spot," says a jewelry vendor, "and I've been doing this for 15 years now."

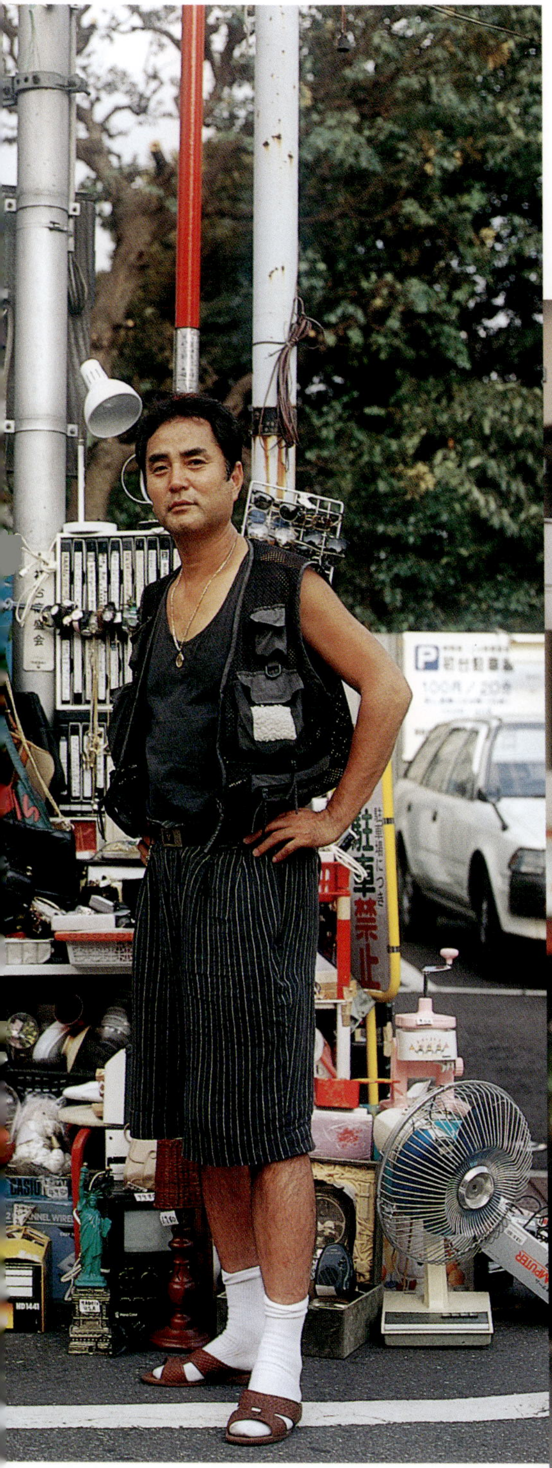

Dusk descends on this vending stall, where sunglasses are sold.
(Better grab a pair while you can still use them!)

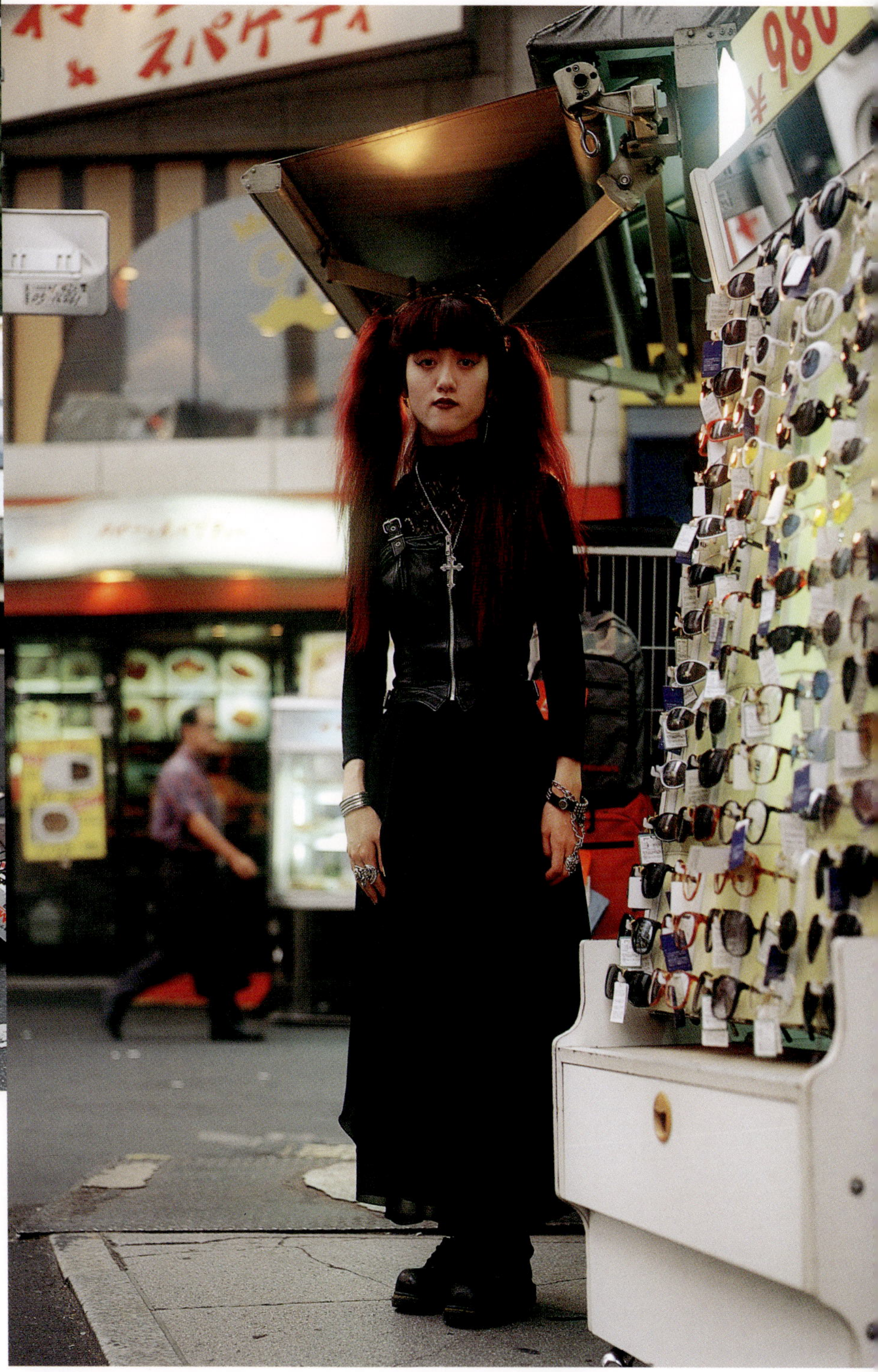

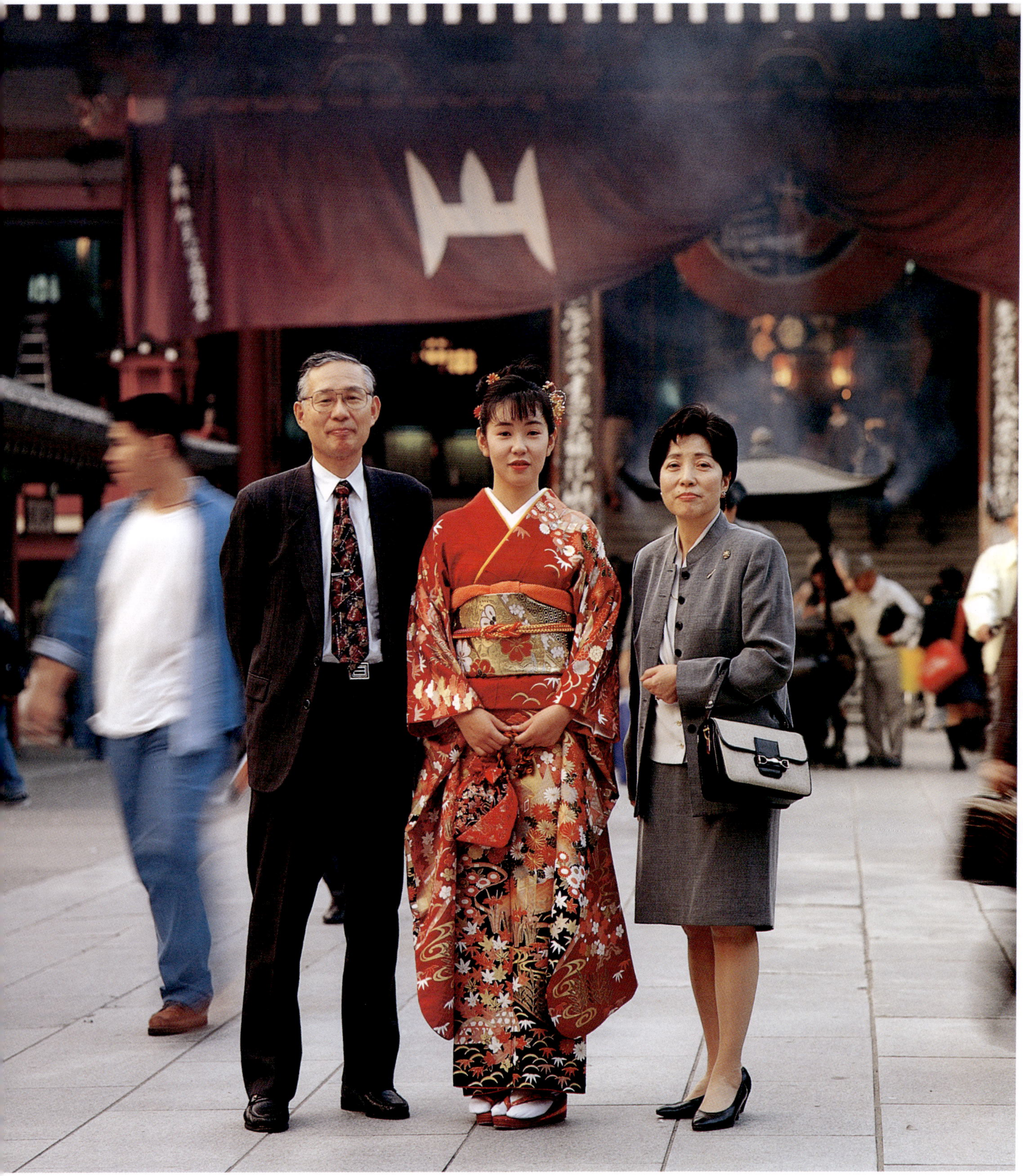

A family visit to Sensoji temple.

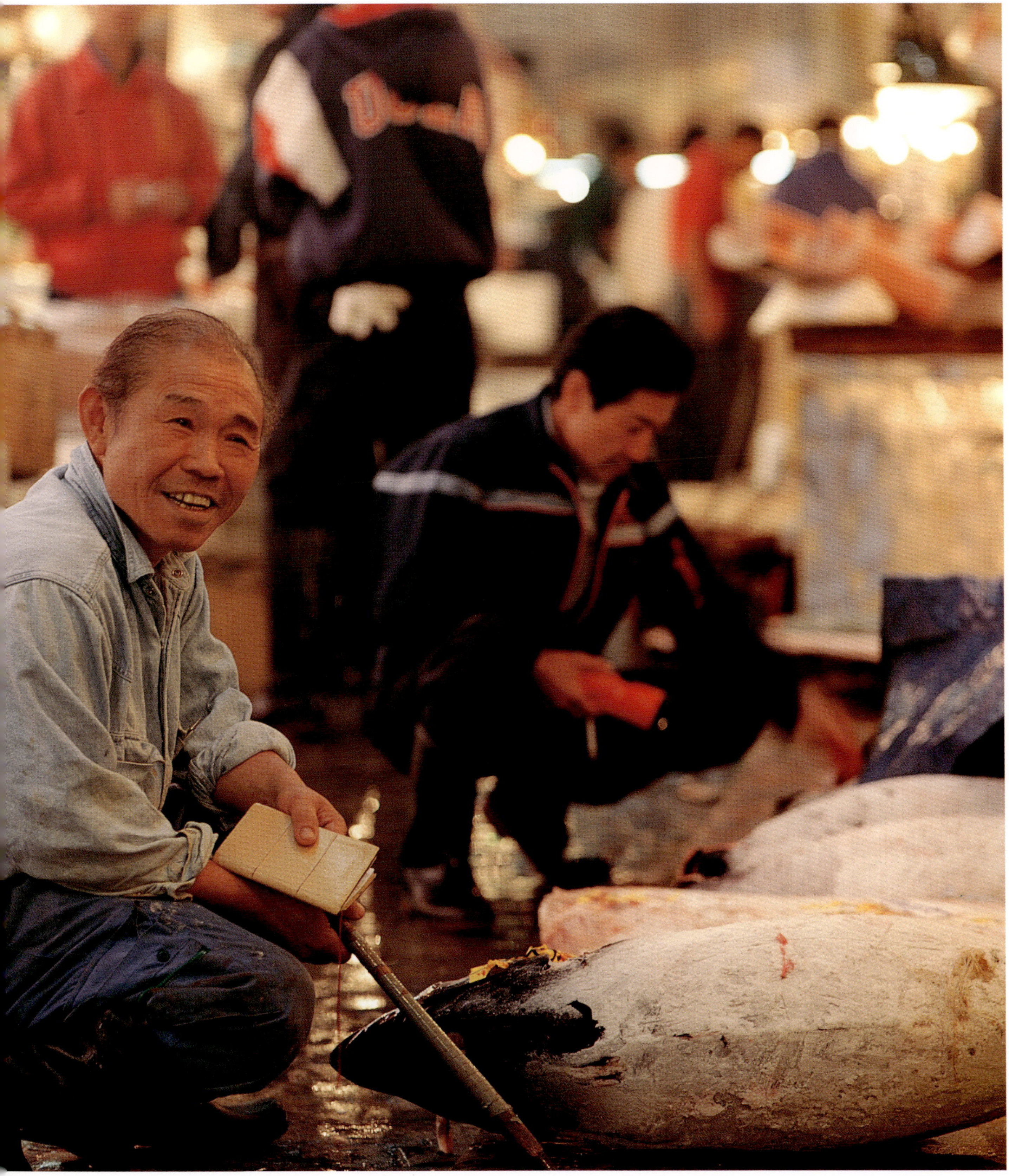

The central wholesale market at Tsukiji is famous for being the largest fish market in the world. Over 400 kinds of fish from 60 countries are sold. About 60,000 people work here, and their energetic shouts fill the air from before dawn until closing time.

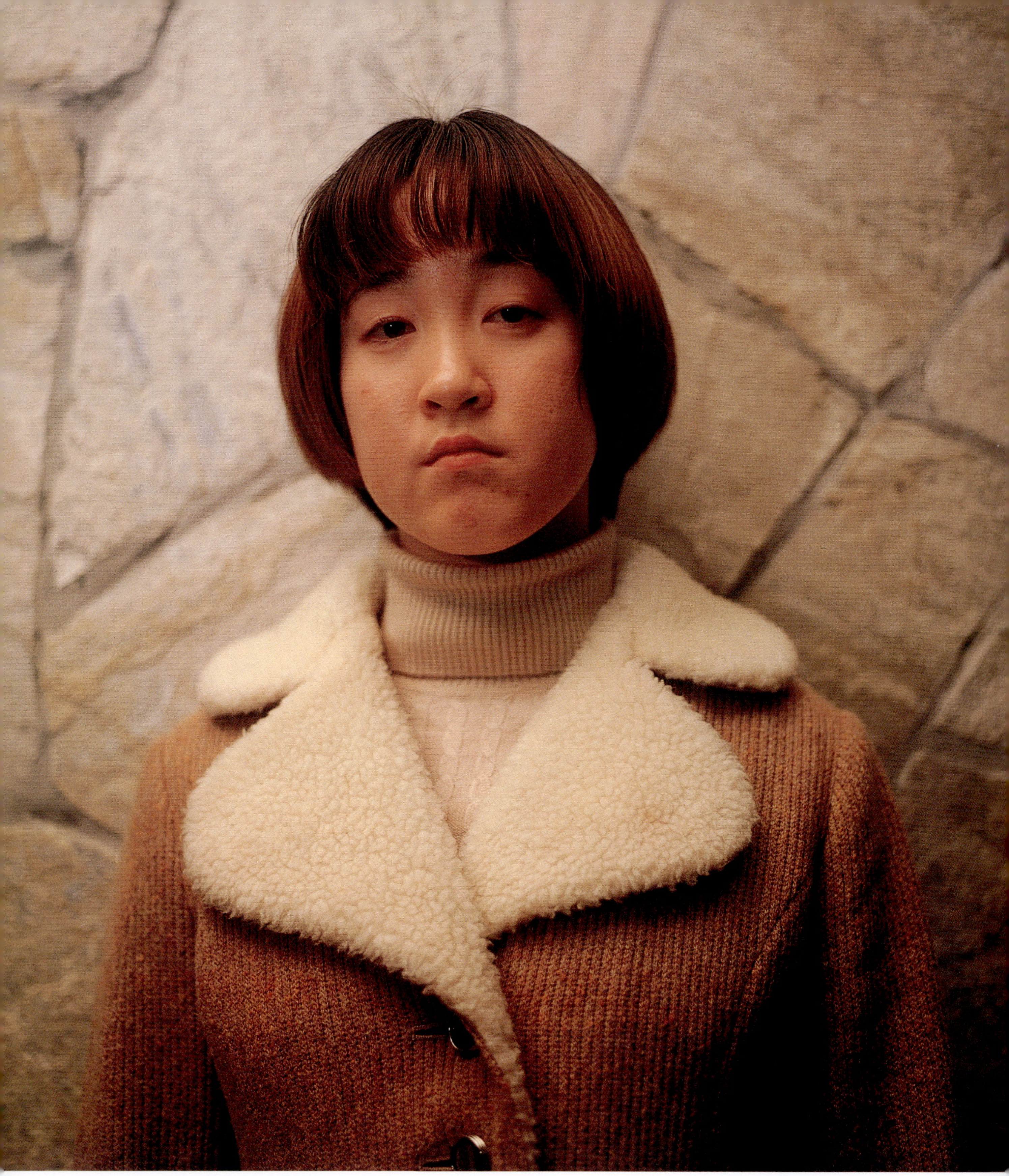

"You only go around once in life, so you've got to live it to the fullest," says this woman, a college student who is on her way to a concert. Today the youth of Japan indulge in leisure activities to a much greater extent than did their forebears; some say this trend represents a backlash against a society that has long devoted itself to the pursuit of efficiency and utility.

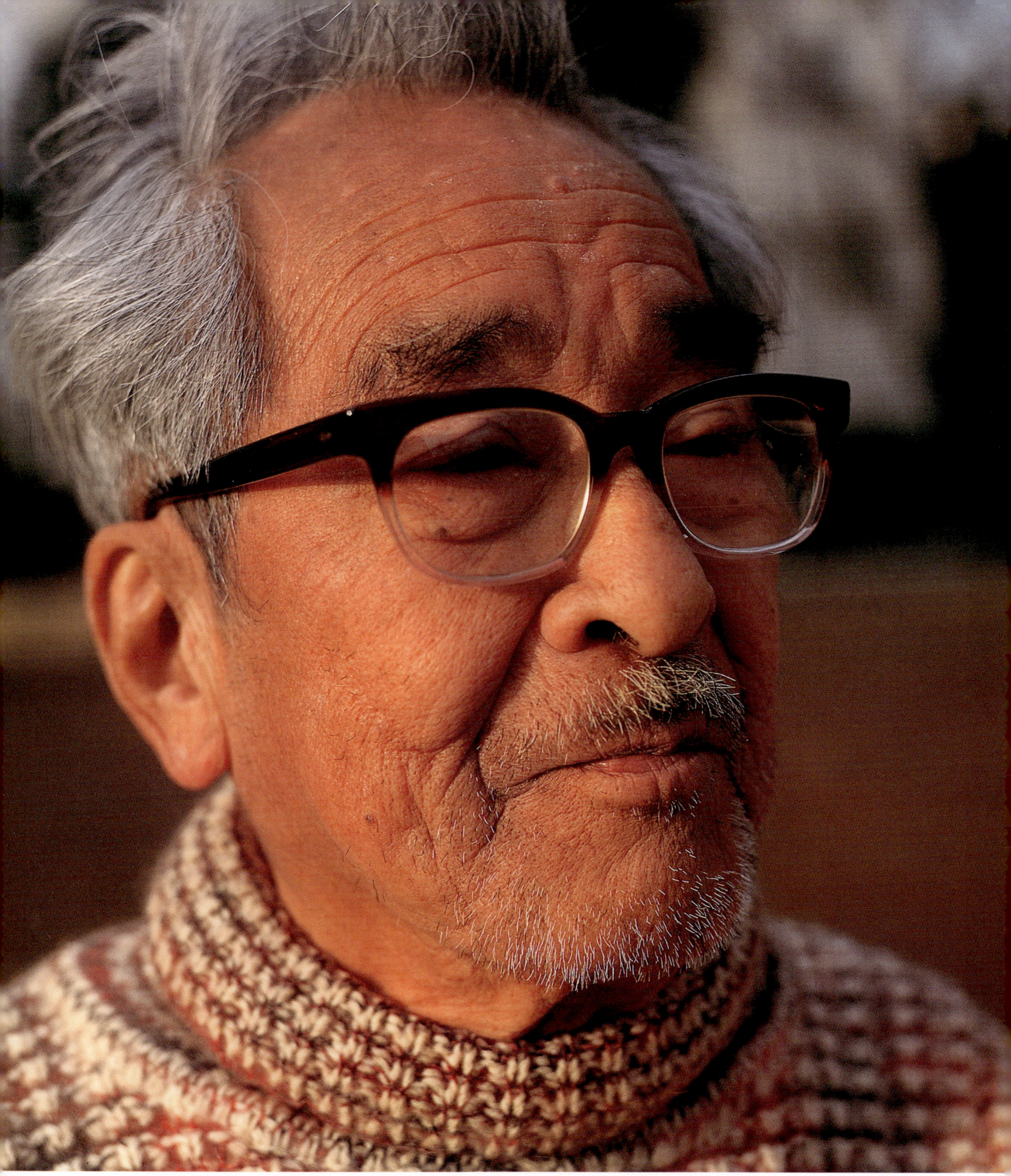

Sitting on a park bench at dusk, an elderly man comments on his life.
"I've done and seen a lot of different things."

This enigmatic statue sits on the sidewalk in front of a shop that sells *manjū* (cakes filled with sweet bean paste).

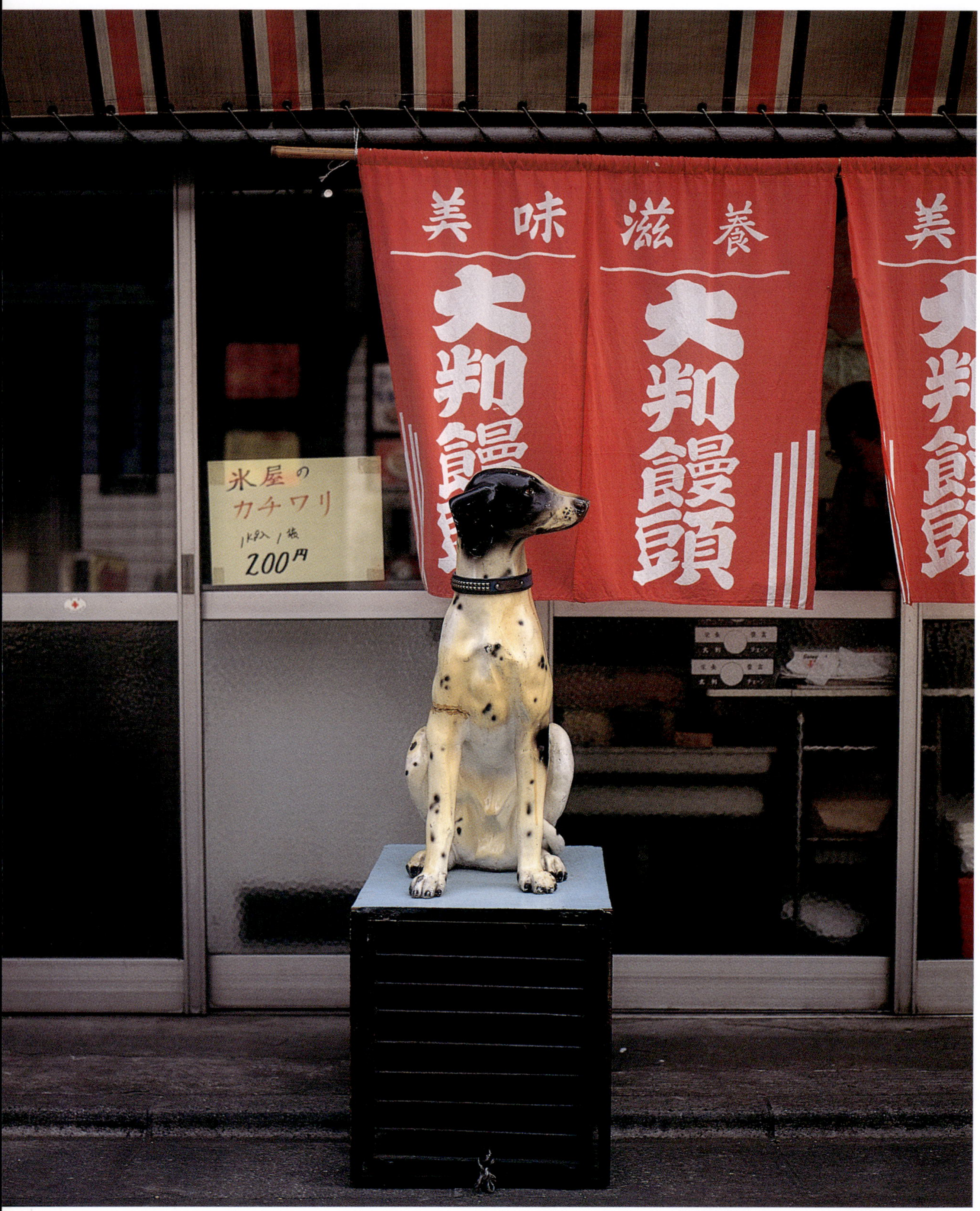


For people seeking eternal bliss in the hereafter, this Buddhist priest shares his advice. "If you want to experience heaven, live a peaceful, heavenly life in this world."

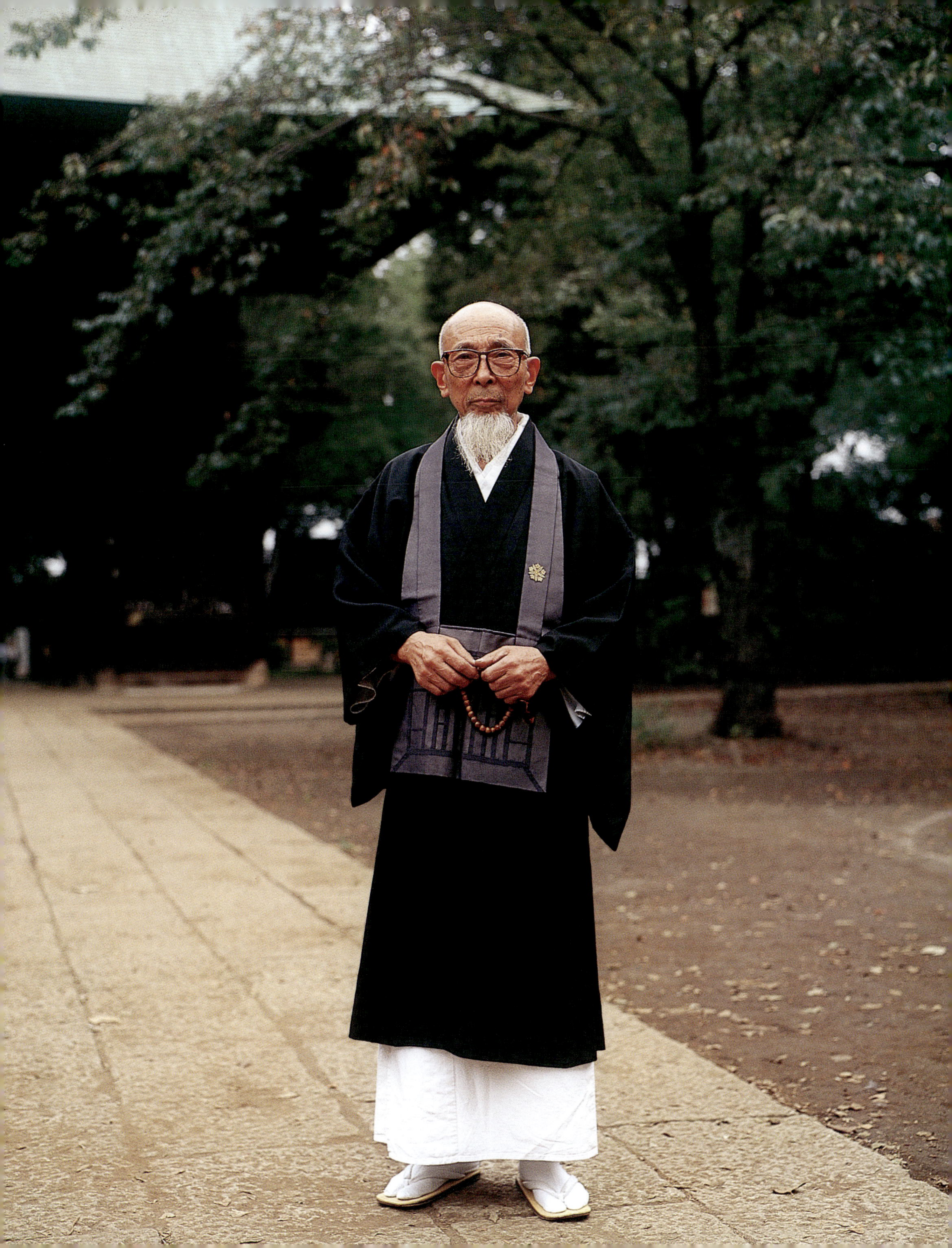

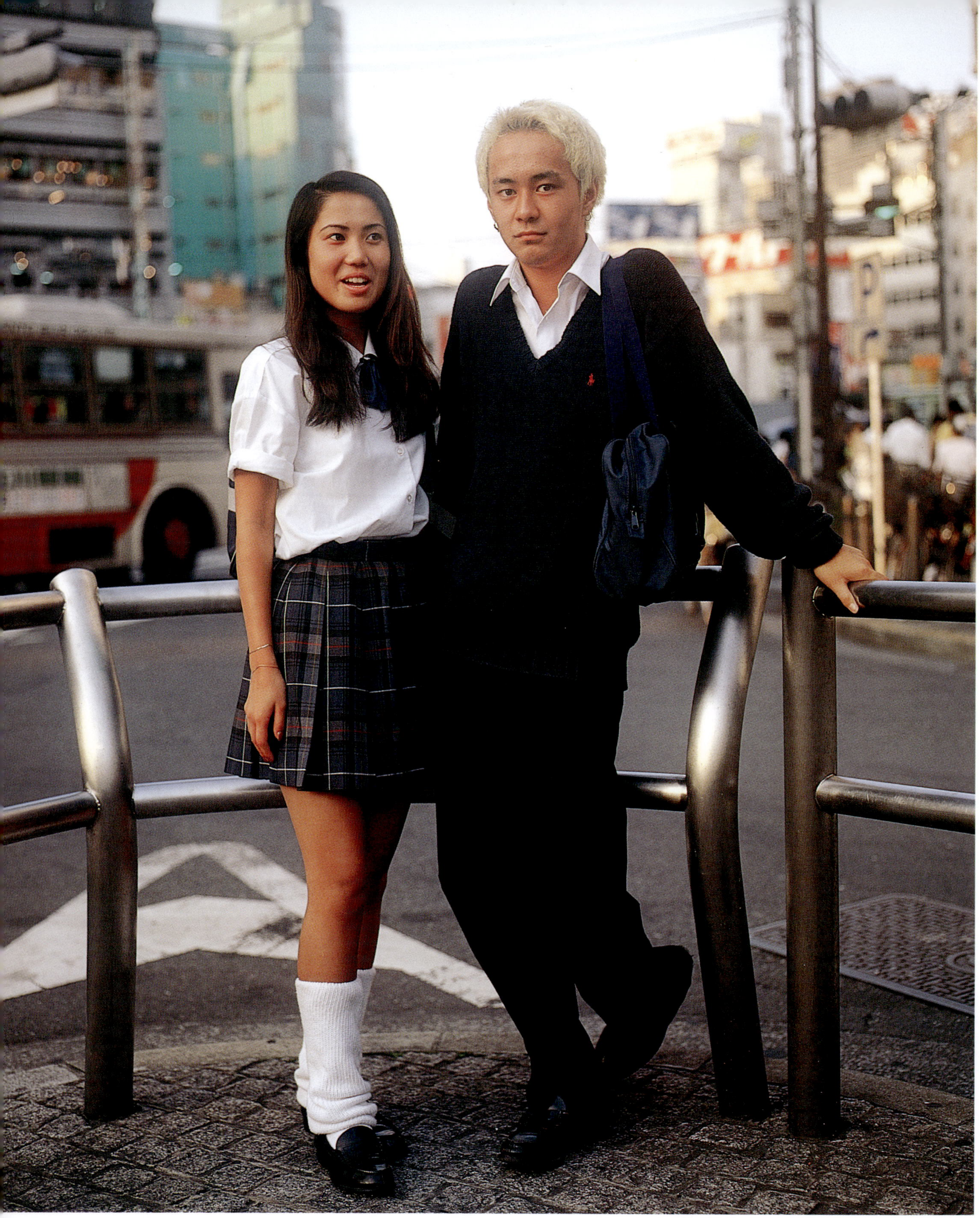

Dyed hair and baggy socks — common signs of teenage rebellion.

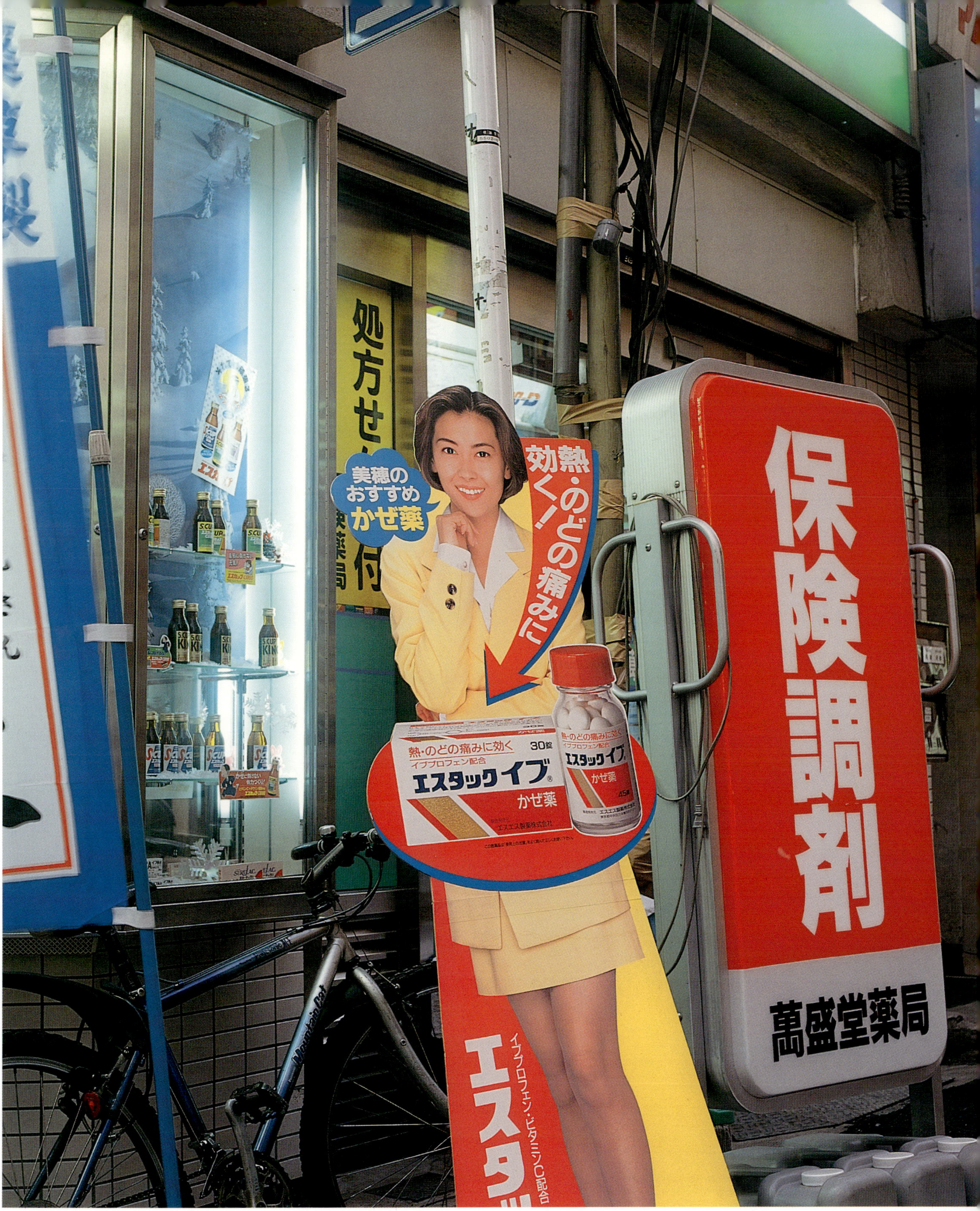


"Posing" in front of a drugstore: a life-size cutout of a pop idol.

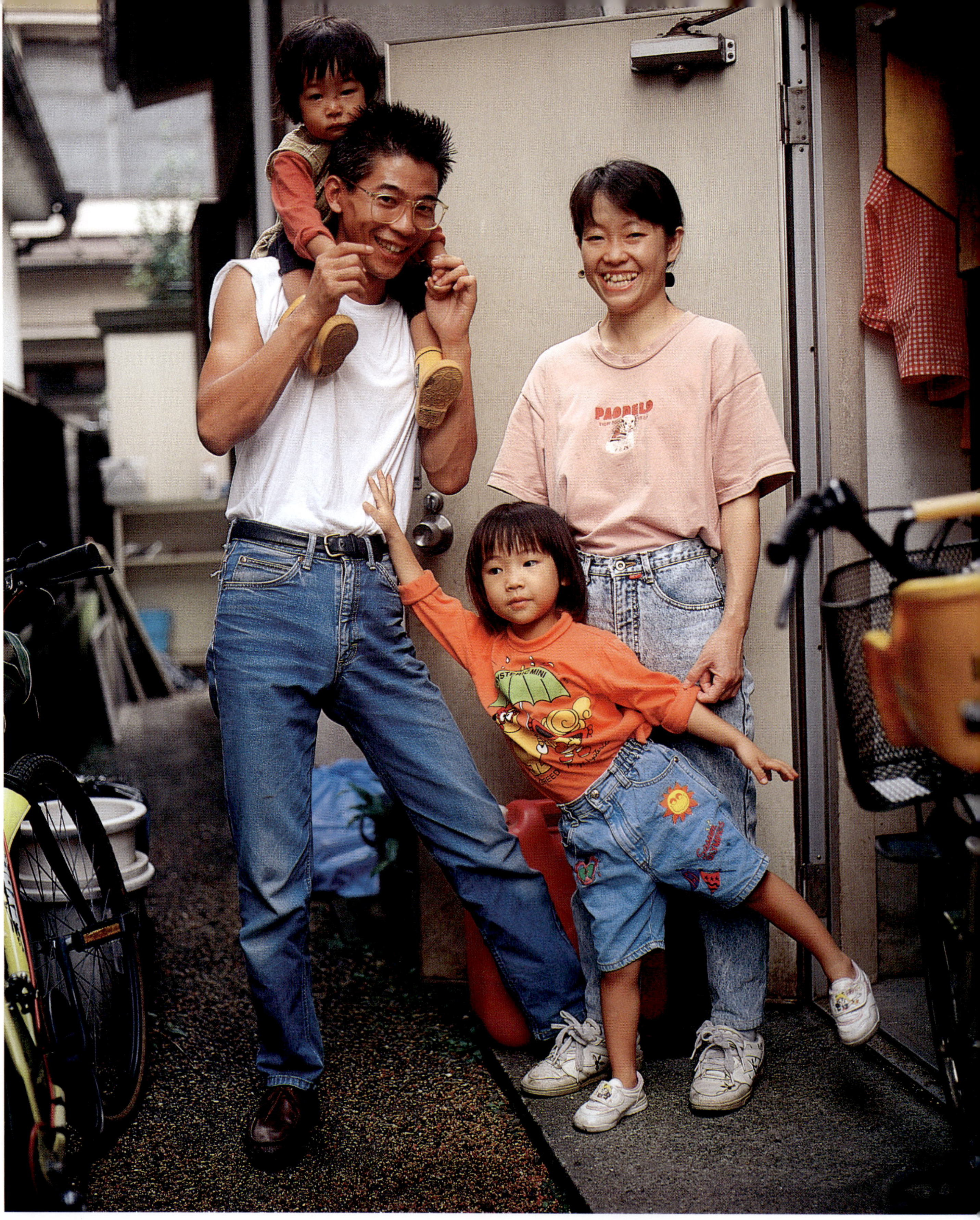

In the space of 10 years, this man moved to Tokyo, got married, and had children, then moved with his family back to his hometown. It's no exaggeration to say that Tokyo has been created by people who originally came from elsewhere. Each day about 1,200 people move to the capital, and about the same number leave.

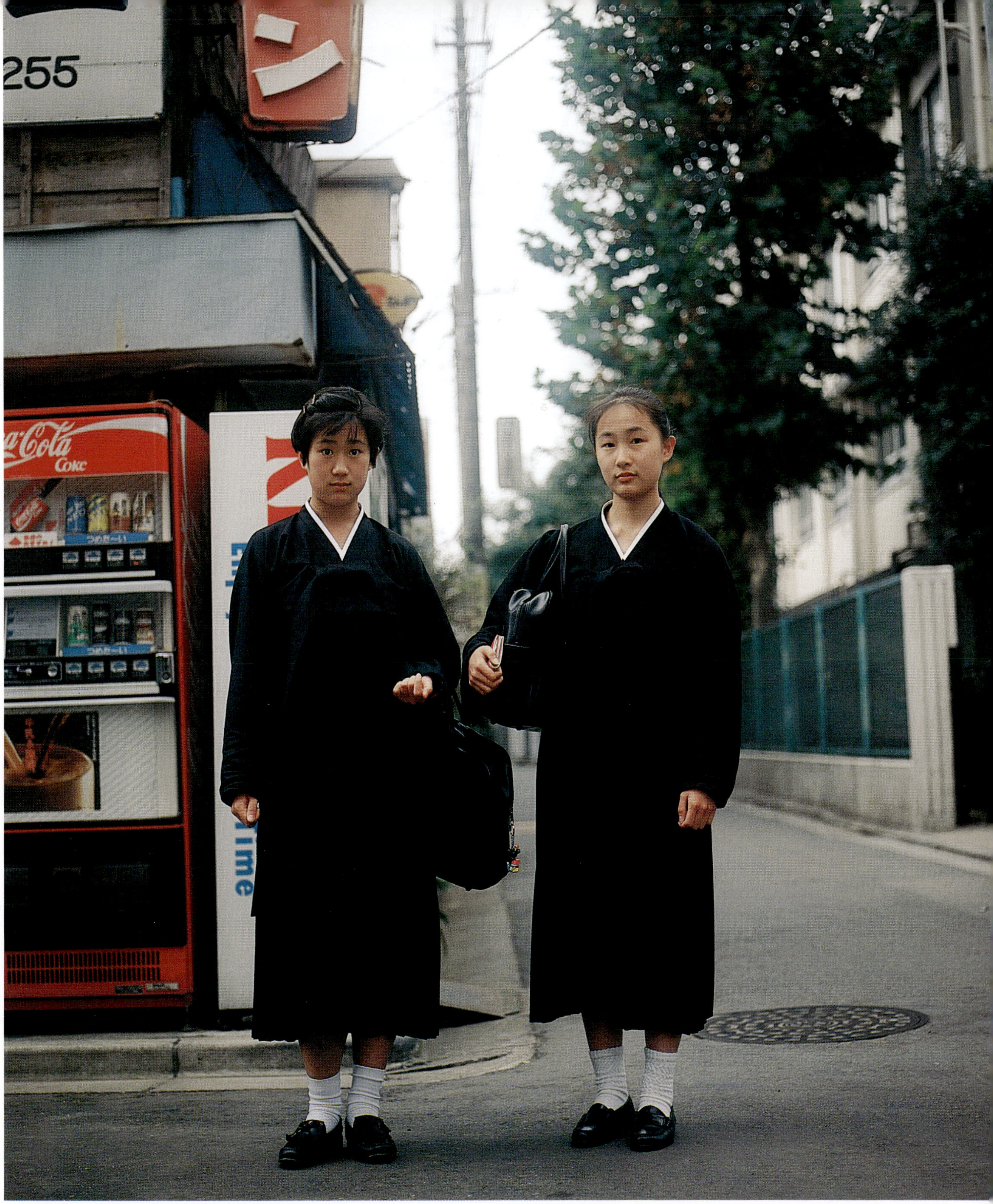


These schoolgirls are the grandchildren of Korean immigrants. North and South Koreans constitute Tokyo's largest foreign community. The girls said they would like to see the Koreans and the Japanese, as well as the two Korean communities, learn to live together in harmony.

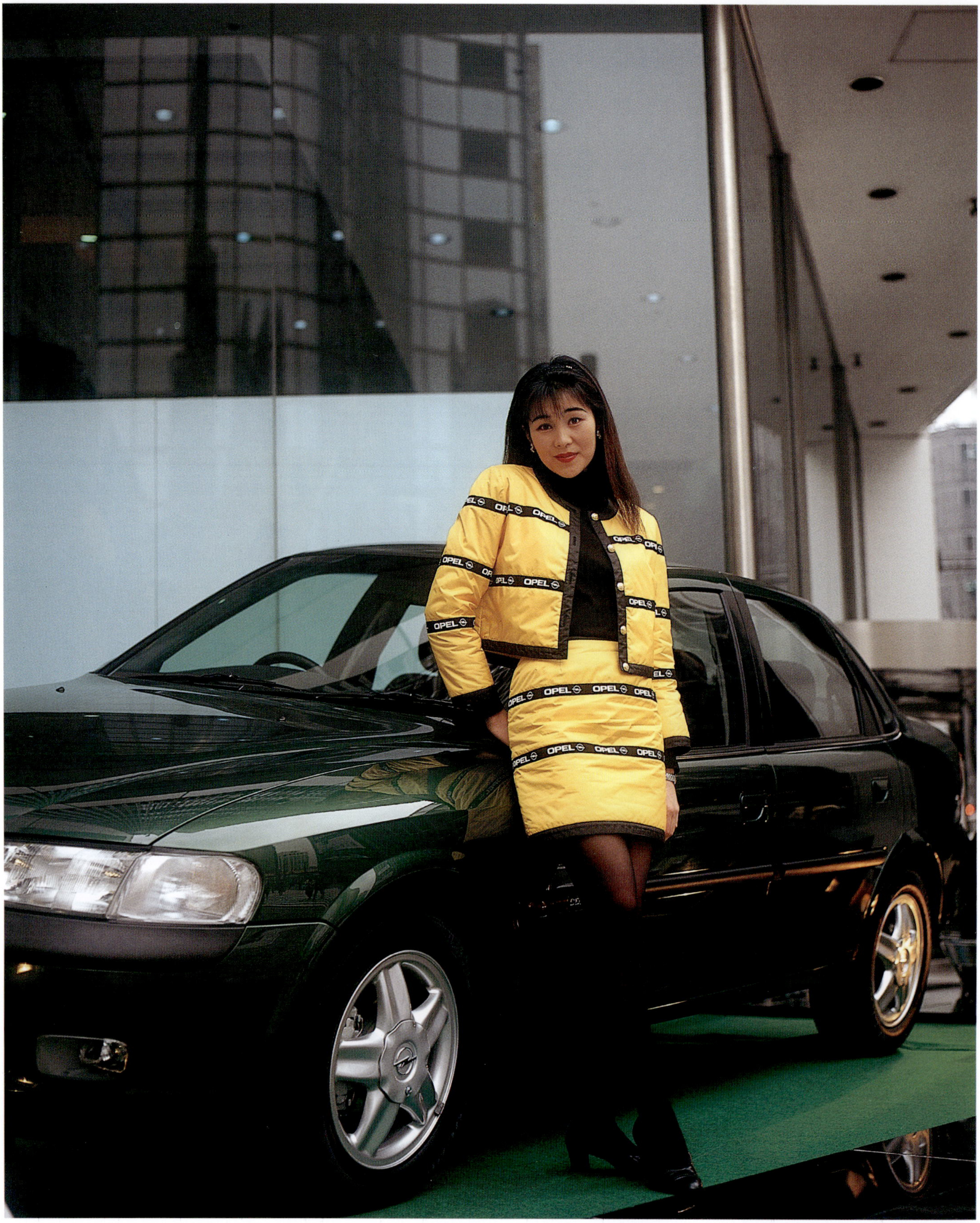


This automobile display in the exclusive Ginza district turns the heads of passersby — some of whom are interested in the car.

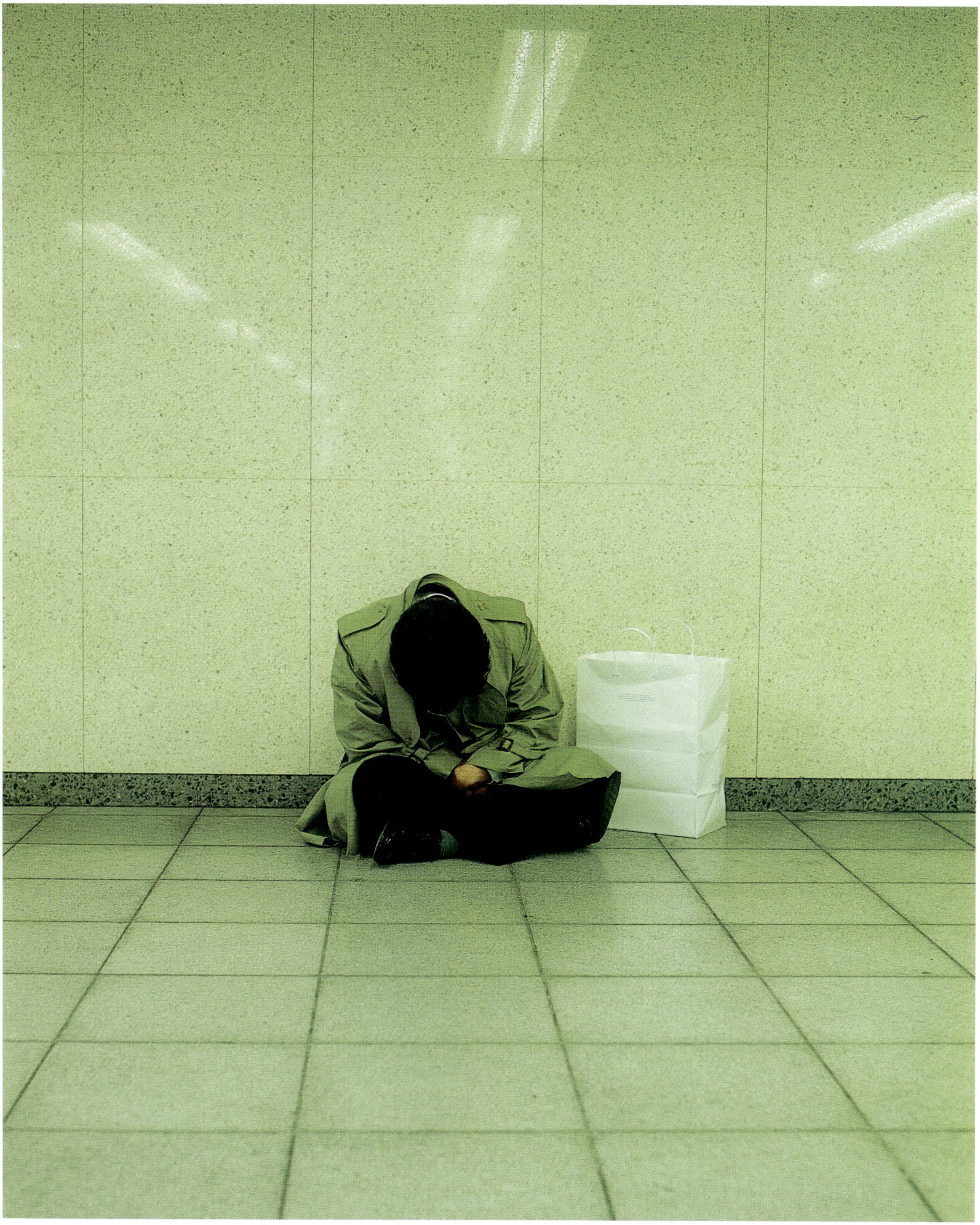

This man is not practicing Zen meditation; he's just had too much to drink at a reception. Dozing off inside the train station, what kind of dreams could he be having?

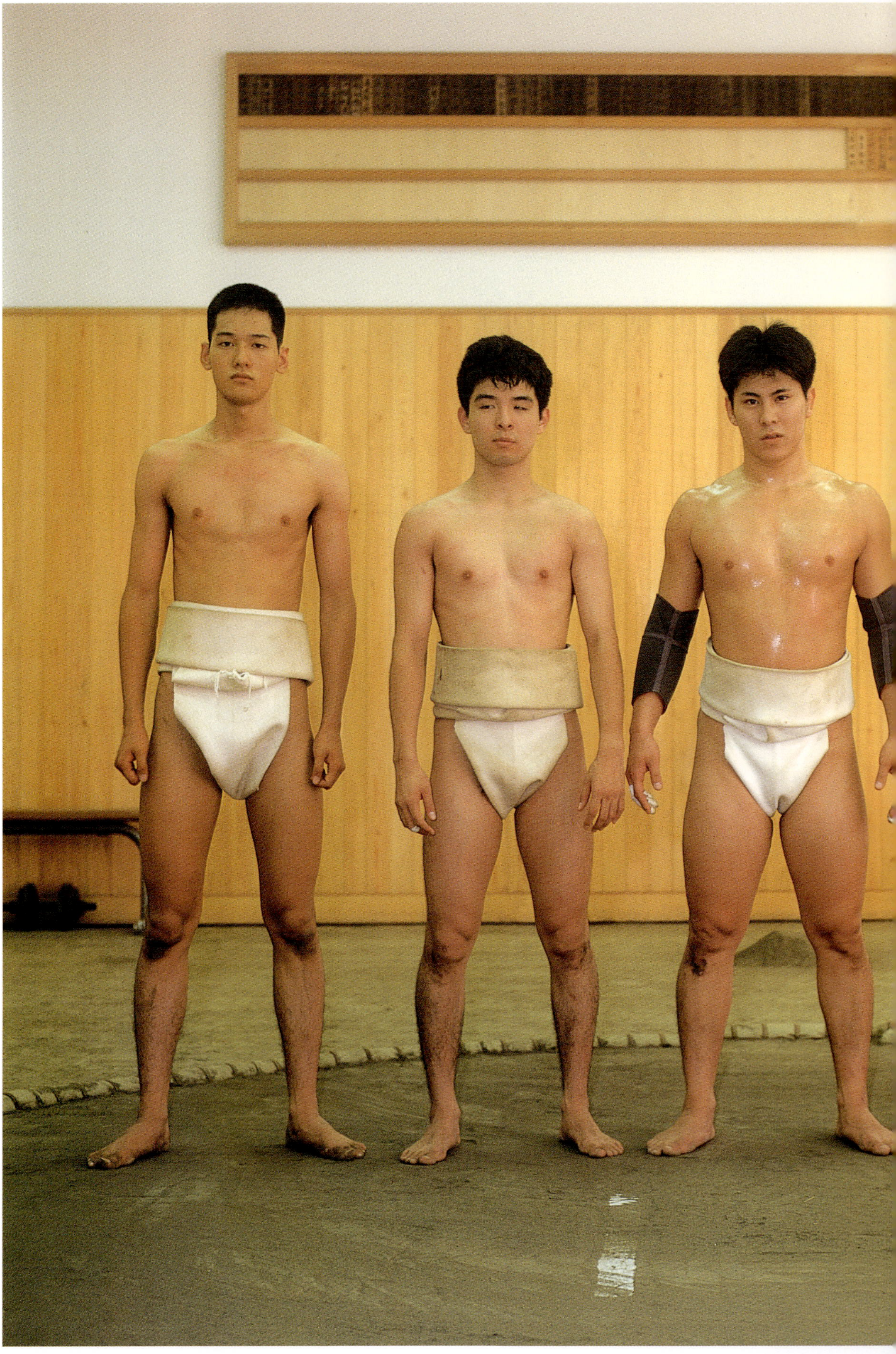

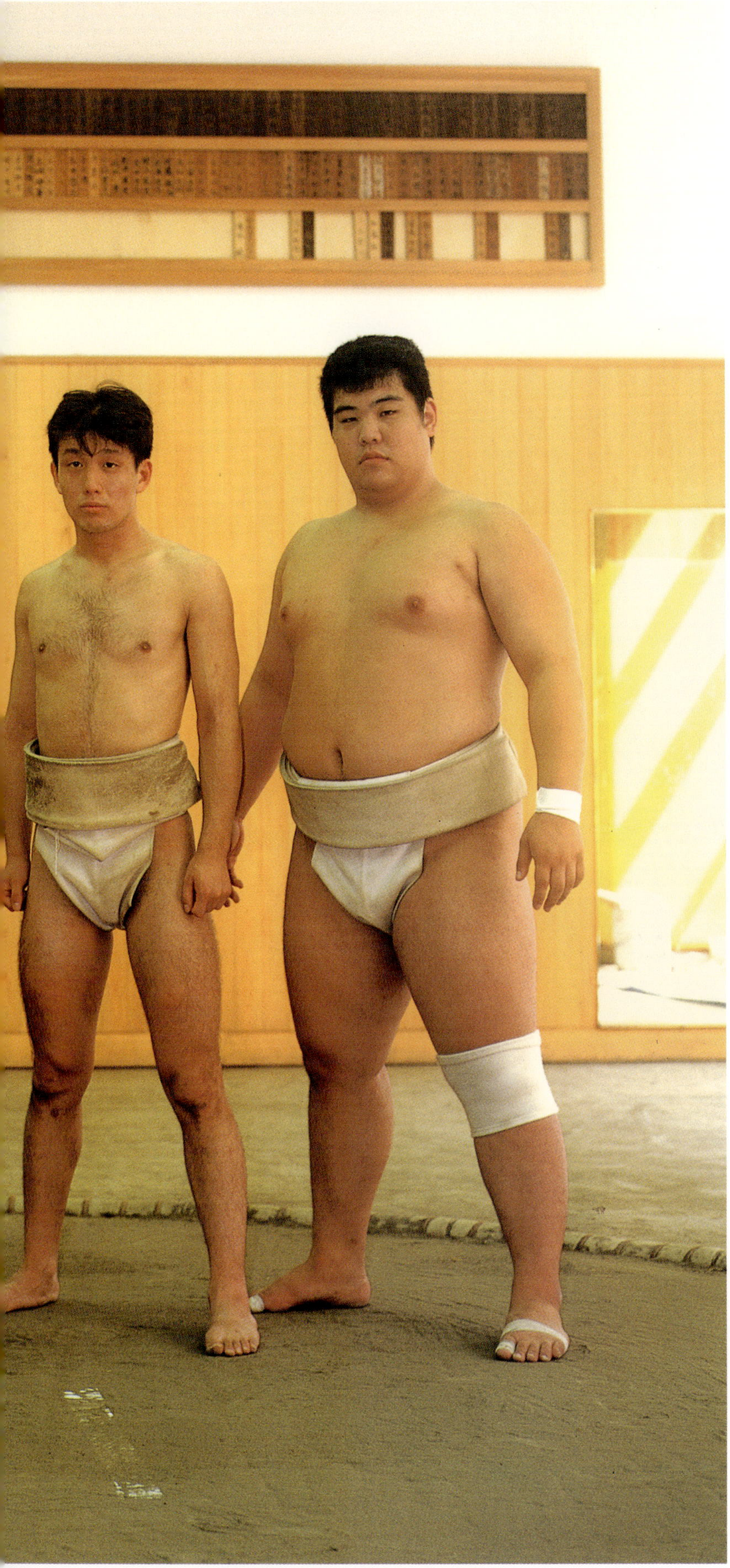

These members of a university sumo club find the sport attractive for a variety of reasons: "Victories and defeats are decided in the span of a moment." "It's the national sport of Japan, and as a Japanese person, I wanted to give it a try." Sumo traces its roots back to Japan's mythical age of the gods. According to the *Record of Ancient Matters* (*Kojiki*), Japan's oldest extant chronicle, the tradition of sumo began when two gods, Takemikazuchinokami and Takeminakatanokami, engaged in a contest of strength.

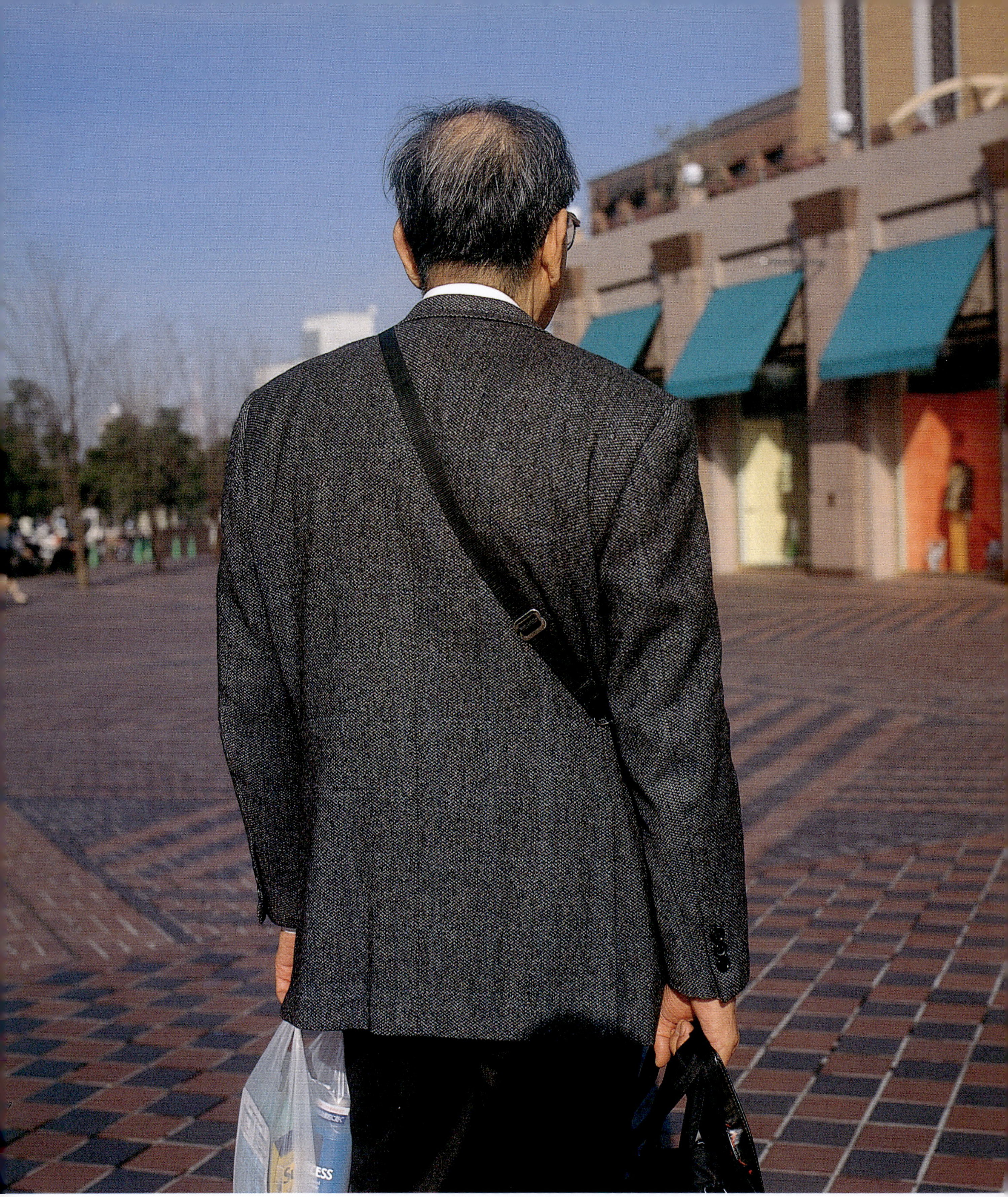

This man is looking at a building in Ebisu Garden Place, a new urban center comprising offices, hotels, department stores, and other facilities. Not long ago Ebisu was characterized by a combination of residential areas and a famous beer factory.

Each day, the Tokyo subway system is used by an estimated 7.25 million people.

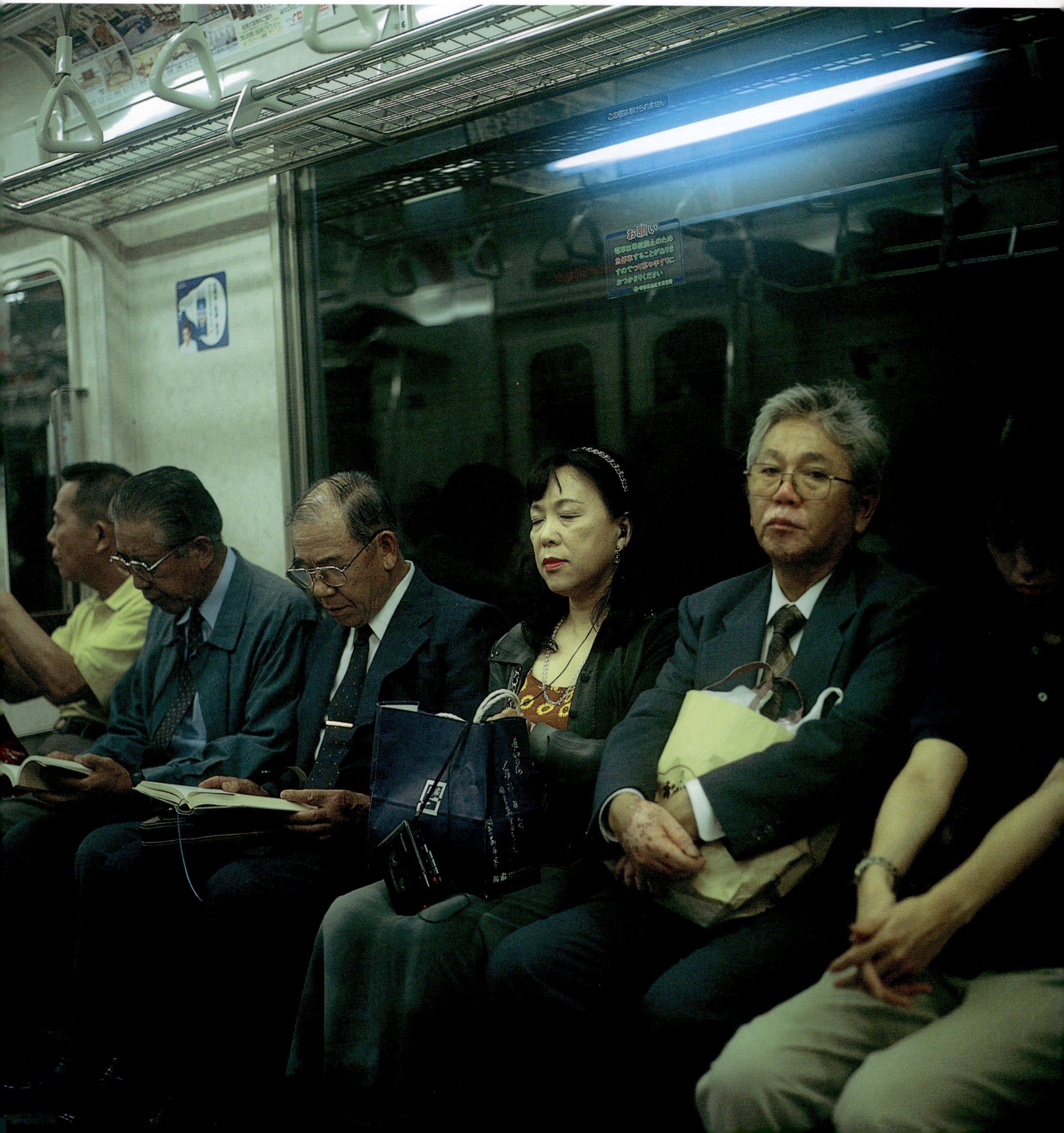

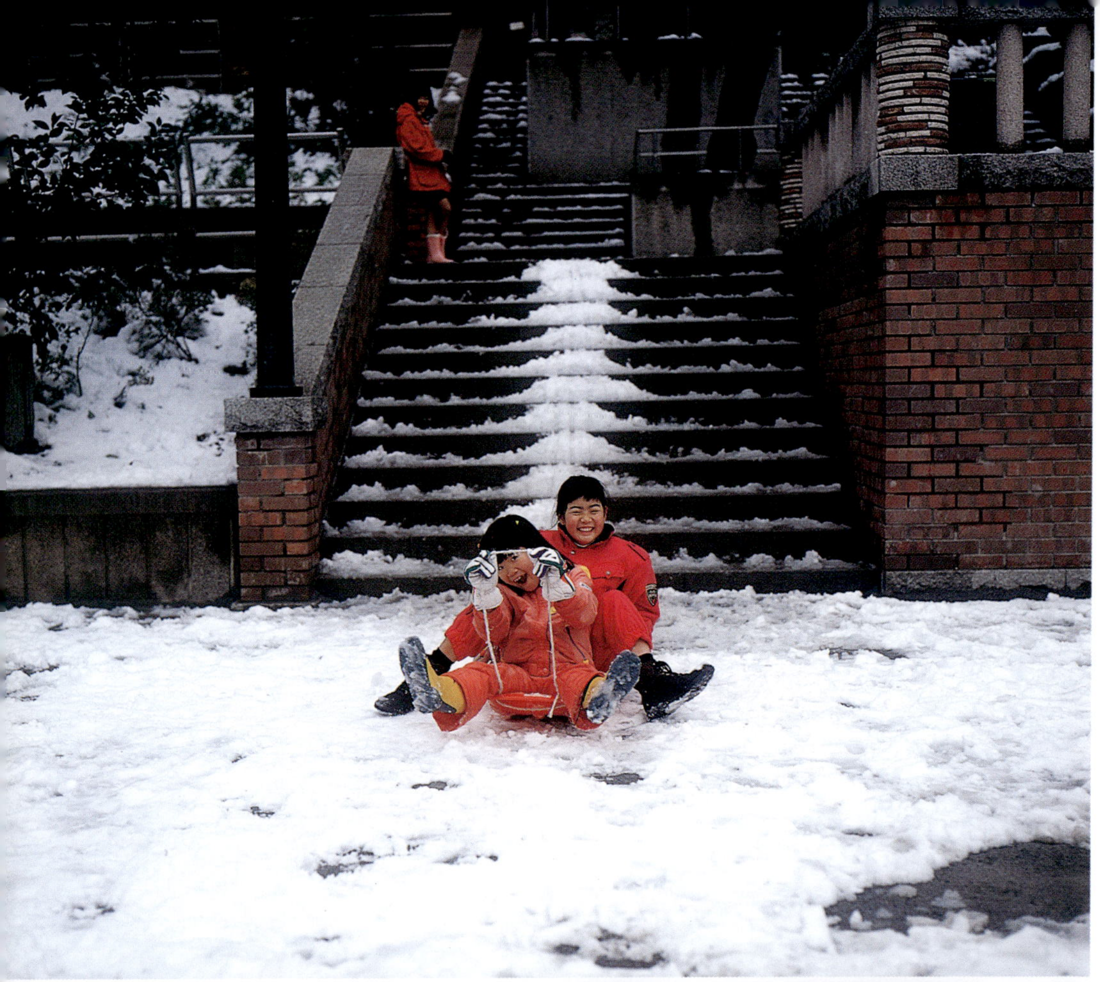

Tokyo isn't known for snowy winters, but snow does fall here two or three times a year.

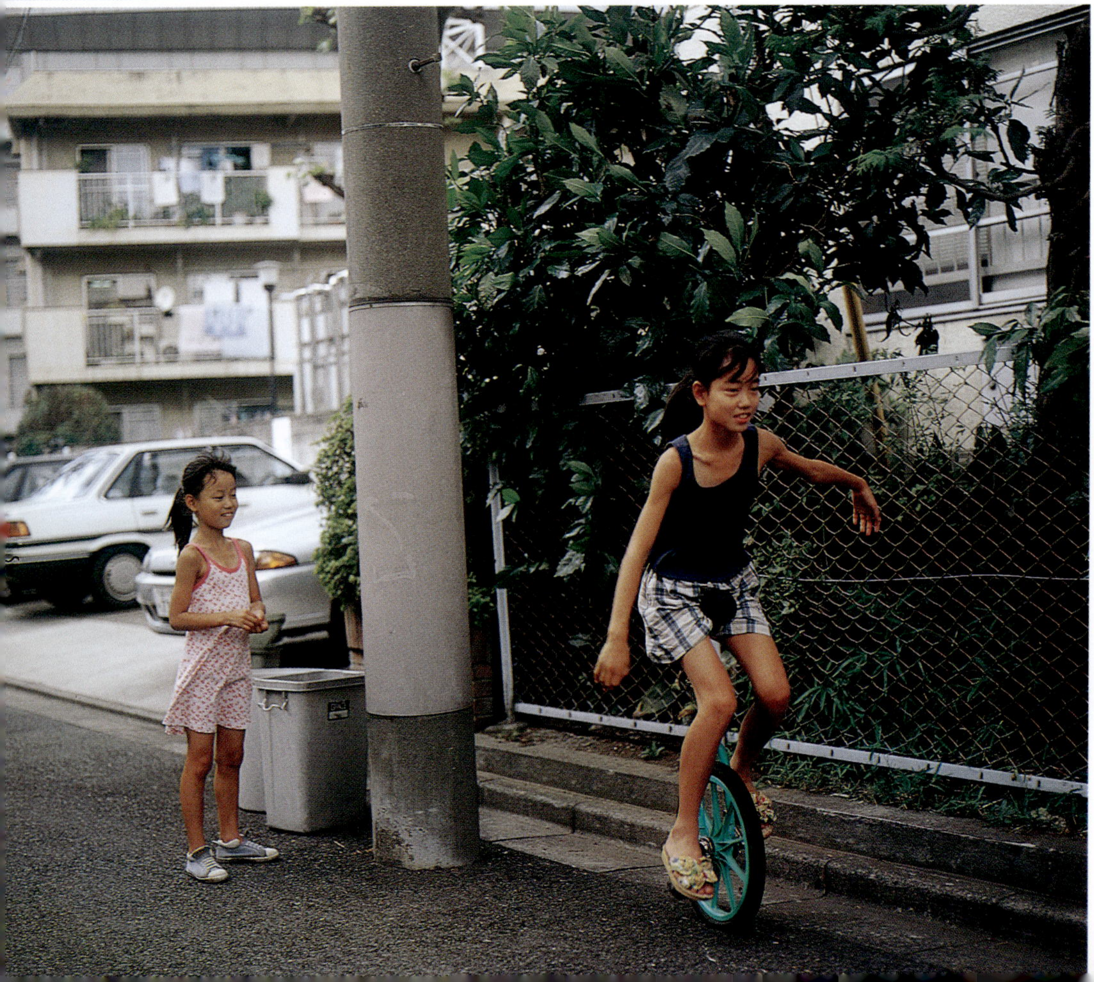

Unicycles are quite popular among Japanese children, like the two sisters pictured here.

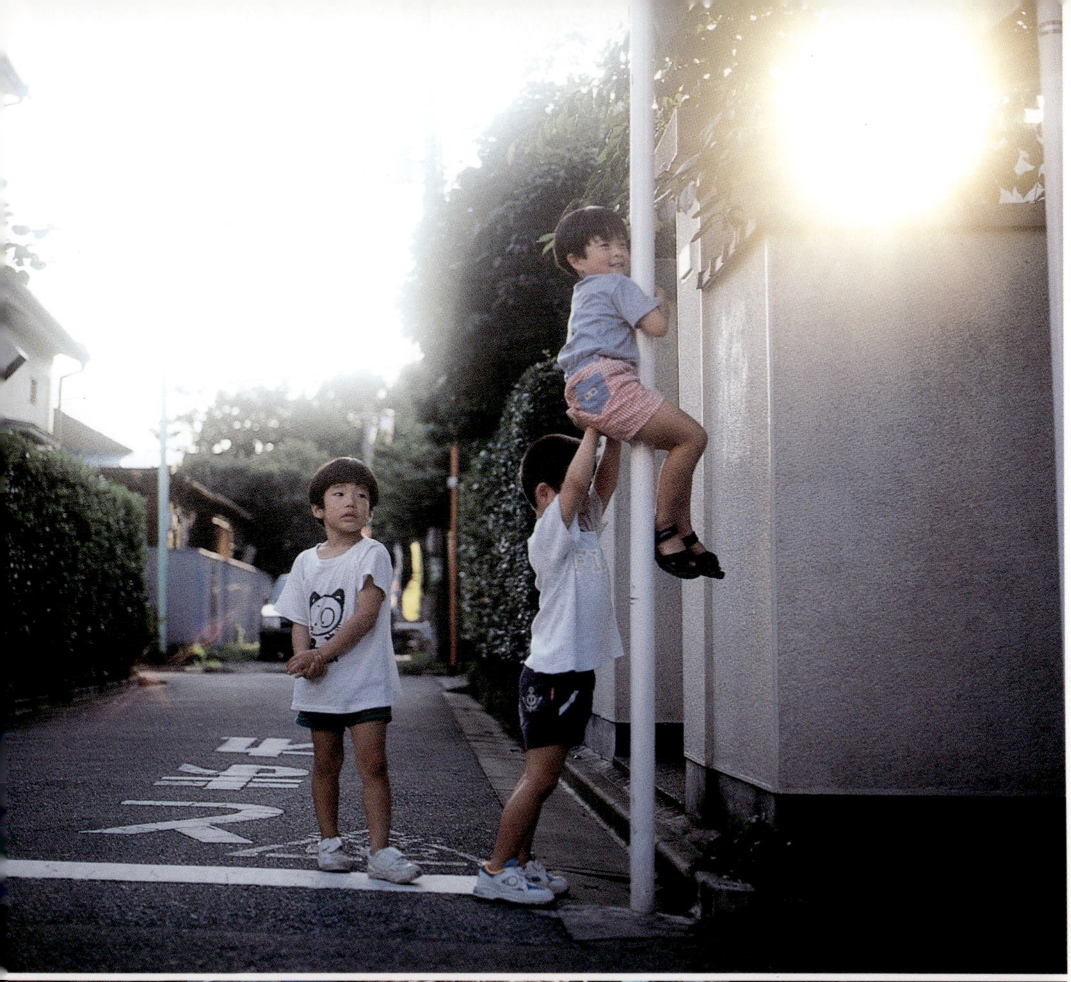

There aren't many trees left in Tokyo to climb, so these kids make do with a sign-post.

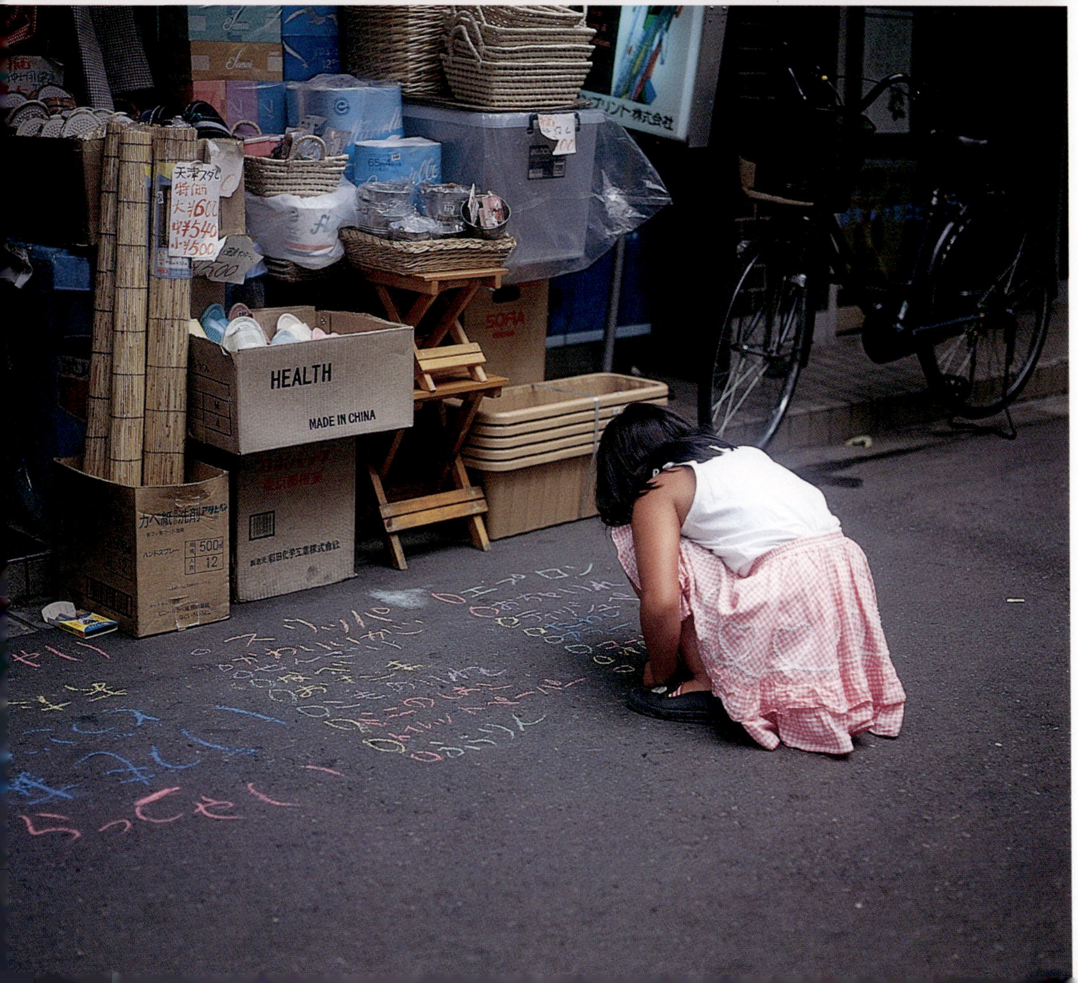


A young girl busies herself with the task of writing a list of the products sold in this shop.

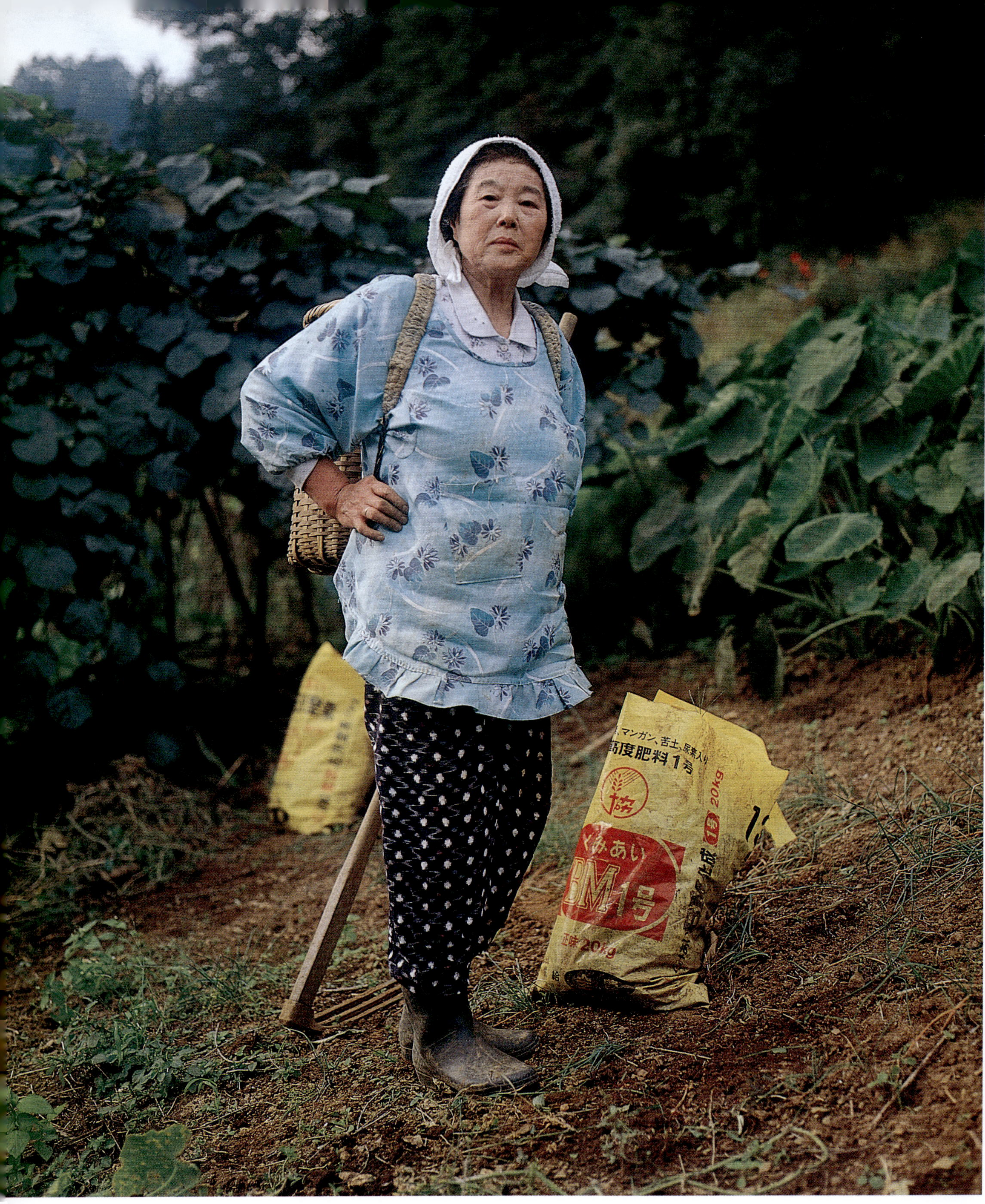


This woman lives in the village of Hinohara, population 3,700, where one in every three residents is aged 65 or older. Only rarely does a new bride come into the village, since most women nowadays aren't willing to marry into the farming life. And most of the younger residents leave as soon as they come of age.

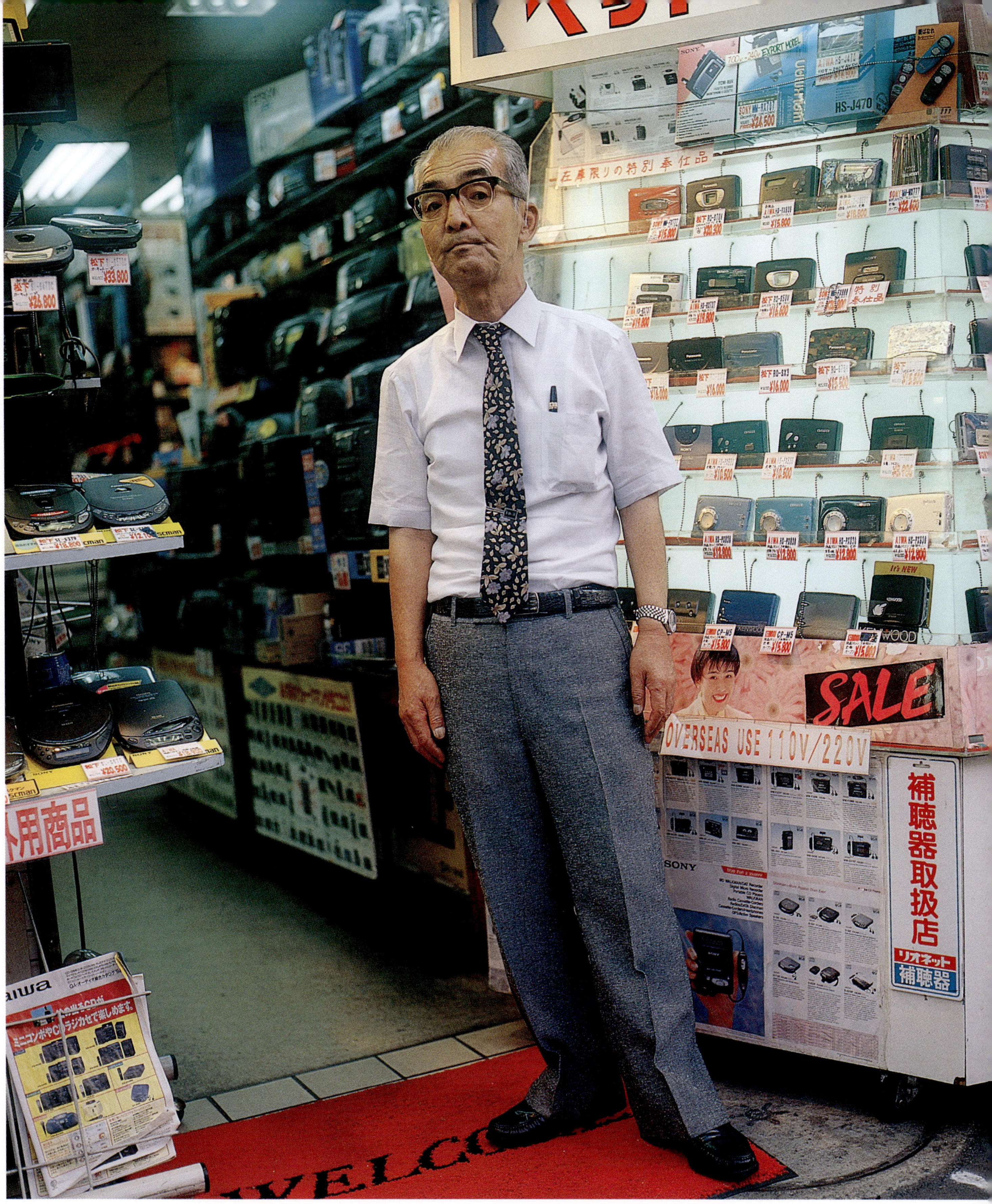


The Akihabara district, located in eastern Tokyo, is a mecca for shoppers looking to purchase electrical and electronic goods. This vast bazaar of high-tech products at bargain prices attracts not only Tokyoites, but also people from other parts of Japan and even from other countries. Personal computers and related products currently account for half of Akihabara's offerings.

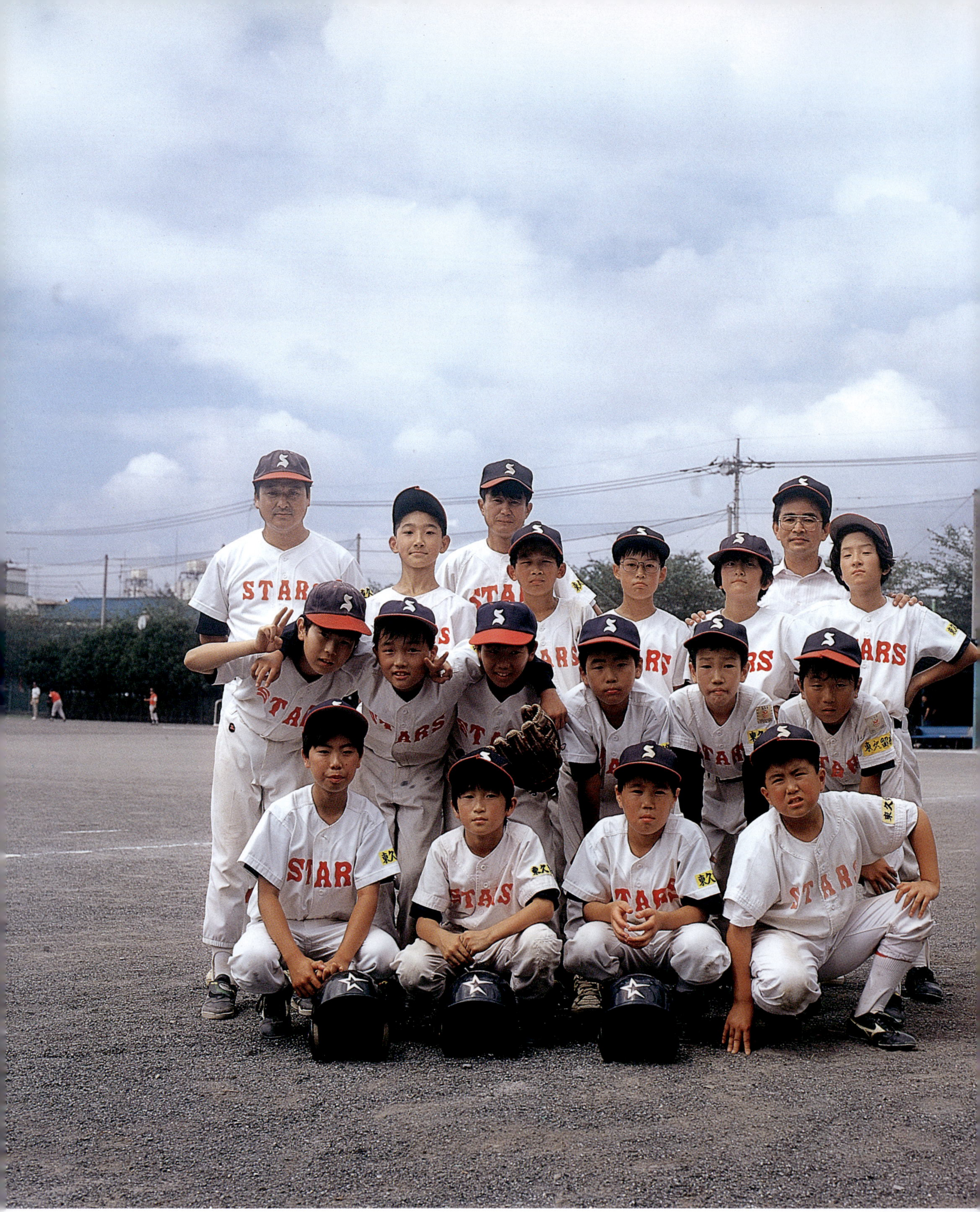


A little league baseball team. Baseball and soccer are popular sports among children.

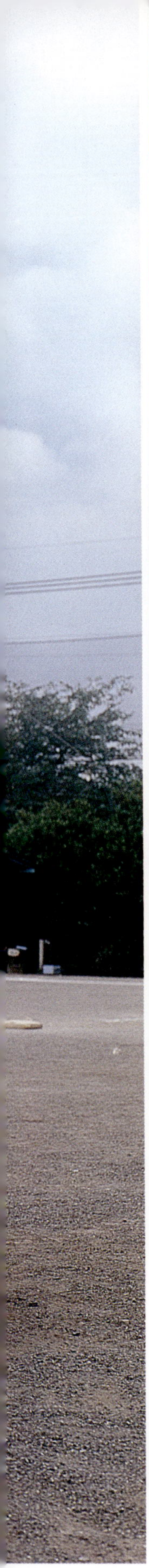

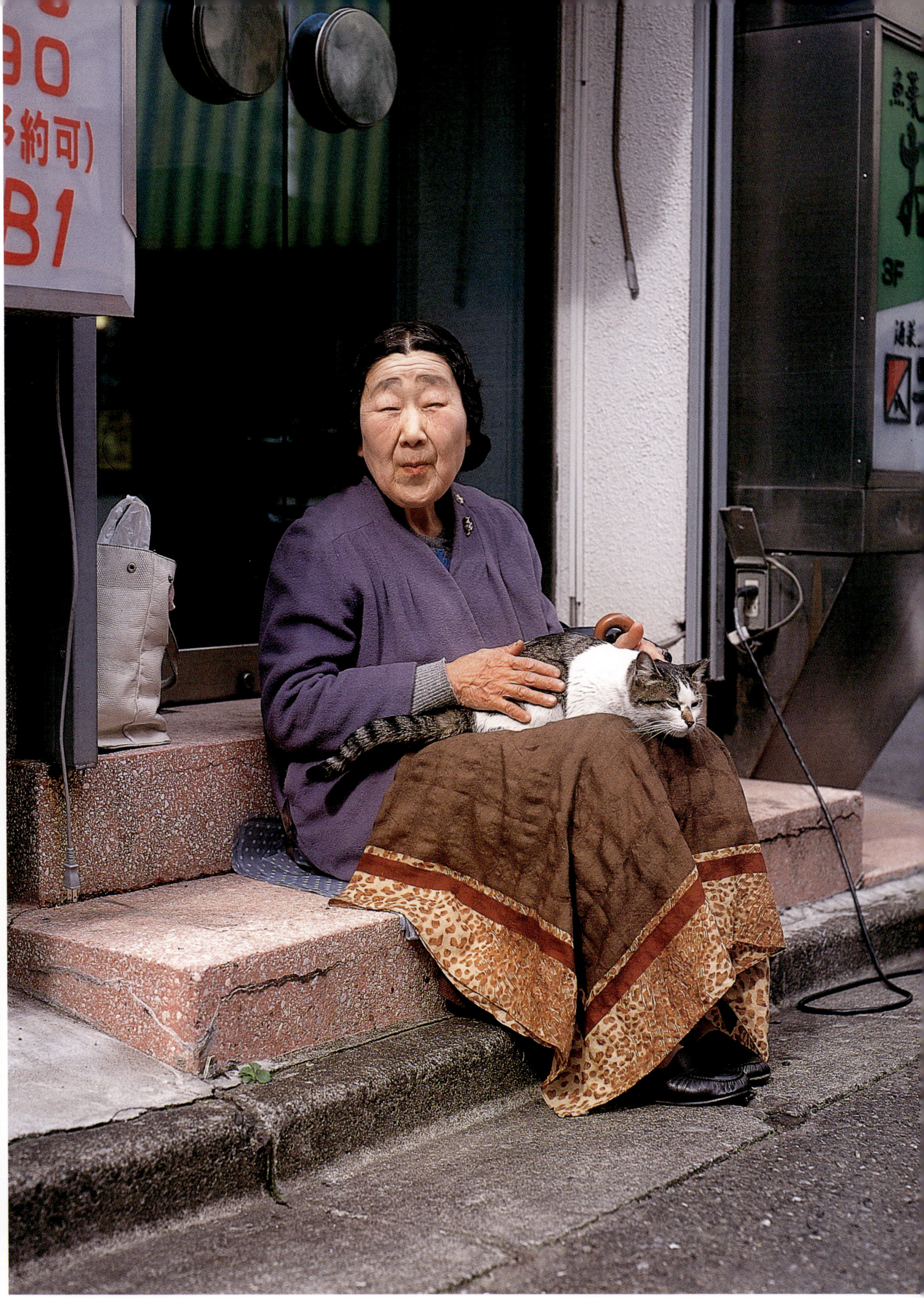


Perched on a stoop, an elderly woman basks in the sun with her cat.

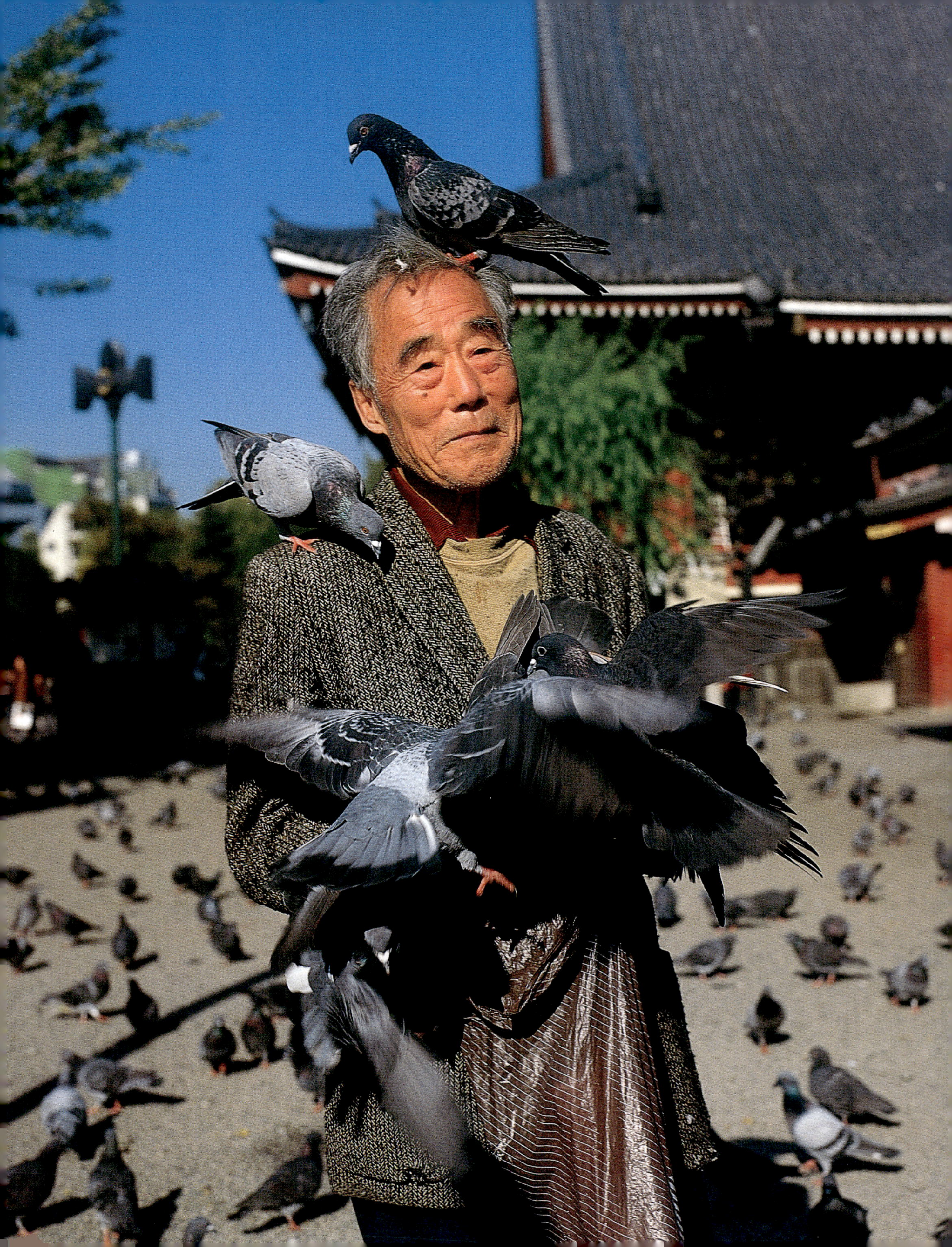

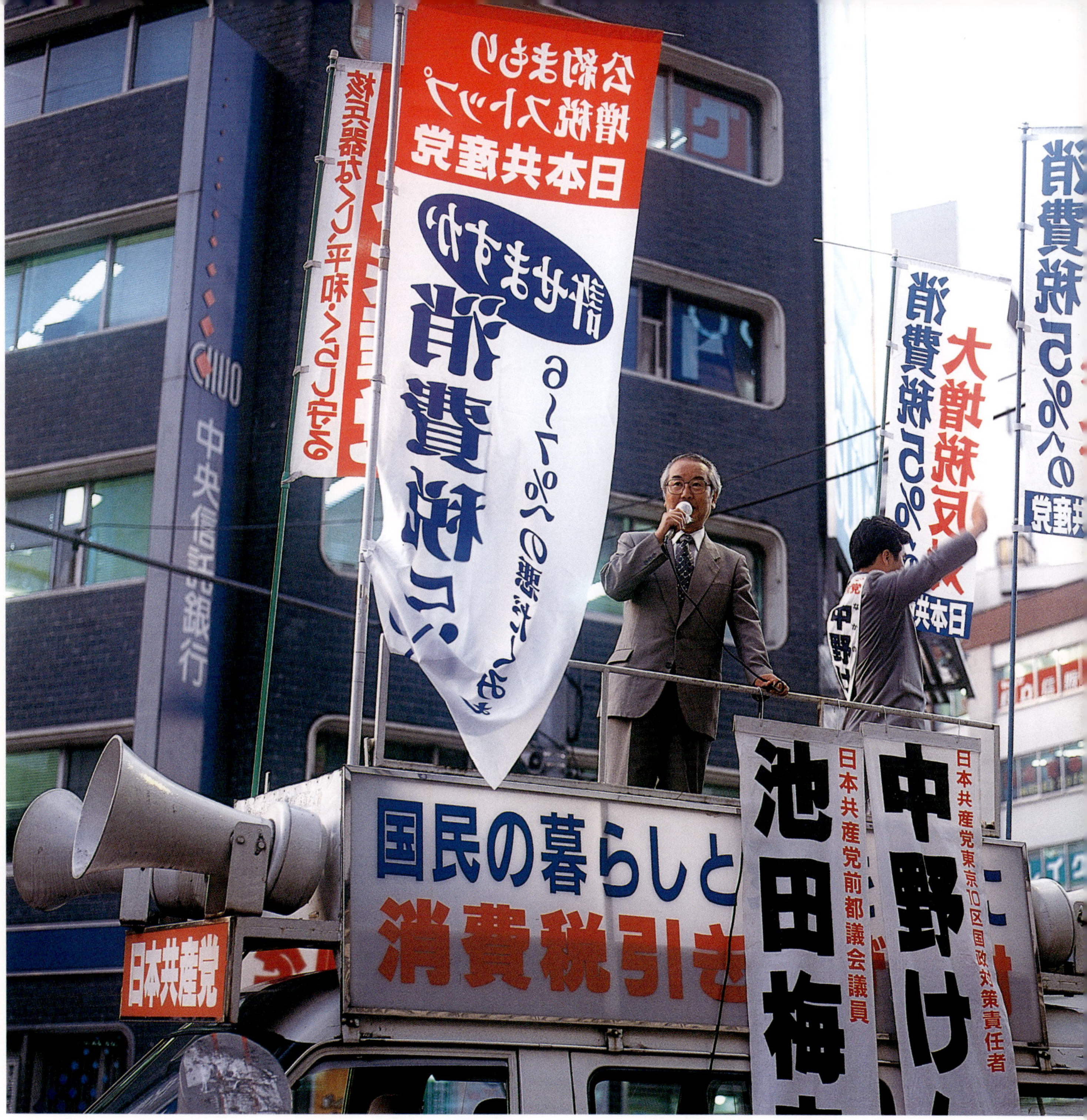


Politicians on a stumping tour. In Japan, election time is marked by a sudden increase in the number of loudspeaker trucks roaming the streets.

Pigeons like to congregate on the grounds of this temple, and this 81-year-old man comes by train every day to see them. "Pigeons have a class-based society just like we do."

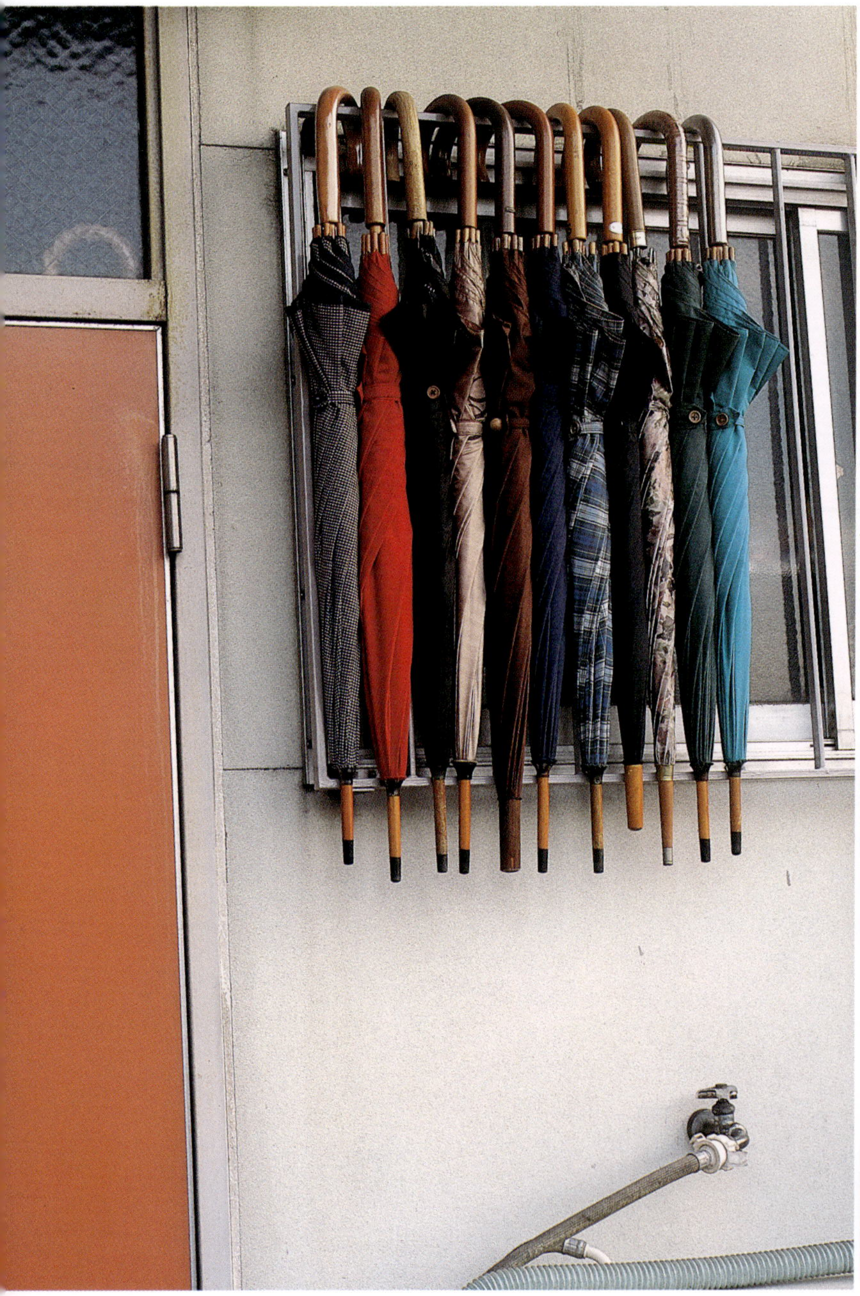

Rain falls in Tokyo on an average of 118 days per year.

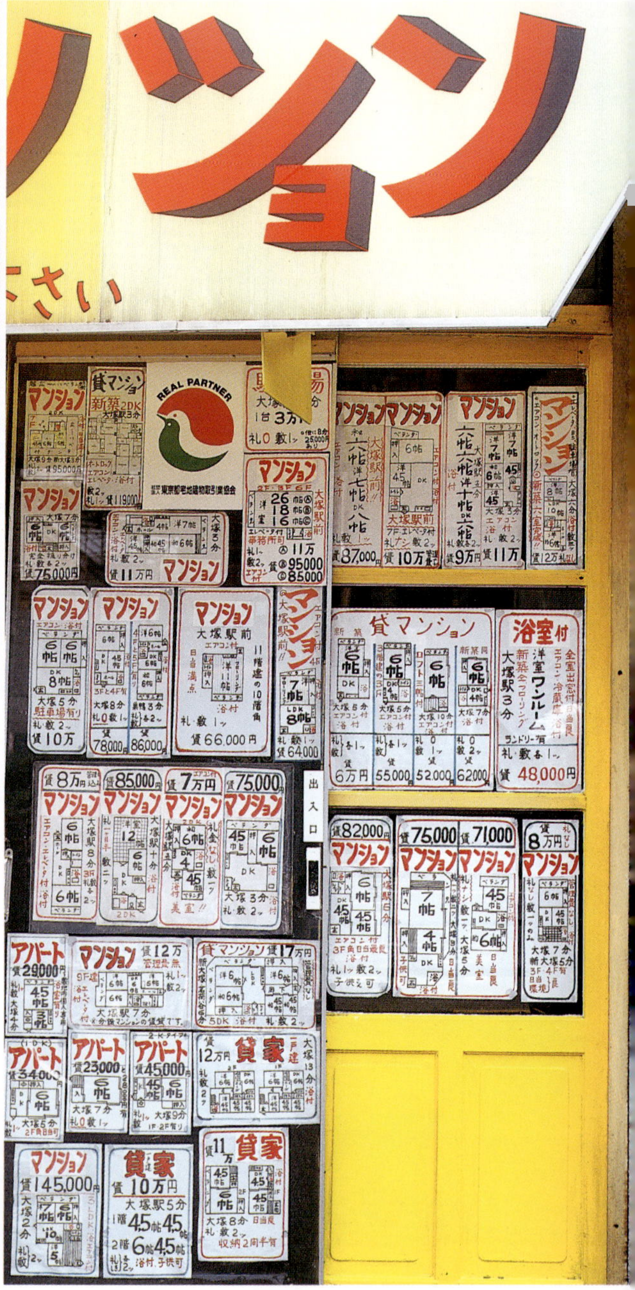


The latest apartment listings are displayed in the window of this real-estate agency. In order to rent an apartment in Japan, it is usually necessary to go through a realtor. Tokyo has some of the highest rents among all the major cities of the world.

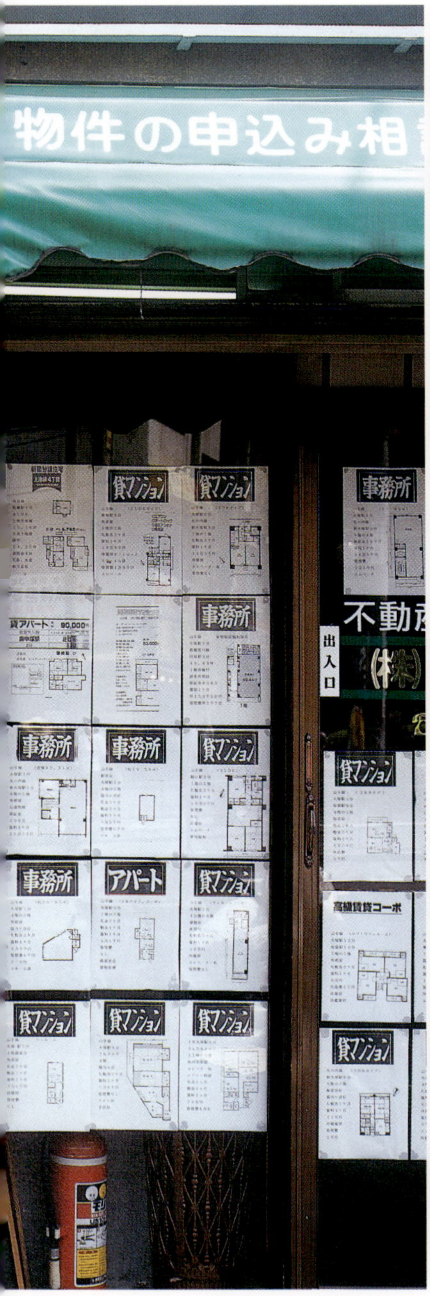


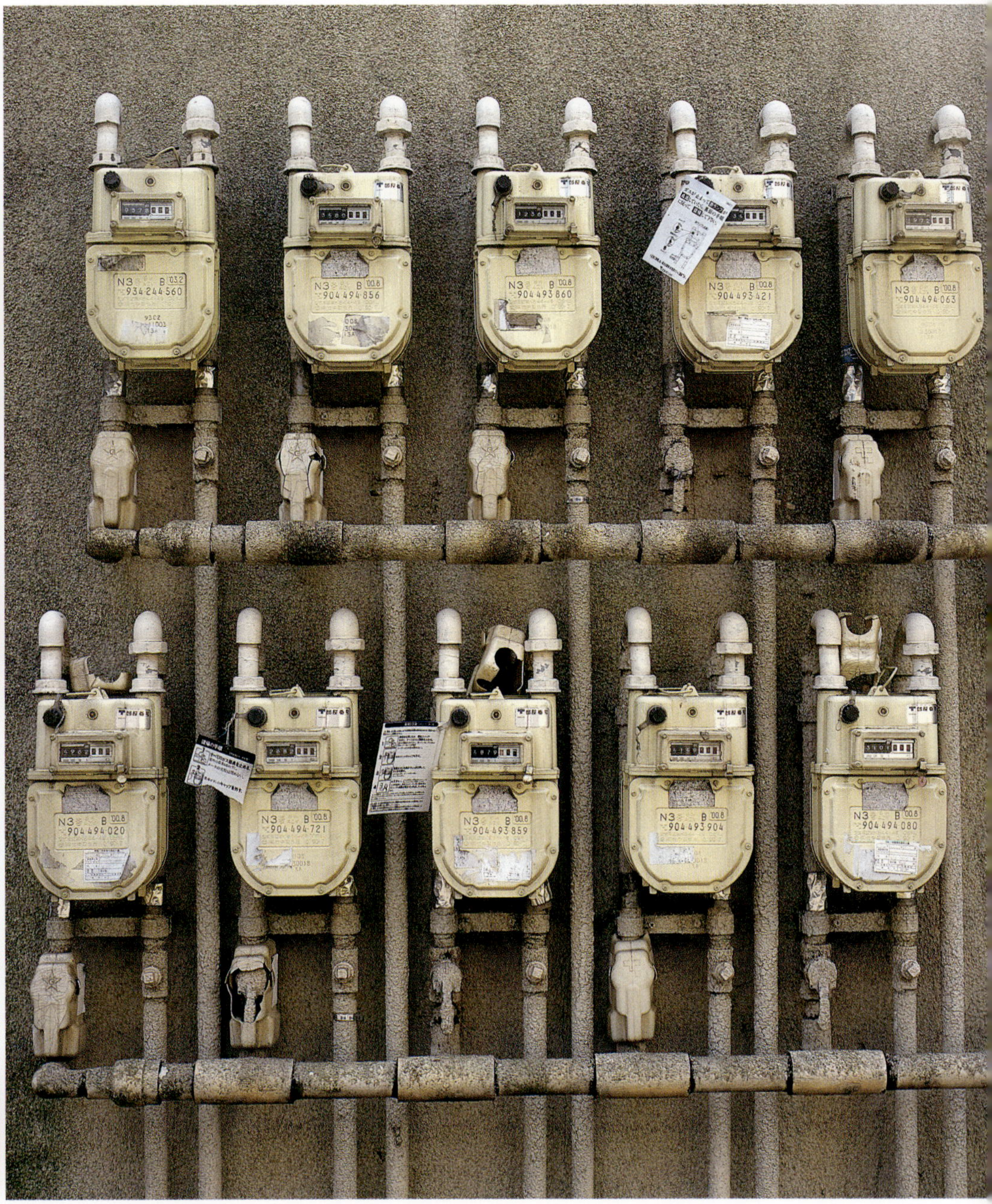

A bank of gas meters.

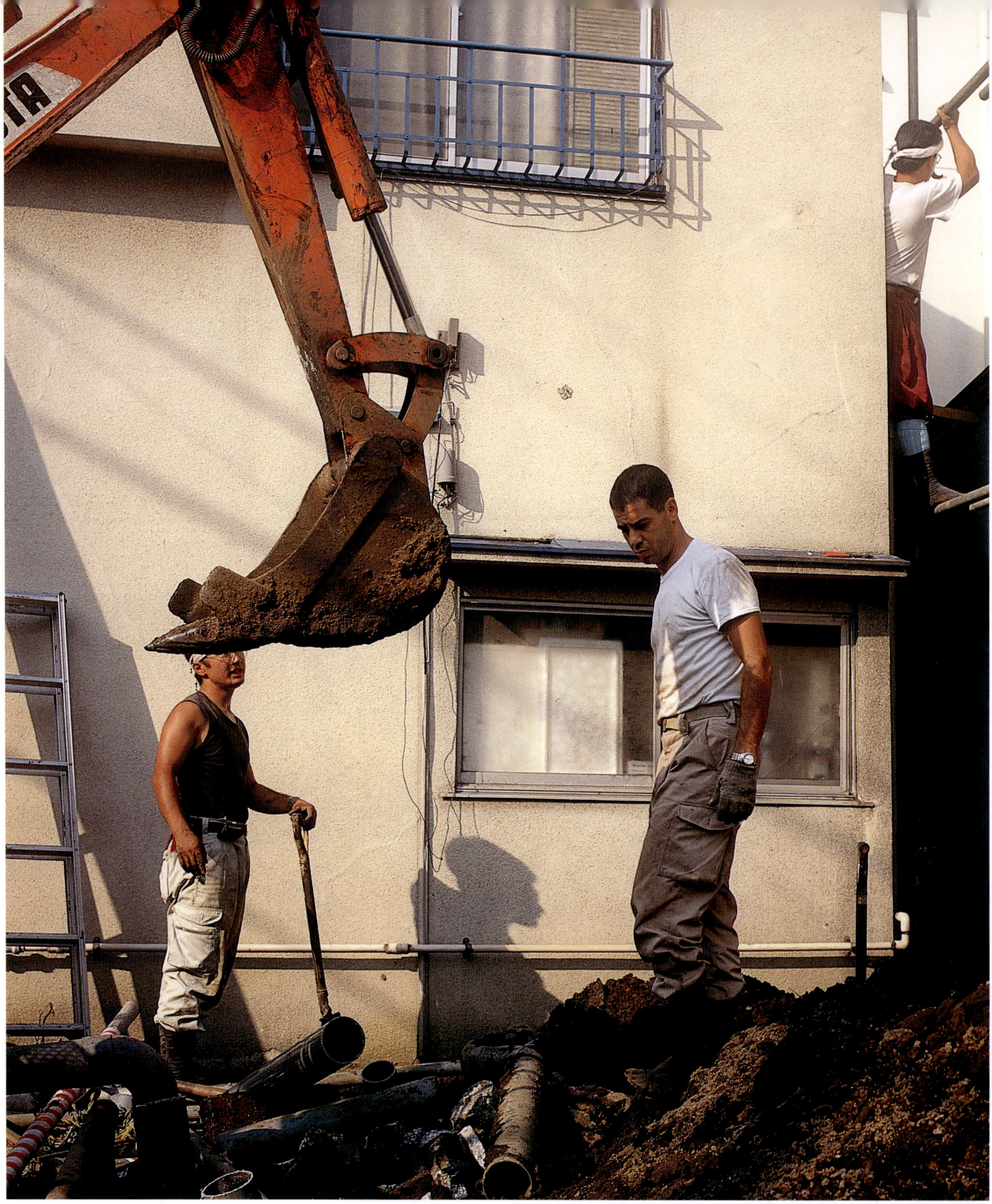

Nowadays, young Japanese people up turn their noses at manual or menial labor such as construction work—work which falls under the term "3-K jobs." The three Ks stand for *kitsui* (demanding), *kitanai* (dirty), and *kiken* (dangerous). The resulting labor gap is being filled by workers from less-developed countries in Asia and other parts of the world who come to Japan to make and save money. The man in the foreground, a North African, tells me, "Tokyo is a strange place, nothing but buildings. If you're going to take pictures, you should photograph nature too."

For the village of Hinohara, the harvest festival is a 230-year-old tradition. In most parts of Japan, this celebration has been abbreviated and simplified. But here in Hinohara, the festivities still continue late into the night.

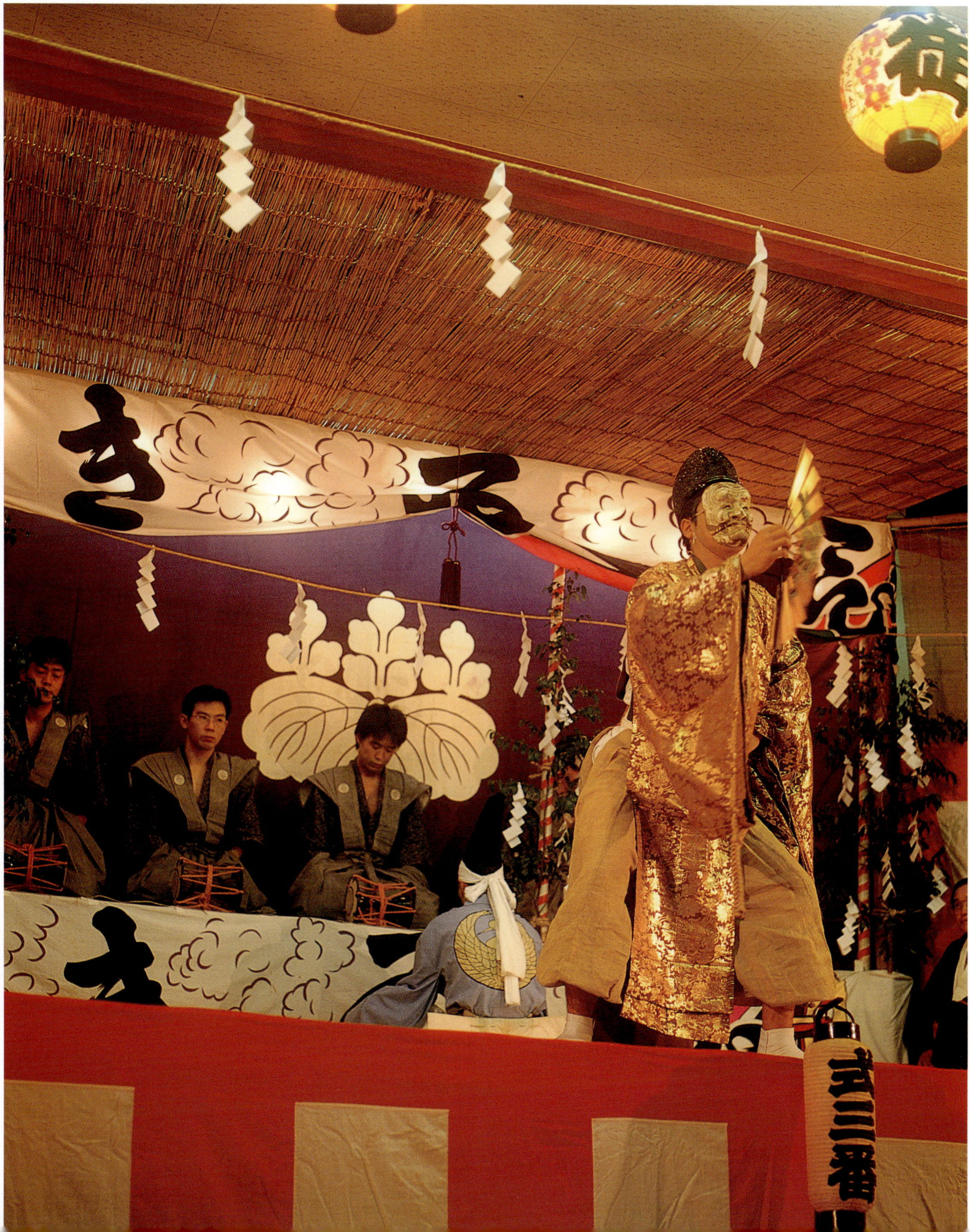

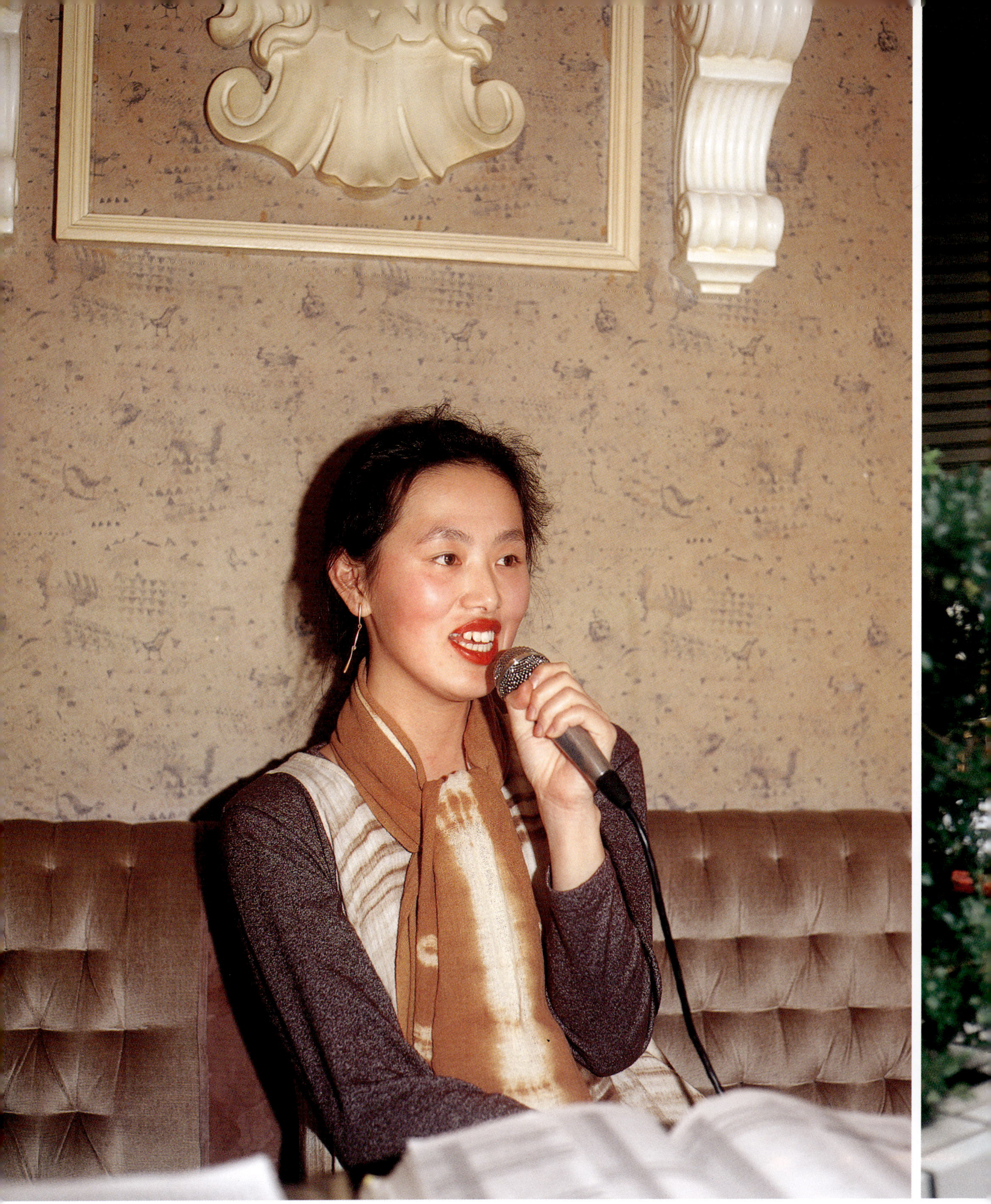

Karaoke is a widely popular leisure pastime among the Japanese, young and old alike. This woman has rented a small private room called a karaoke box, where she can indulge her songstress fantasies with unselfconscious abandon.

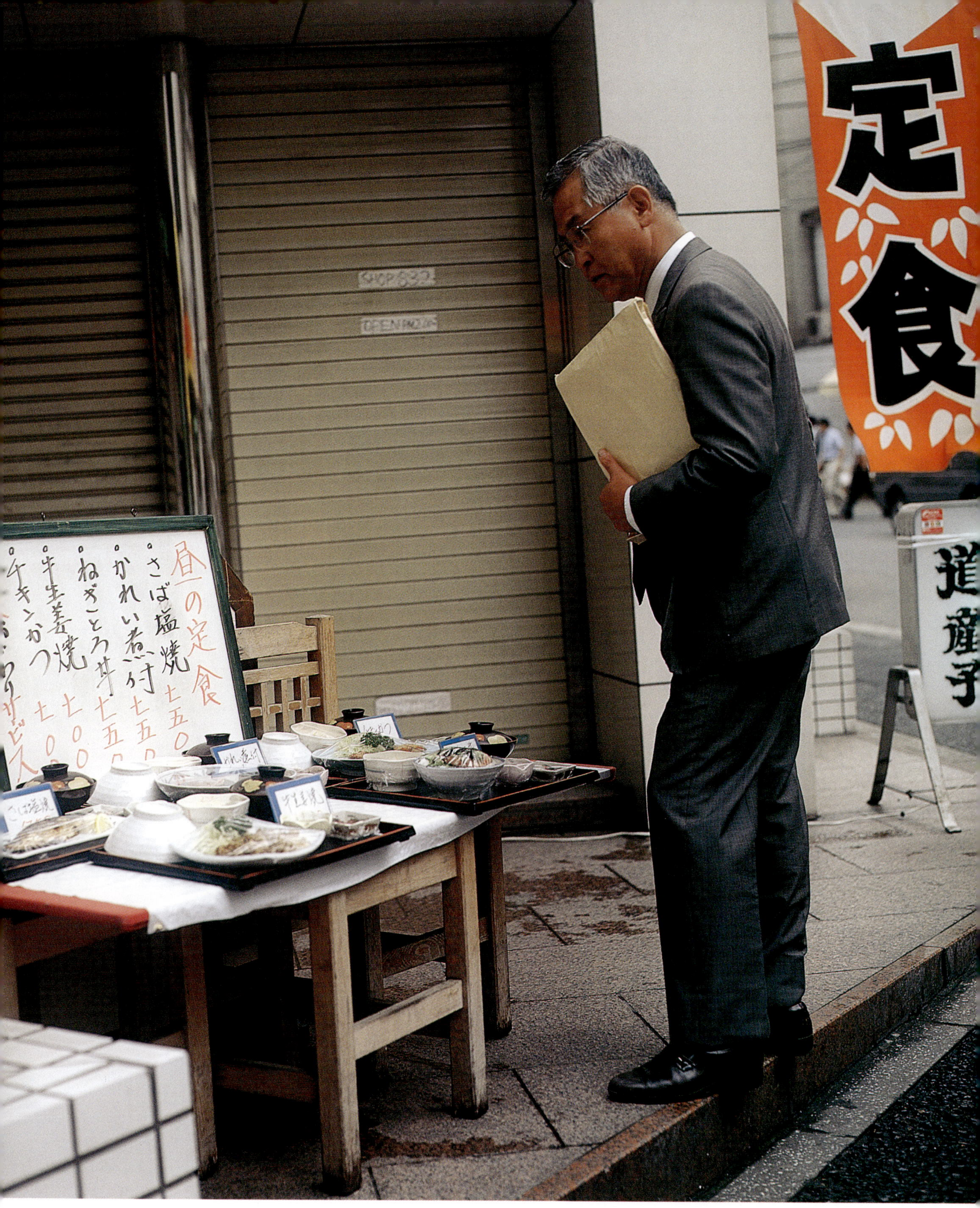


Lunchtime confronts this customer with yet another in life's endless parade of choices.

This photo was taken in front of the train station at Ogikubo, one of Tokyo's inner suburbs. In Tokyo, urban development inevitably proceeds in a disorderly fashion, but the ability to assimilate all the changes with aplomb is one of this city's defining characteristics.

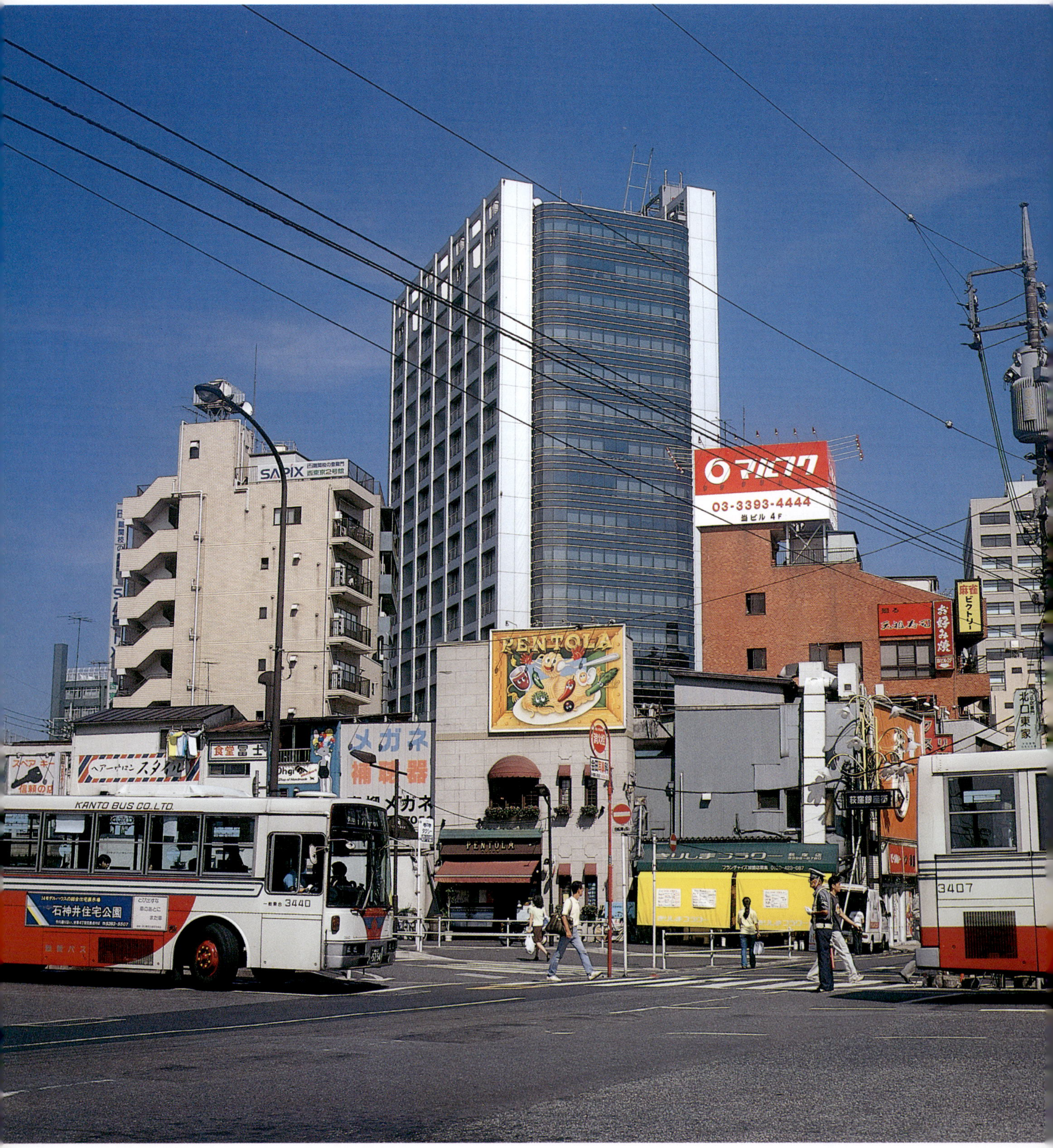


As this taxi driver knows, Tokyo's horrendous traffic jams, together with its narrow alleys and one-way streets, make the city one of the toughest places in the world to navigate.

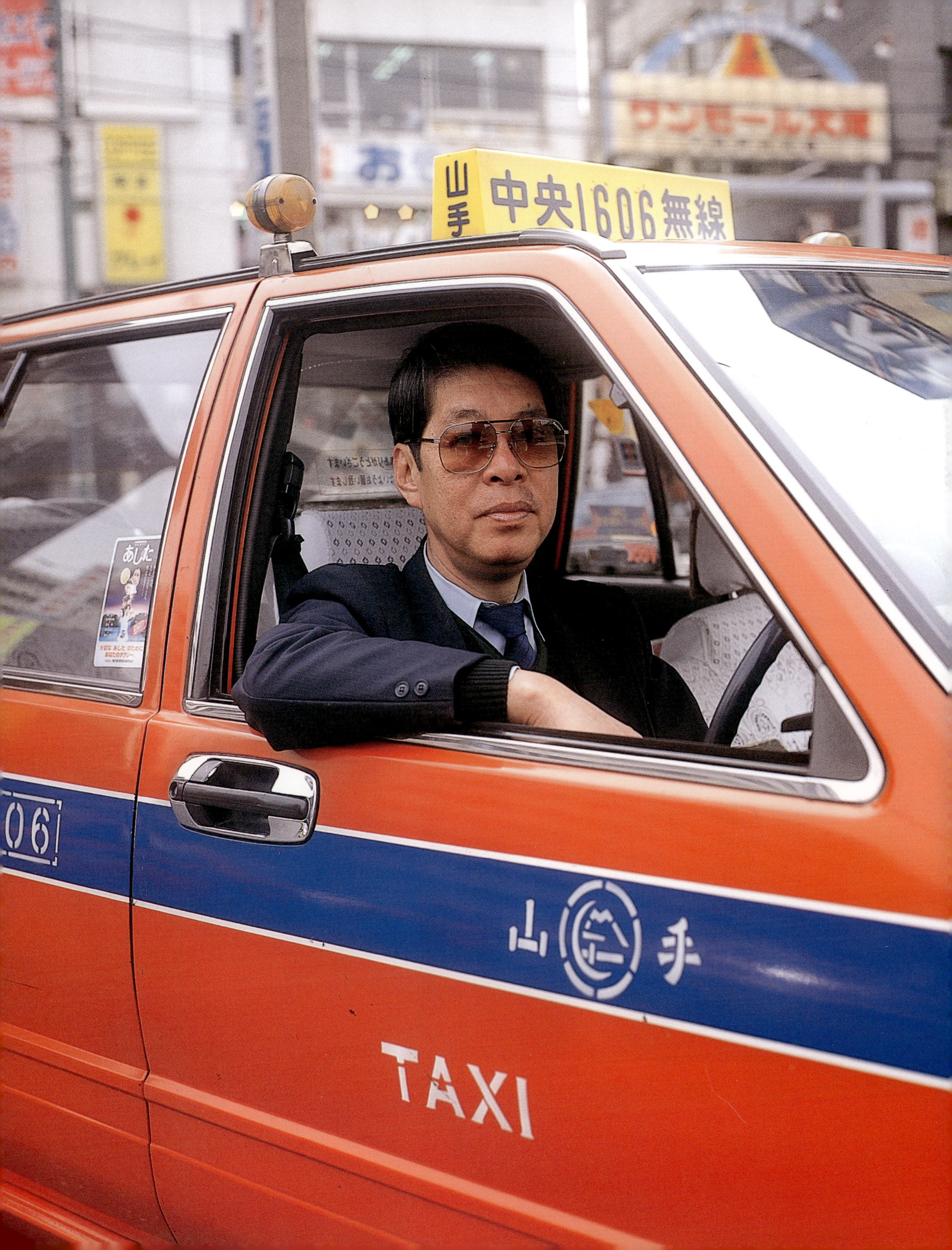
山手
中央1606無線
06
山 手
TAXI

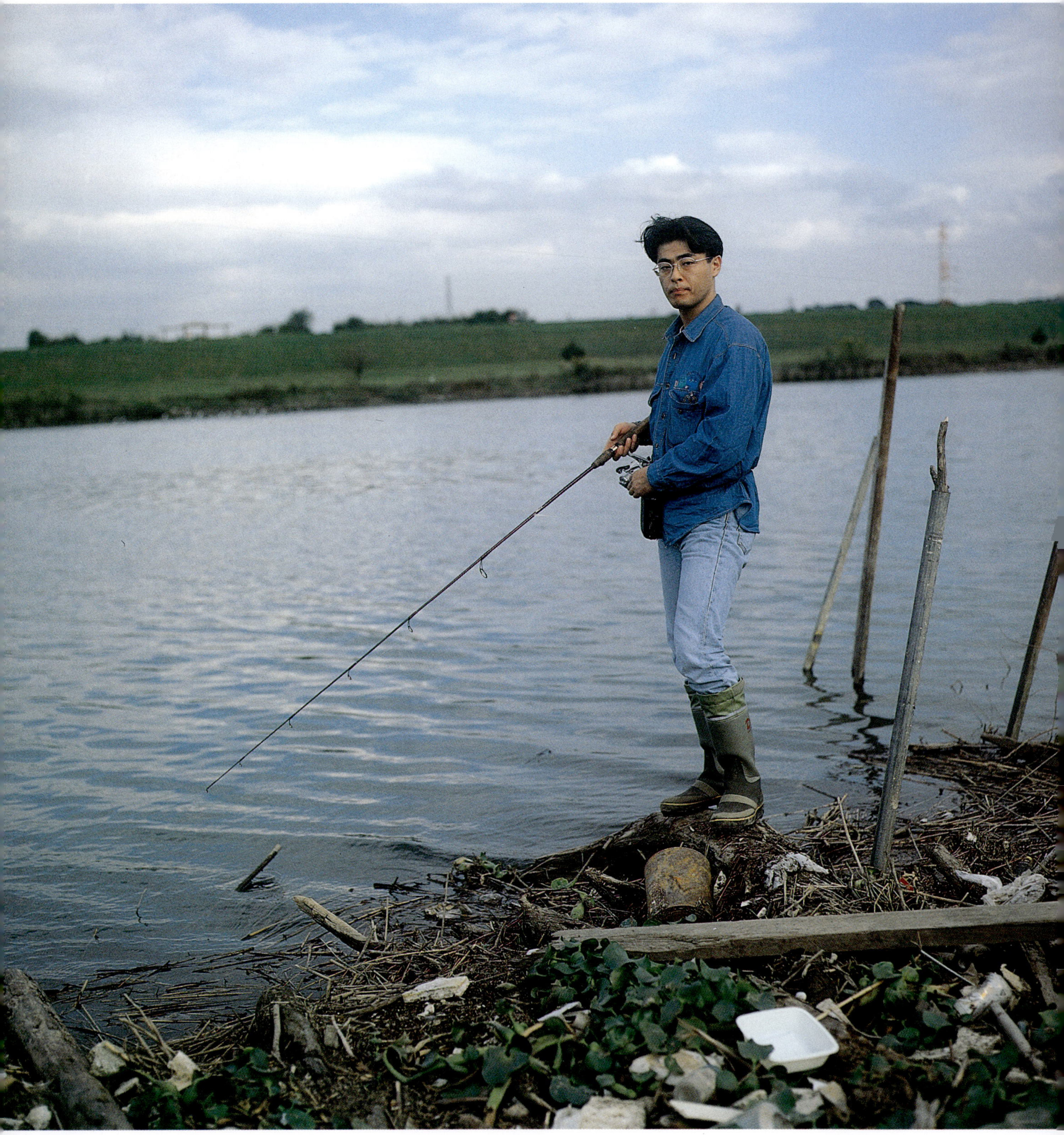

Fishing on the Edogawa. "When I was a kid," says this man, "this river was clean. I used to swim to the other side." Japan has begun to take a serious look at the problems afflicting its natural environment.

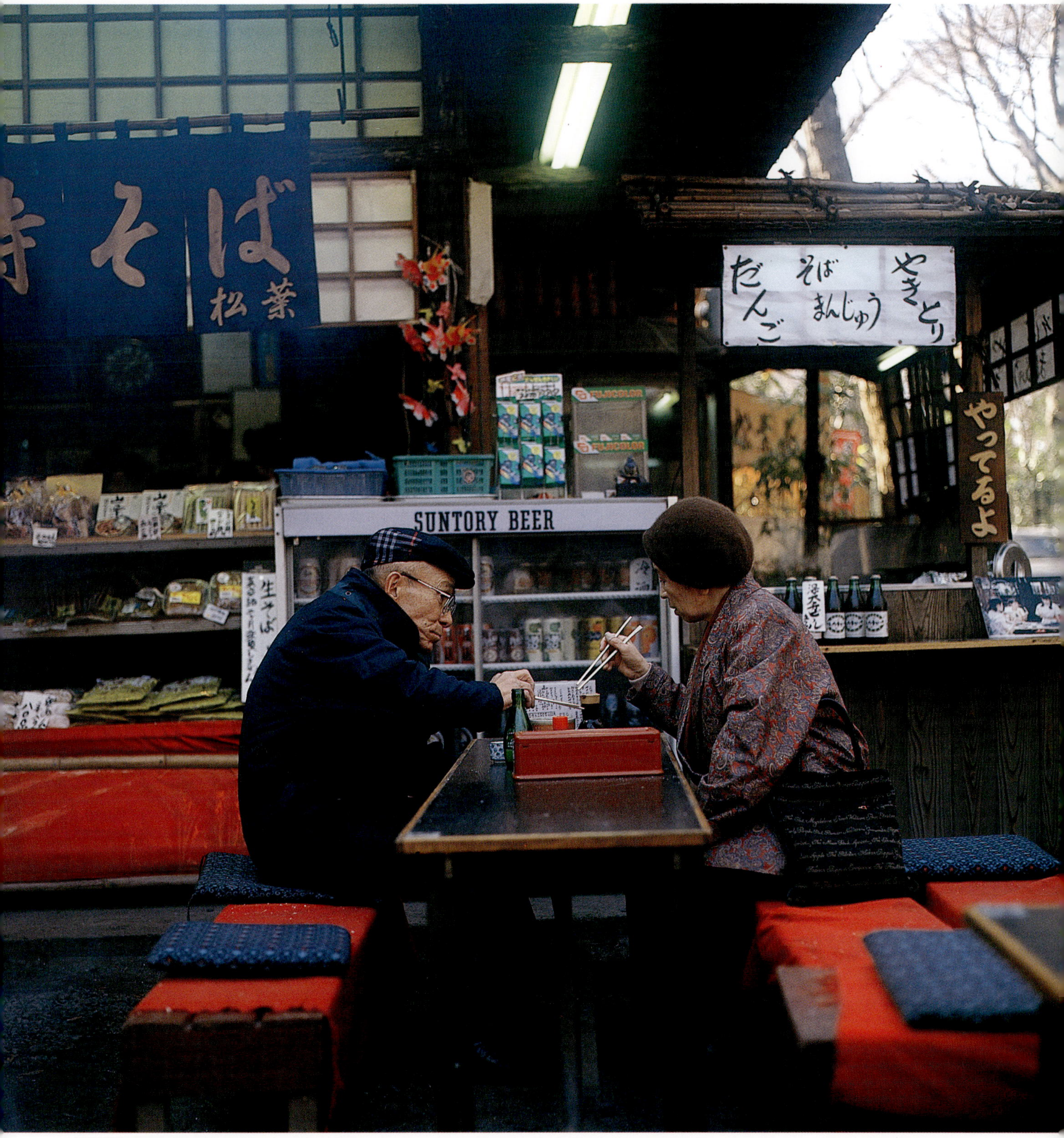


This couple are taking tea at a shop near Jindaiji temple. Jindaiji is located in the western suburbs of Tokyo, on the Musashino Plateau — an upland once characterized by woodlands and fields but now dominated by factories and housing projects. A trace of the old Musashi Plateau survives in the neighborhood around Jindaiji, which is dotted with wooded areas.

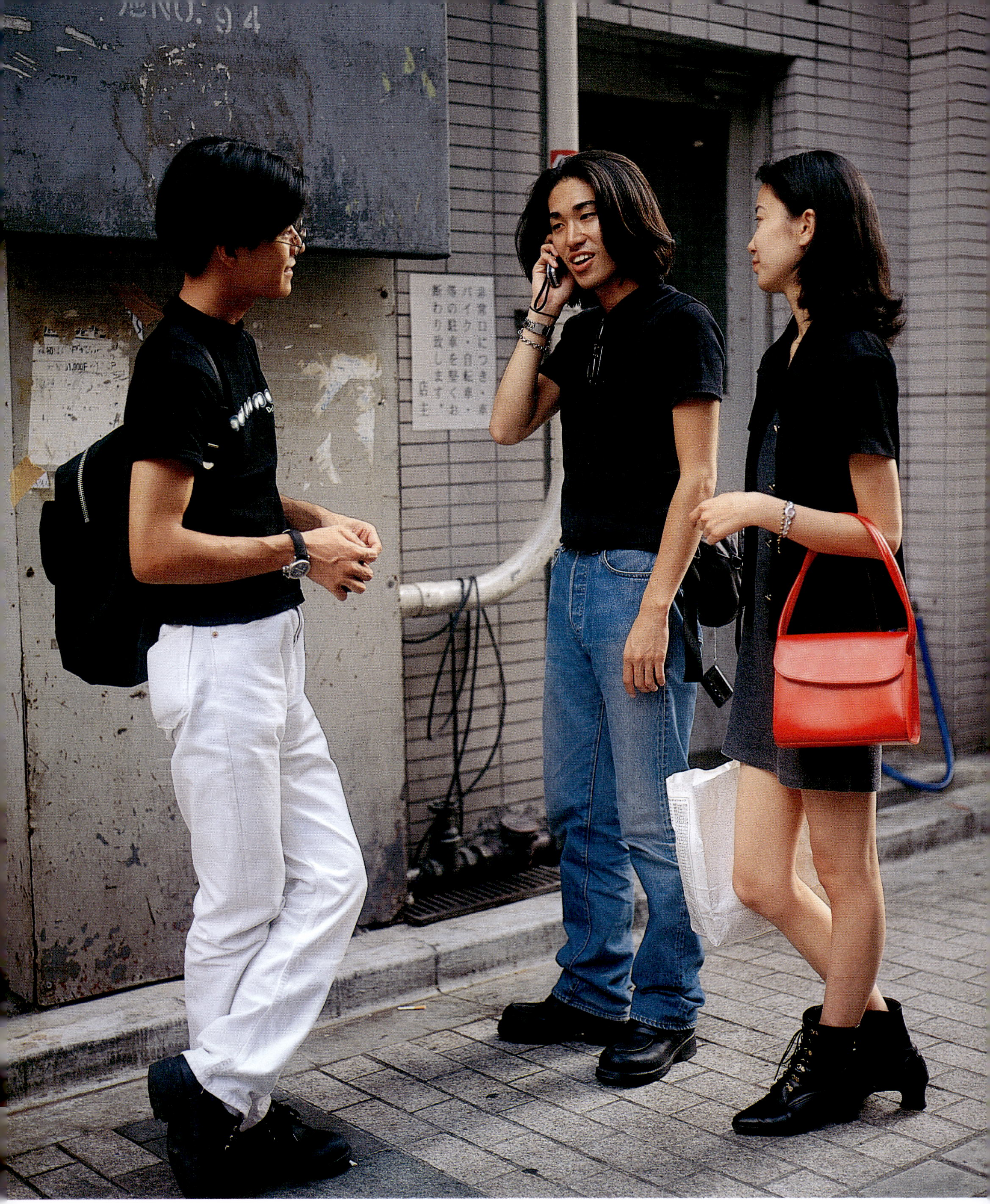


Young people these days wouldn't dream of leaving home without their cellphones or pagers.

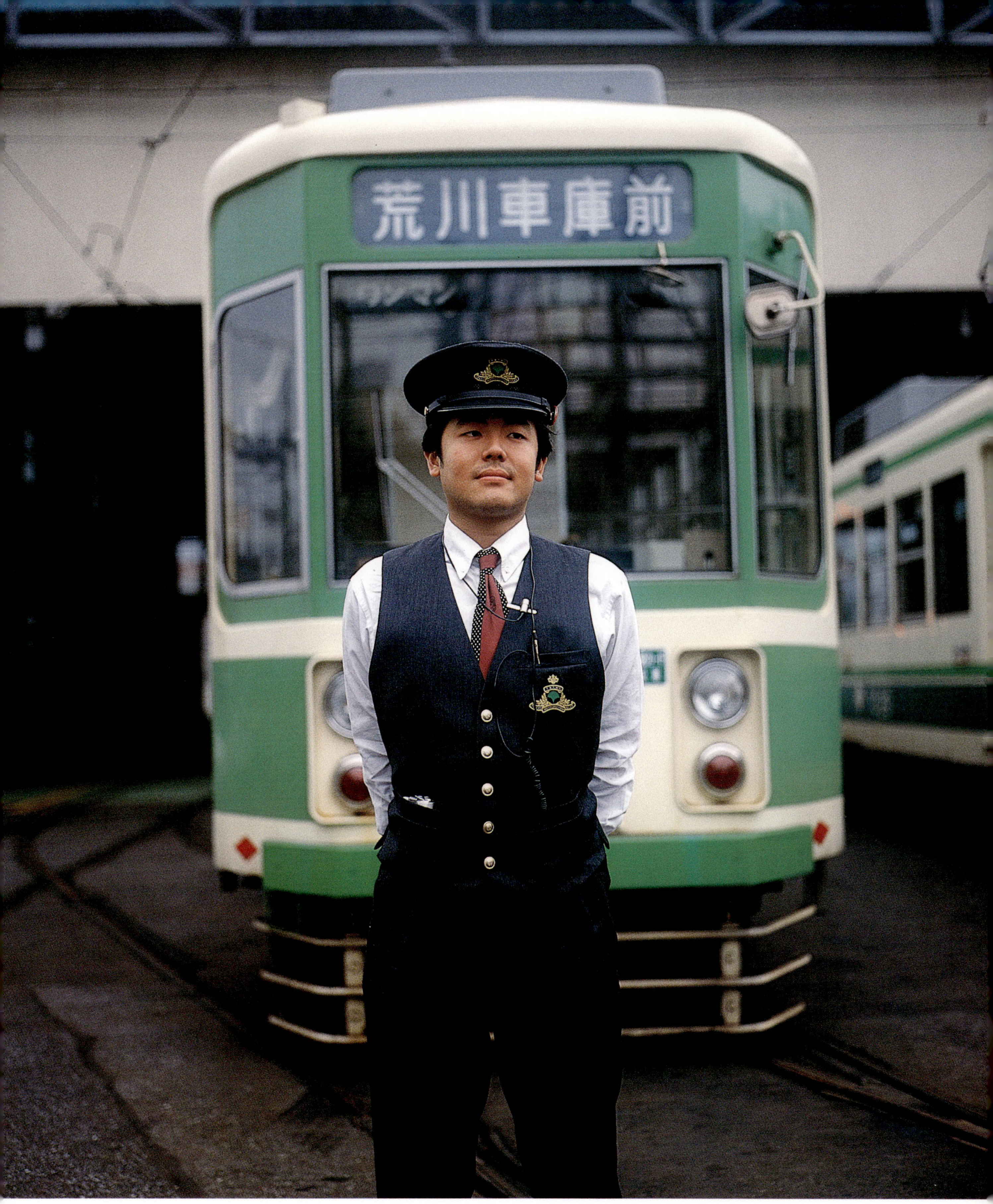


This man is a conductor on Tokyo's only remaining streetcar line, the Toden Arakawa Line. The train passes through some of the city's older neighborhoods — moving slowly, so you can enjoy the view.

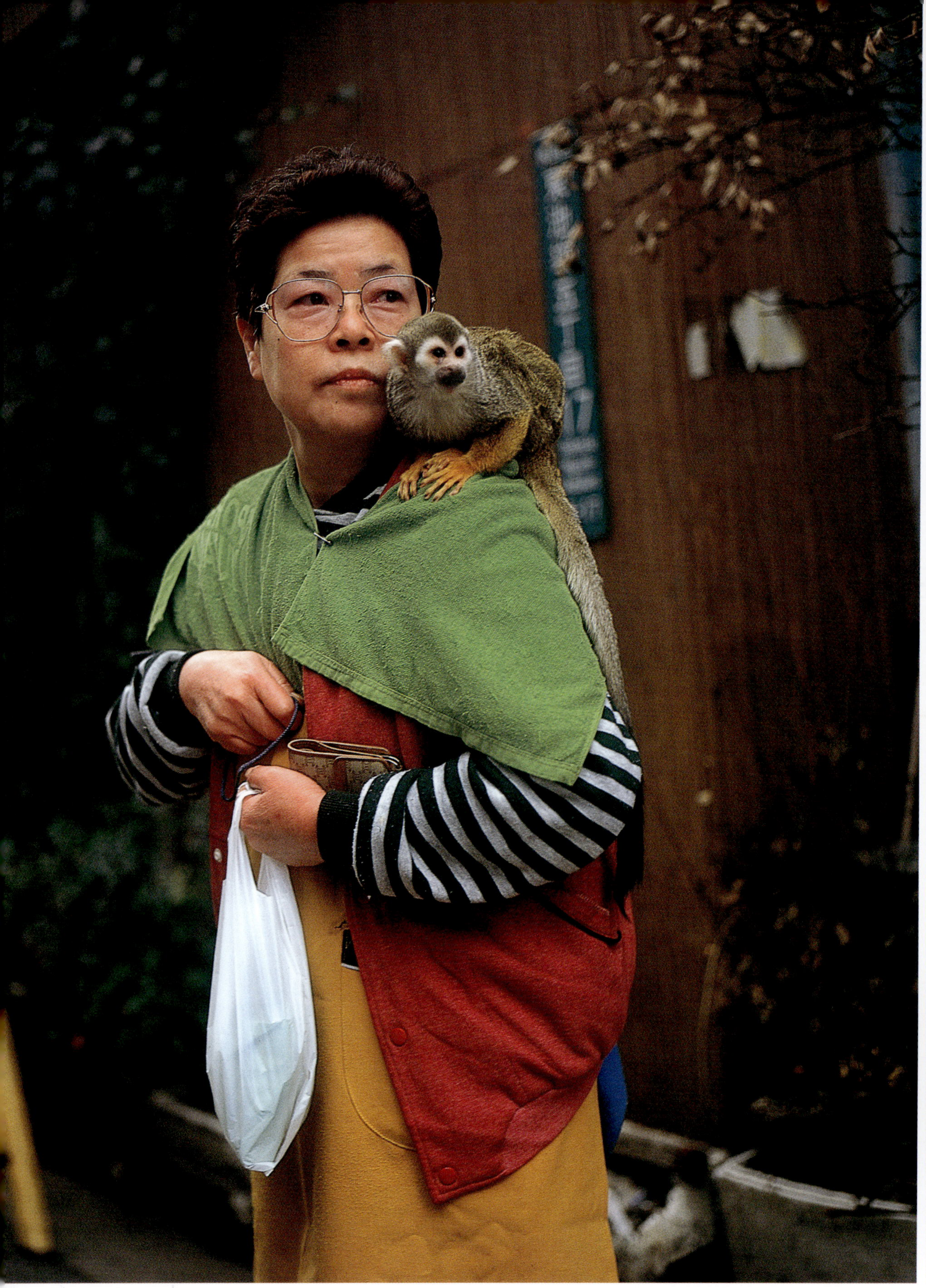

This beloved pet monkey accompanies its owner even on shopping trips. In the cities, where ties between human beings have grown tenuous, an increasing number of people are keeping pets.

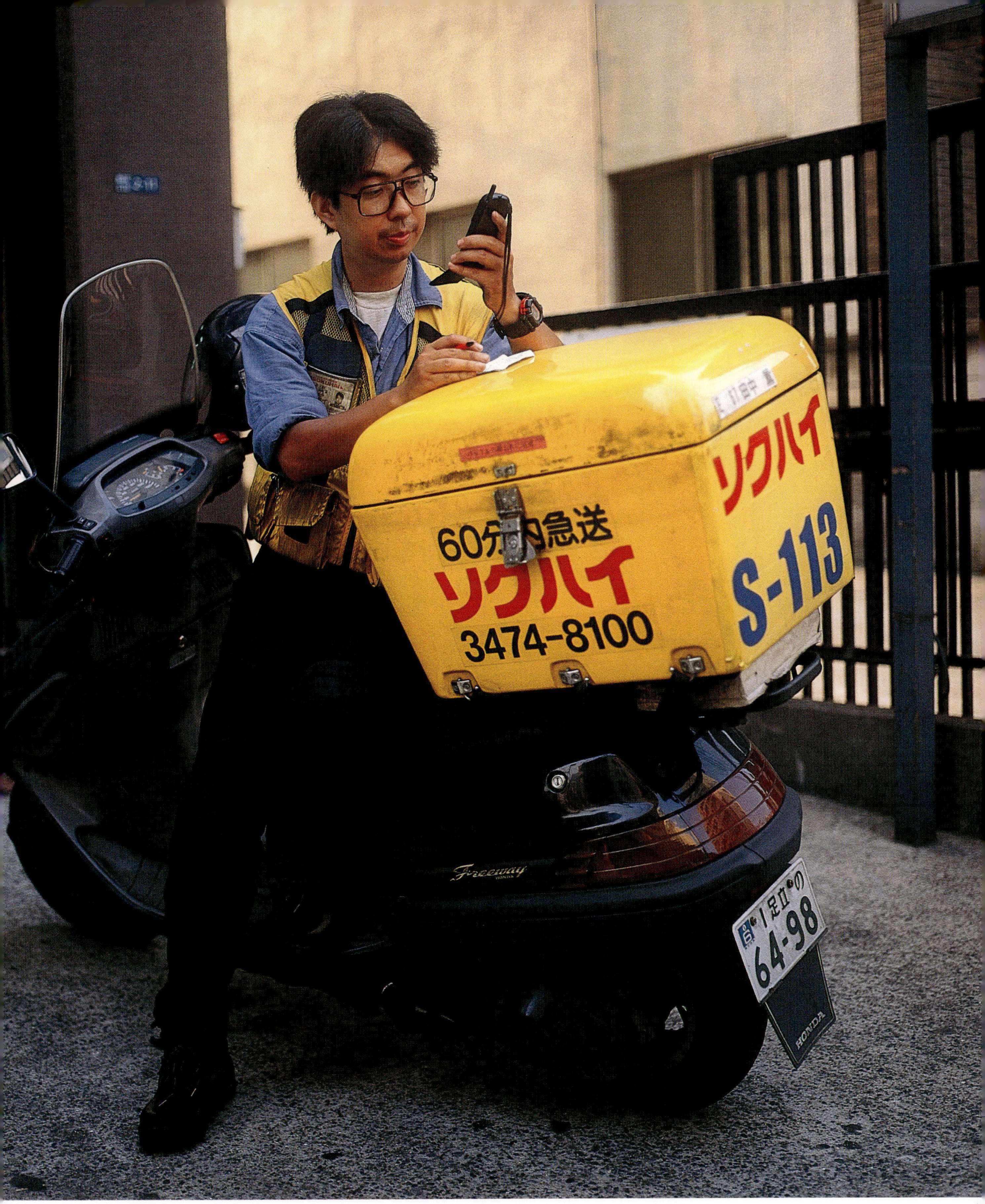


With the business world operating at an ever-increasing pace, motorbike couriers have become indispensable. The scooters sail triumphantly past endless columns of backed-up traffic as they whisk small packages to their destinations.

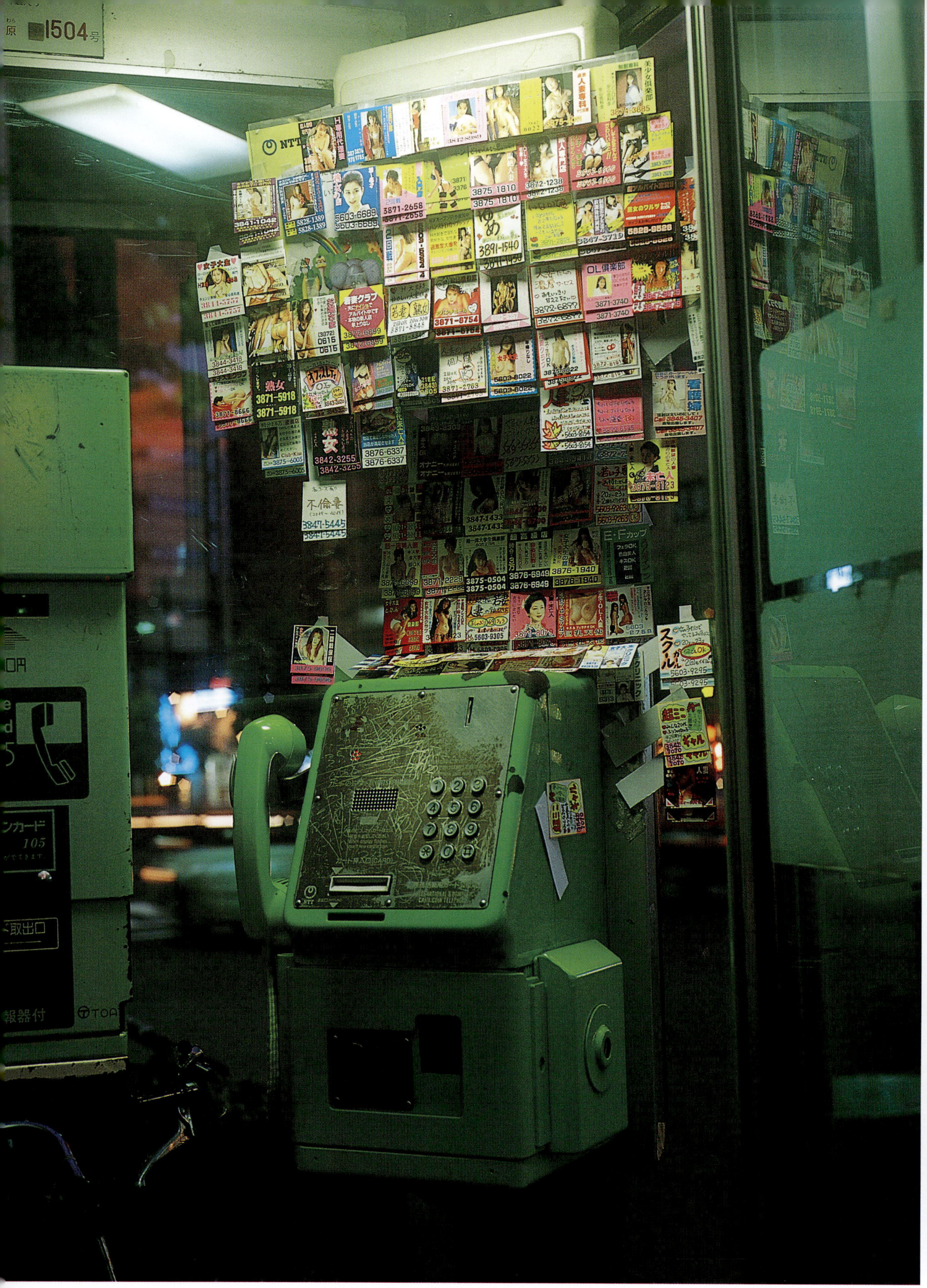

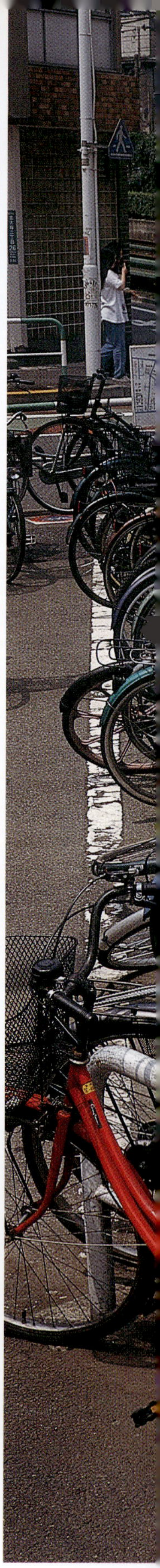

Inside this public phone booth lurks temptation. The walls are plastered with leaflets touting an array of illicit pleasures. As a wise philosopher might say, life offers us two paths: We can be true to reason, or we can blindly follow our baser instincts.

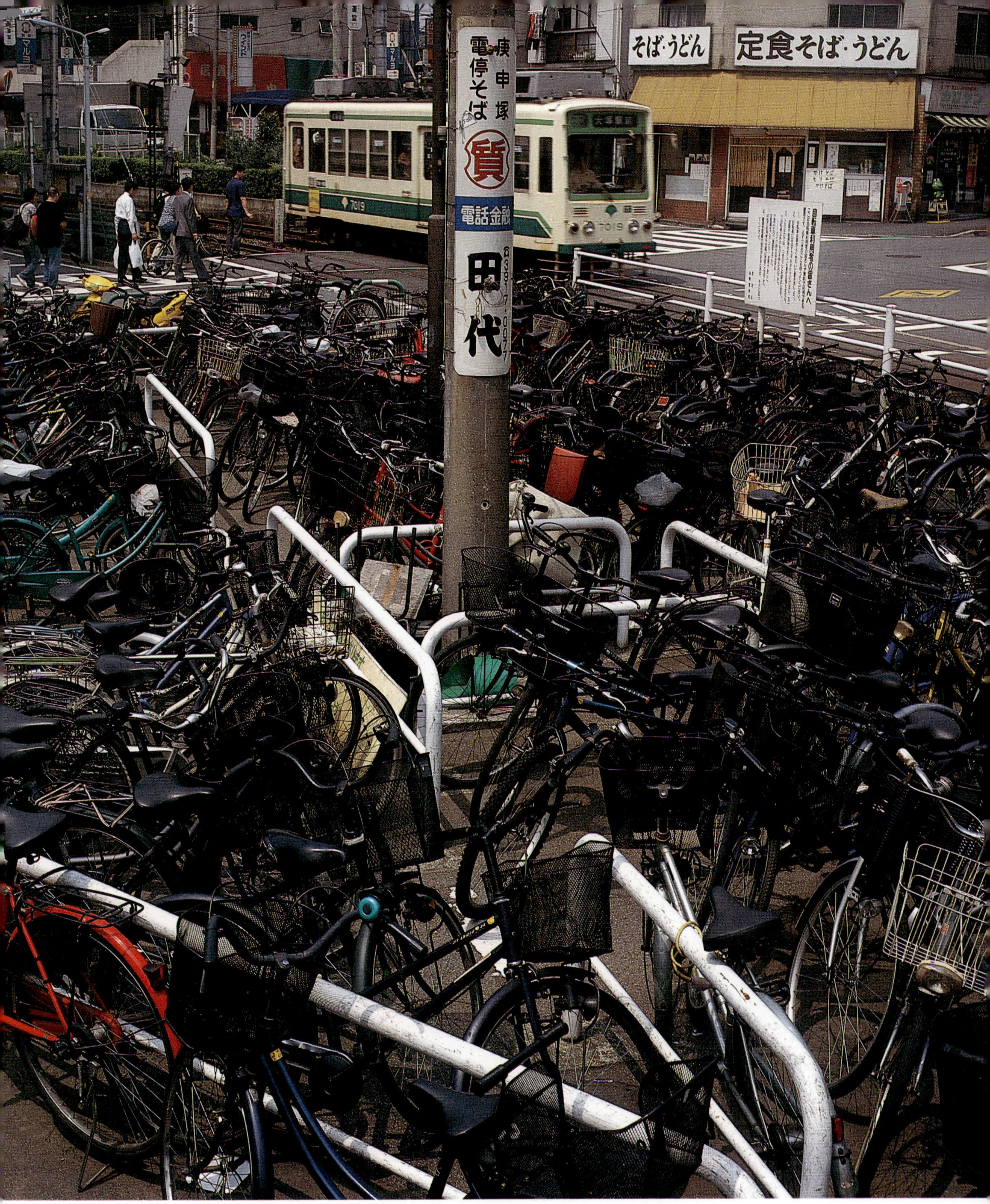


Bicycle parking areas near train stations are often full to the point of overflowing, so that the bikes encroach on streets and sidewalks — a phenomenon so severe and widespread that the term "bicycle pollution" has been coined to describe it.

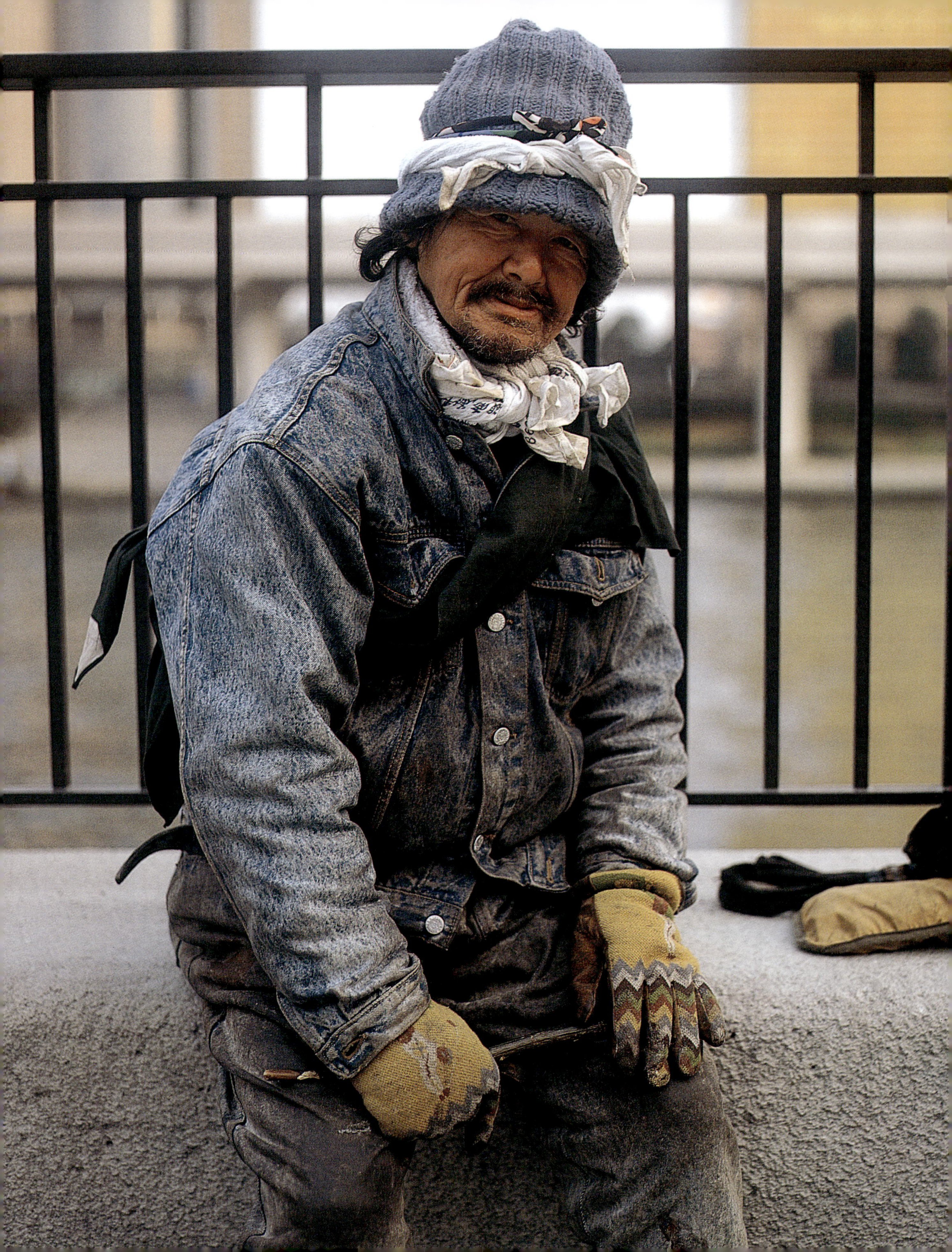

“It’s cold again today, so I’ll sleep inside the station,” says this man. “I’ve been living like this for two, three years now. Someday I want to leave the city and go back to the country.”

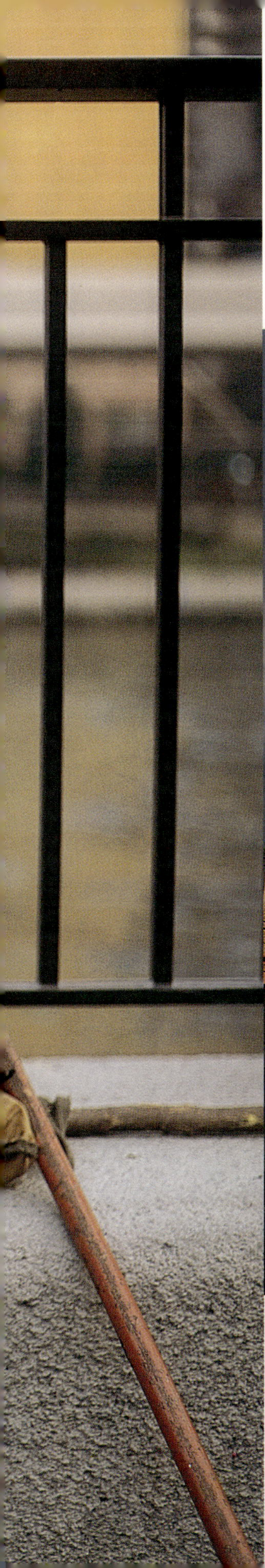

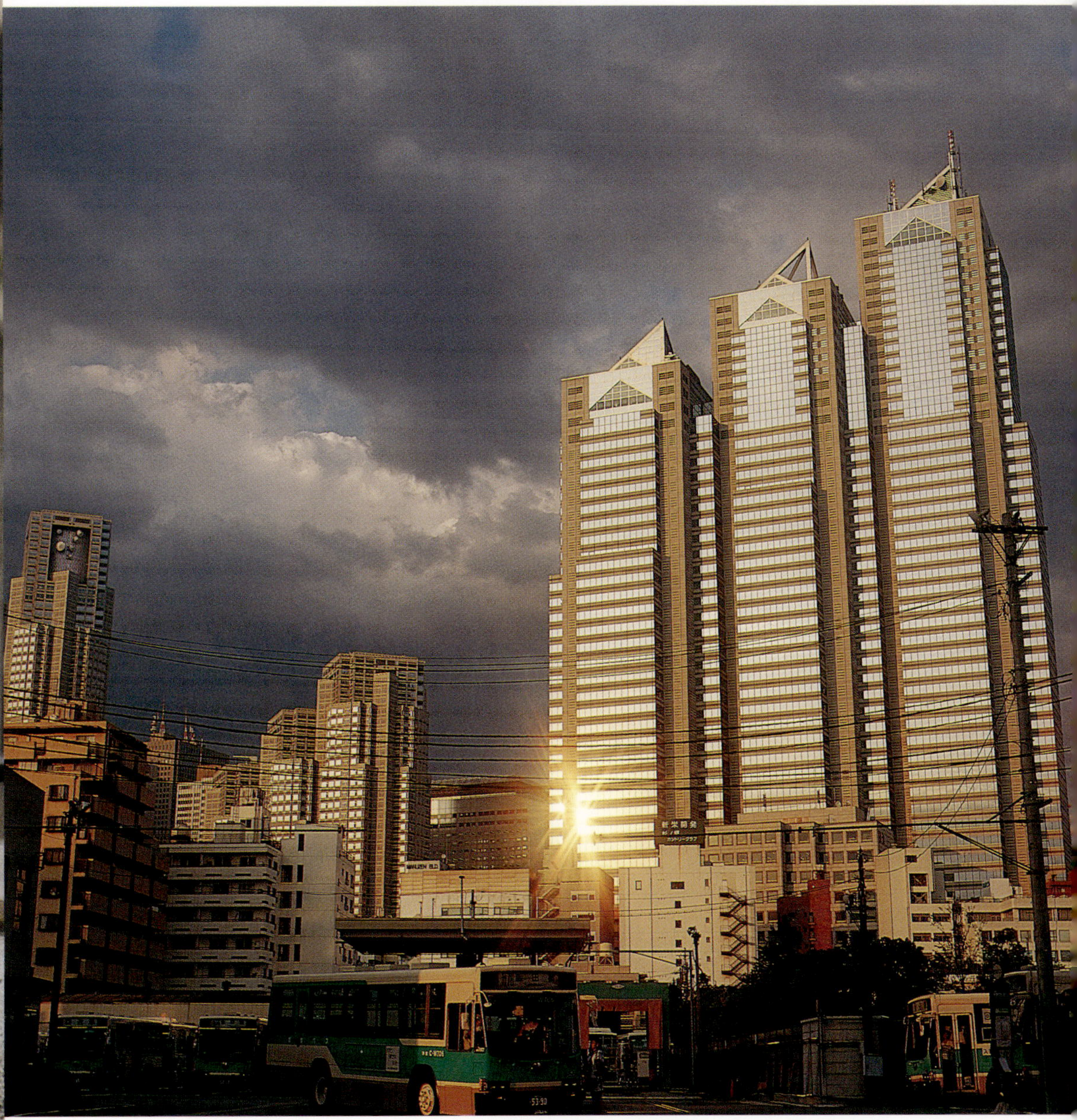

Tokyo serves a variety of roles for Japan. Government functions, for instance, are highly concentrated in the capital. In this photo, the sun sets on skyscrapers in Shinjuku, home to many new high-rise office buildings.

This Shinjuku street, ordinarily clogged with traffic, is closed to cars on Sundays. It is a pedestrian's paradise, attracting many different types—which also makes it a people-watcher's paradise.

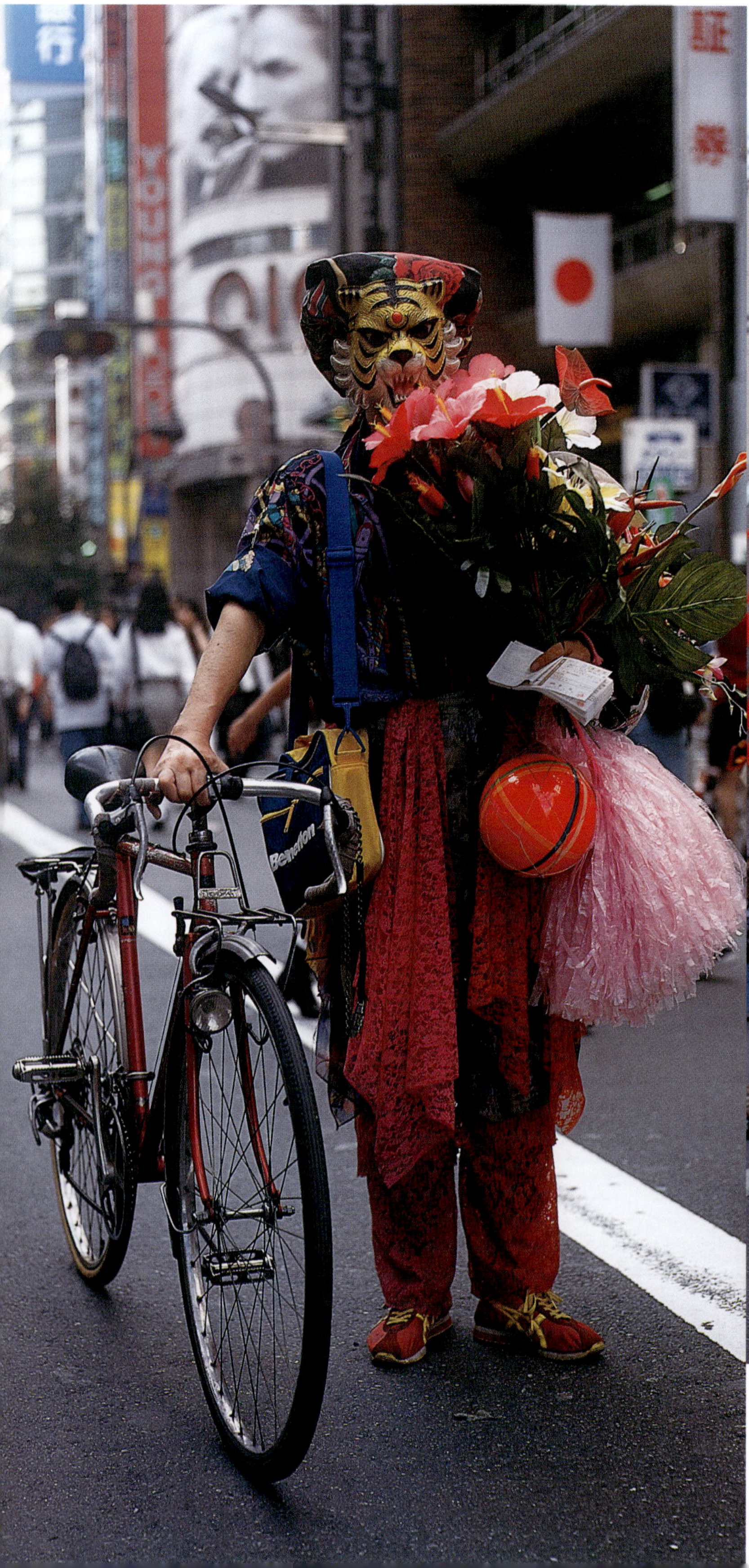


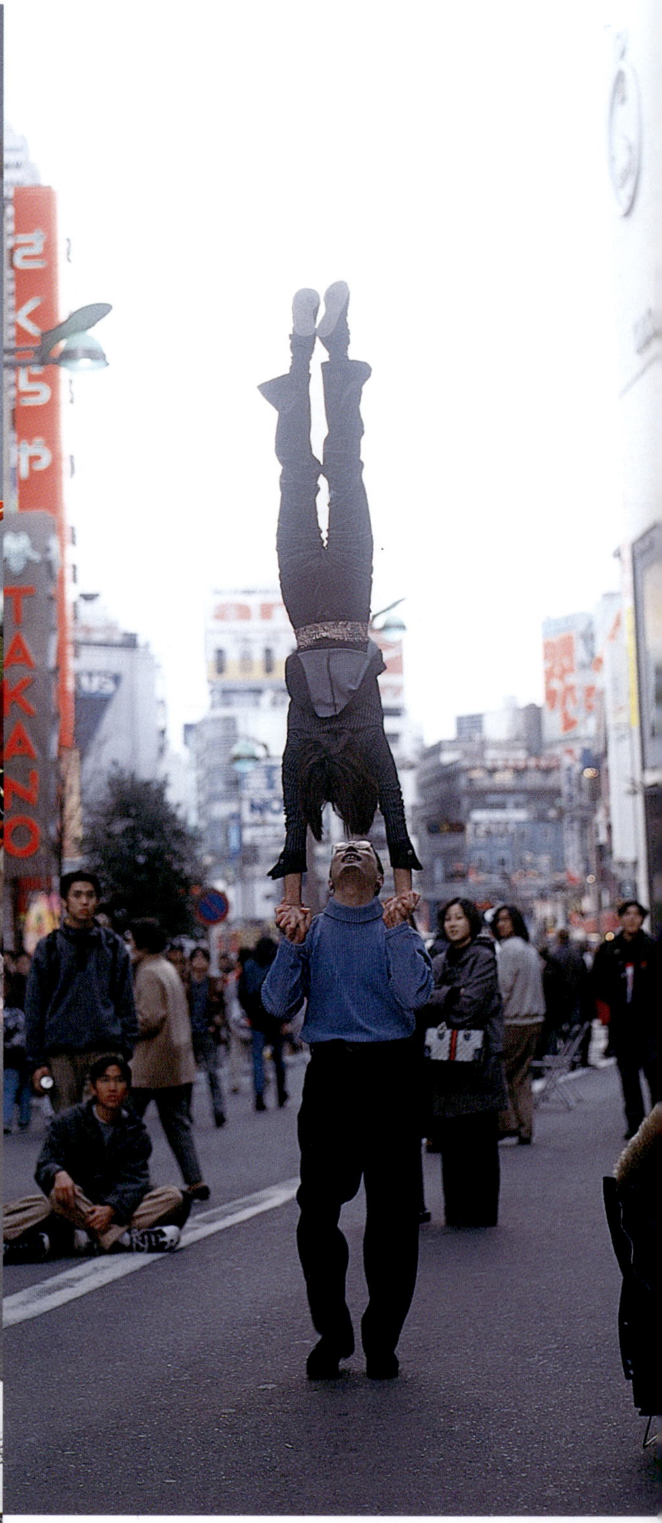

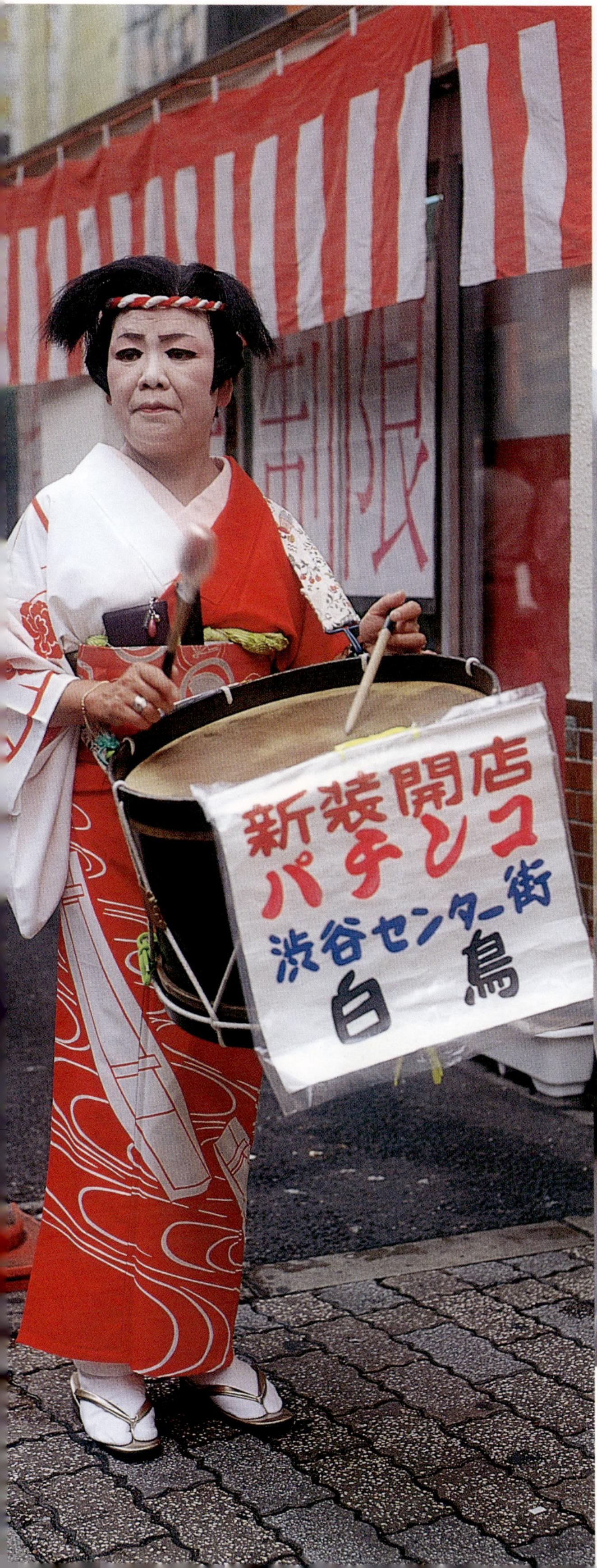


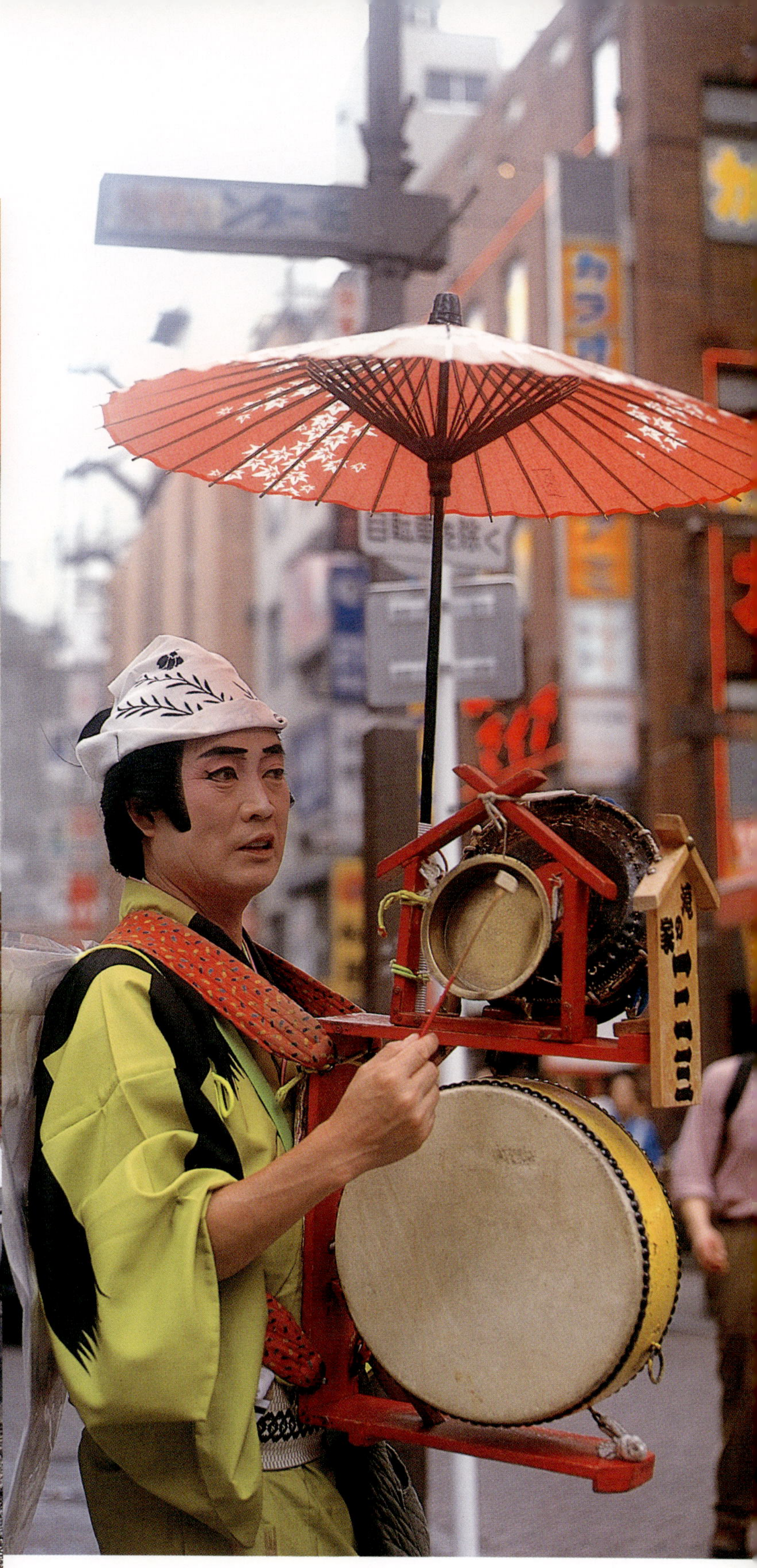

These people are *chindon-ya*—street entertainers employed to act as walking advertisements for store openings and other events. Banging their gongs and beating their drums, they dance through the streets creating a festive atmosphere.

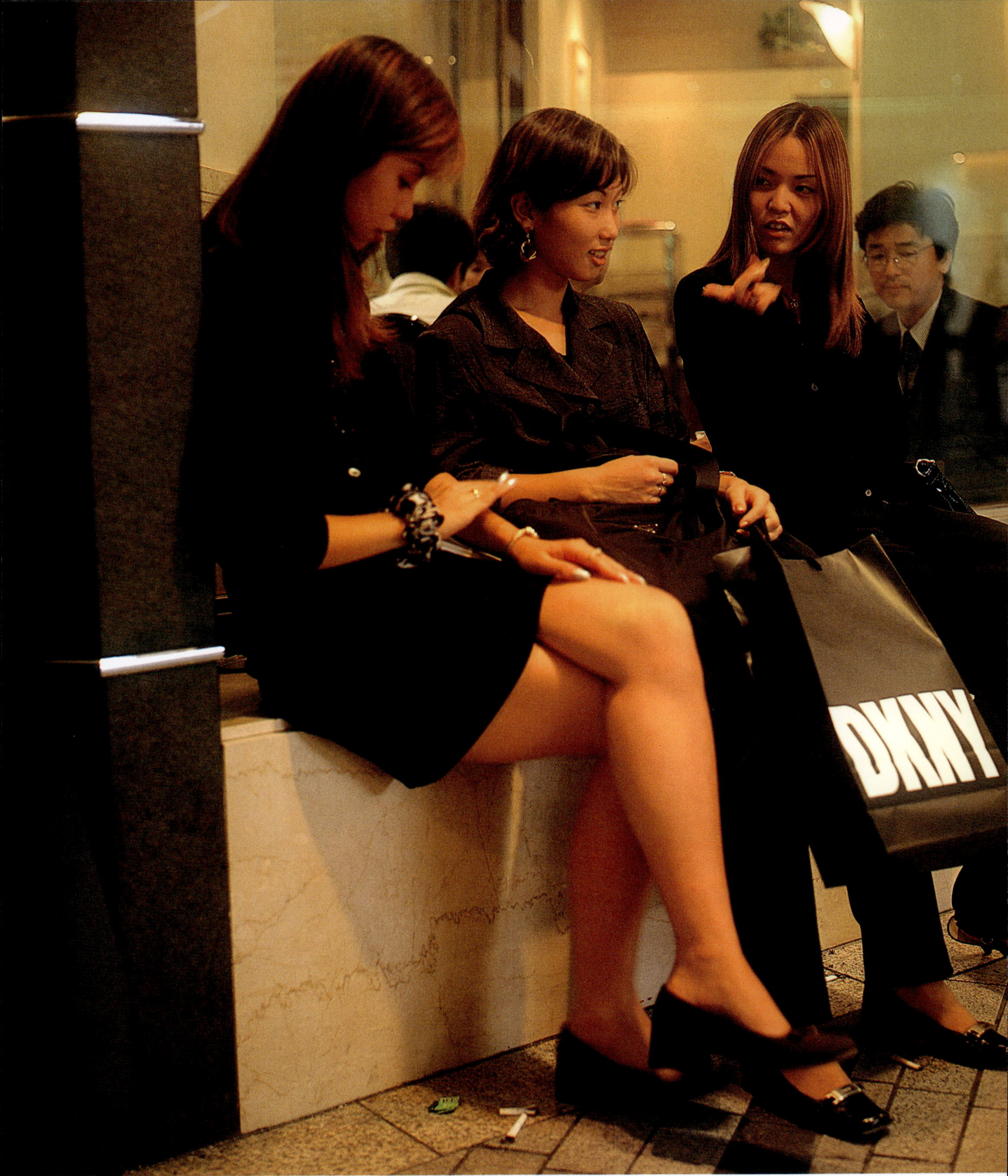


Young women out shopping. Among Japanese consumers, single women are reported to have the greatest purchasing power.

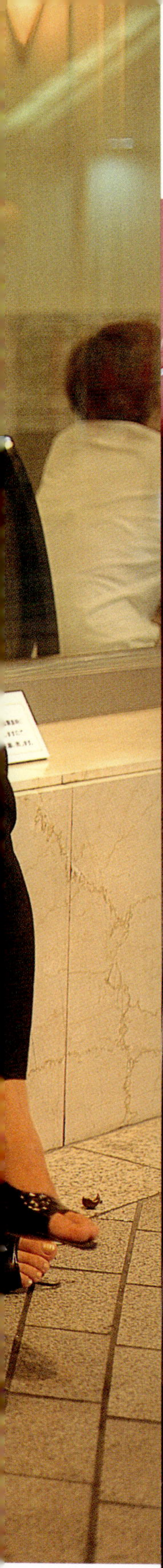

With the display window of a leading department store in the background, a couple stop to catch their breath during a shopping expedition.

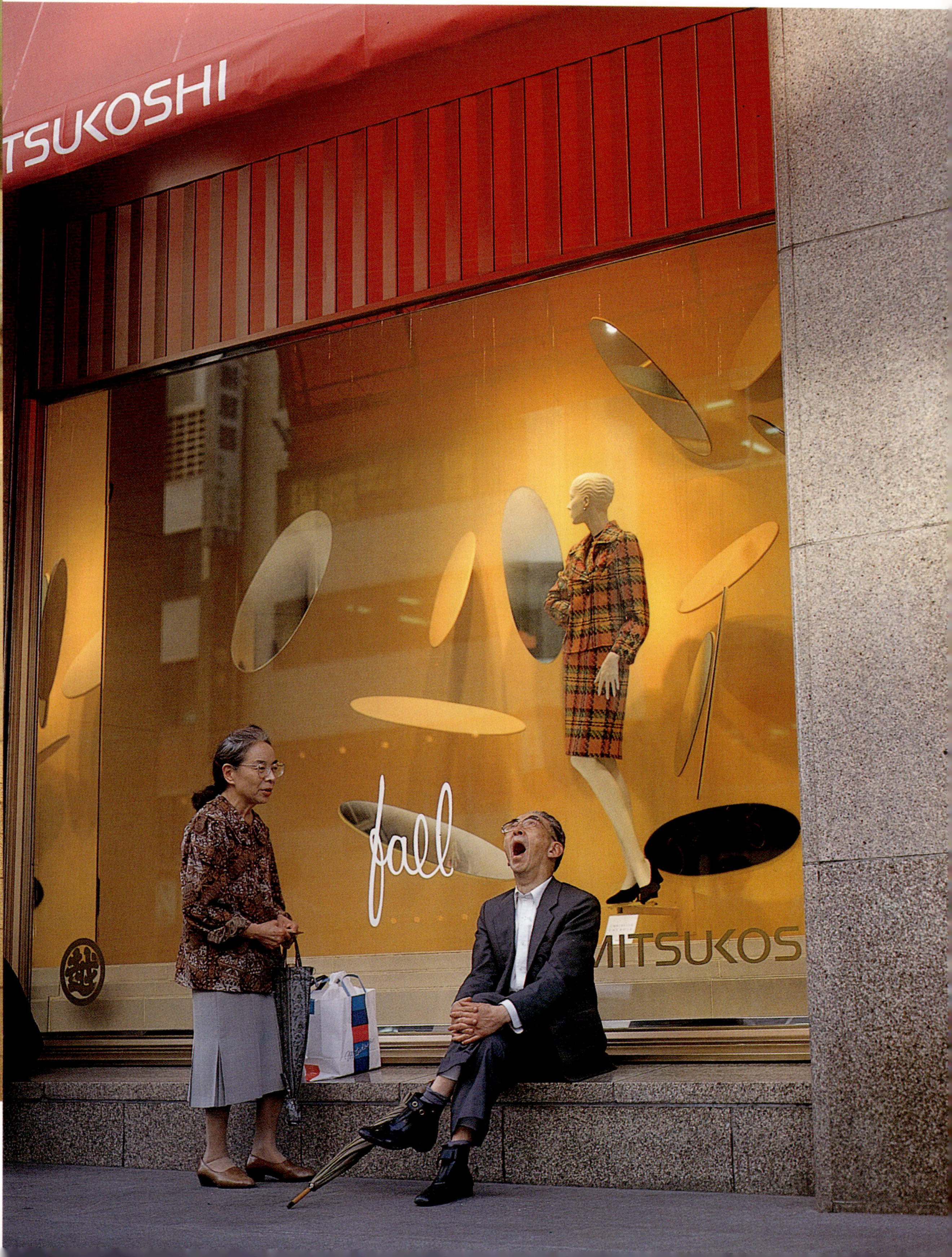

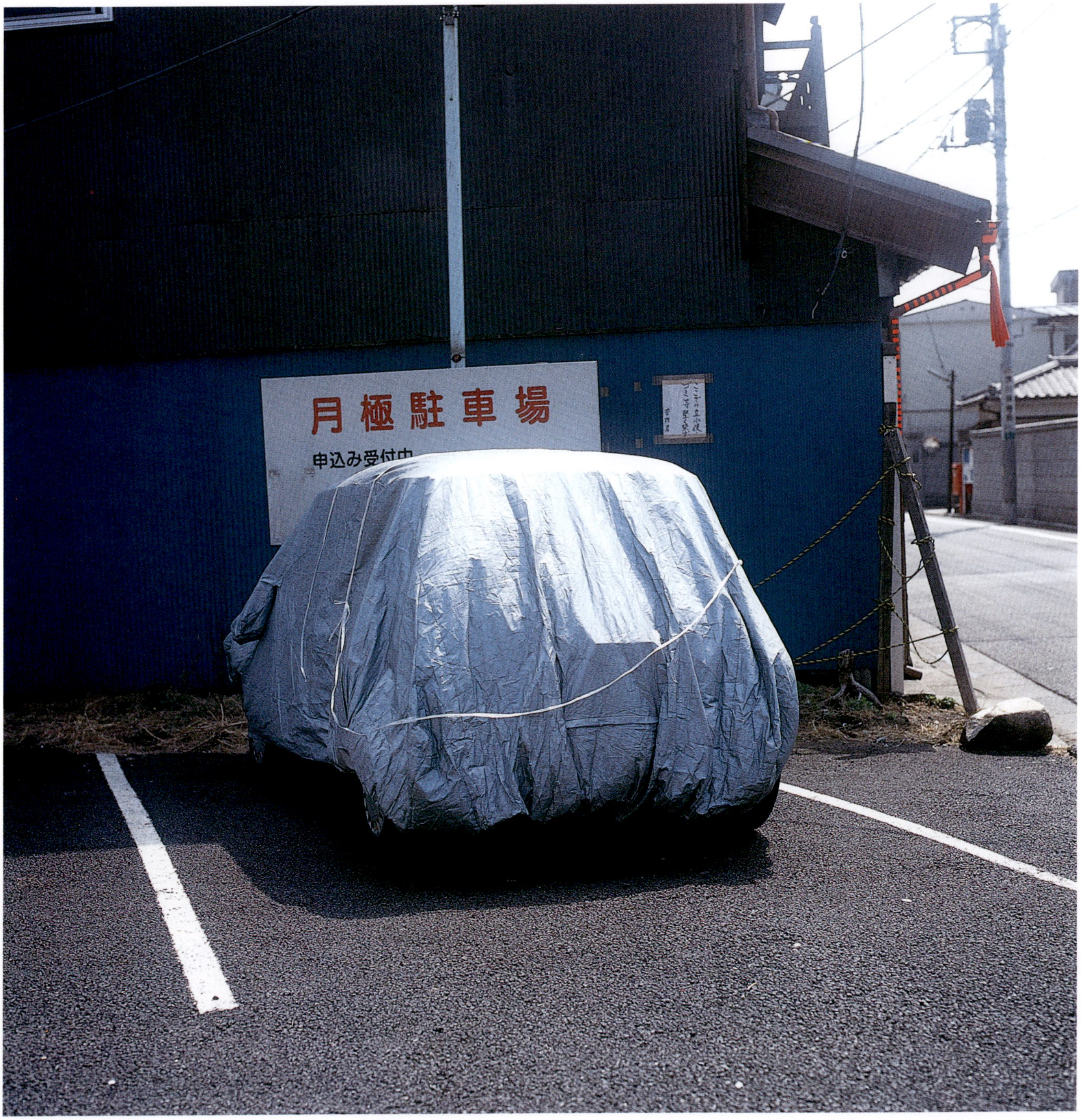


Where there's a sliver of idle real estate—no matter how tiny—there's room to build a parking lot. In central Tokyo, it's not unusual to pay over $450 a month for a parking space. There are now about 3.7 million cars in the metropolitan area.

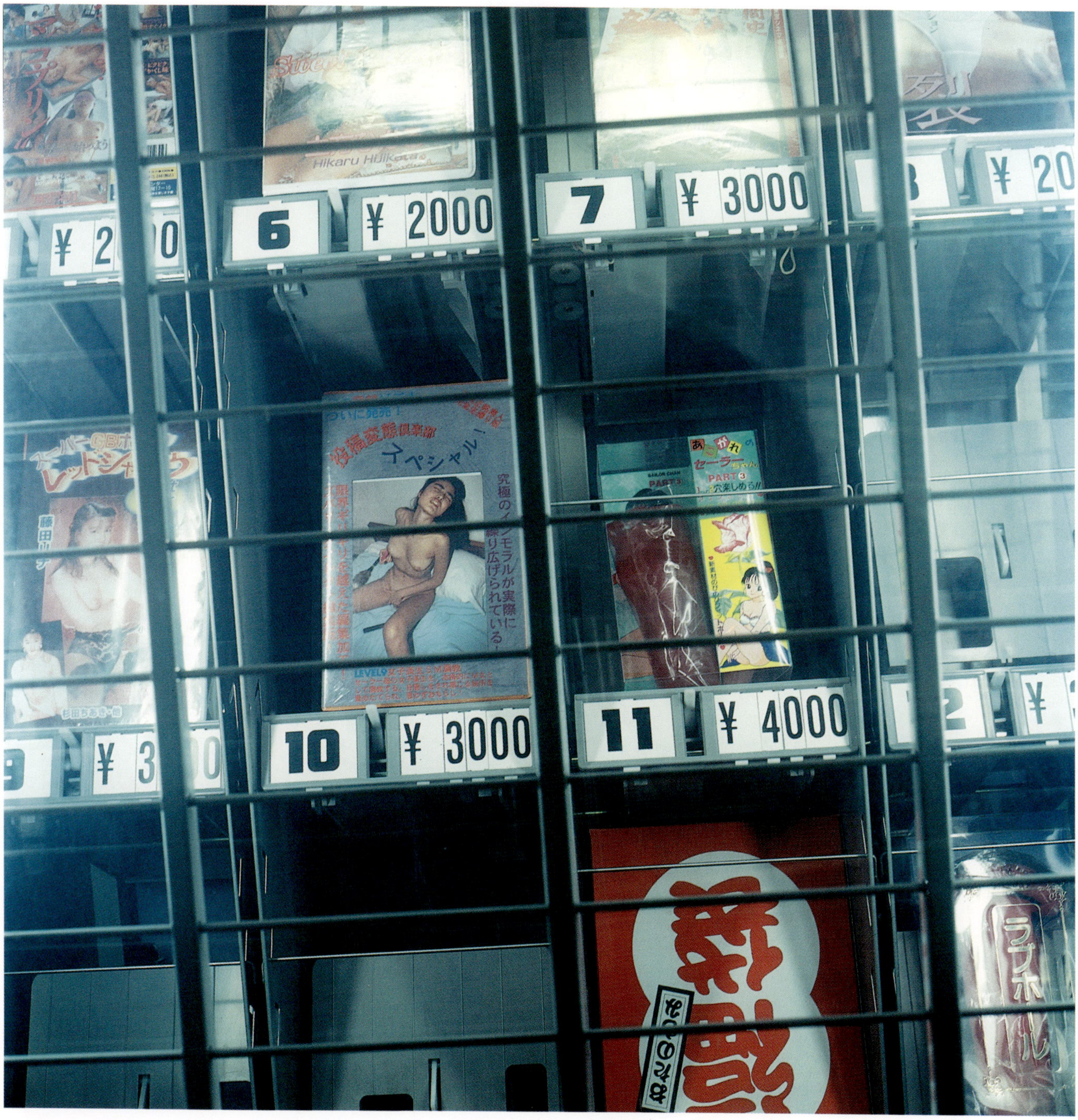


Even pornographic videos and other sex-related merchandise can be purchased from vending machines.

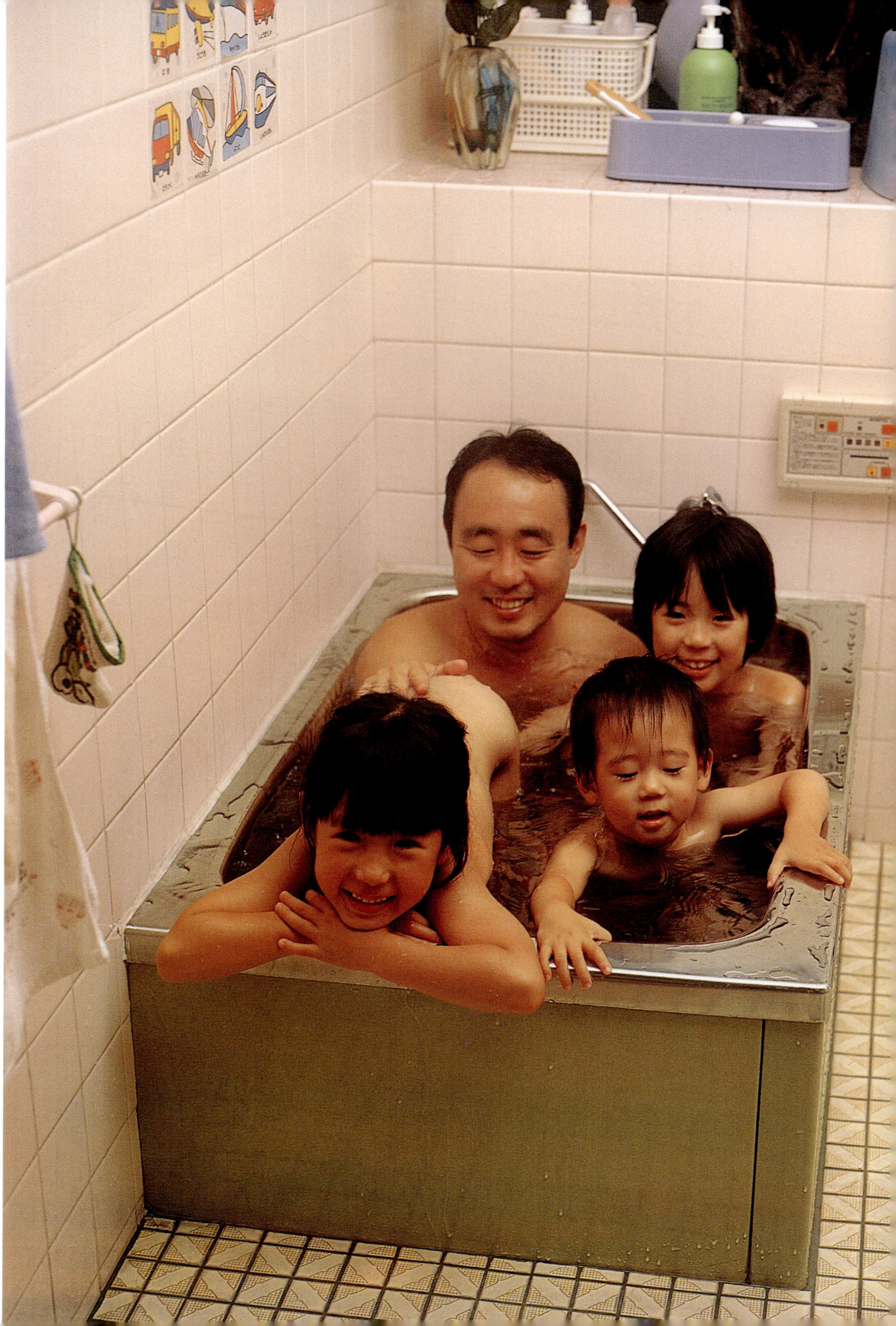

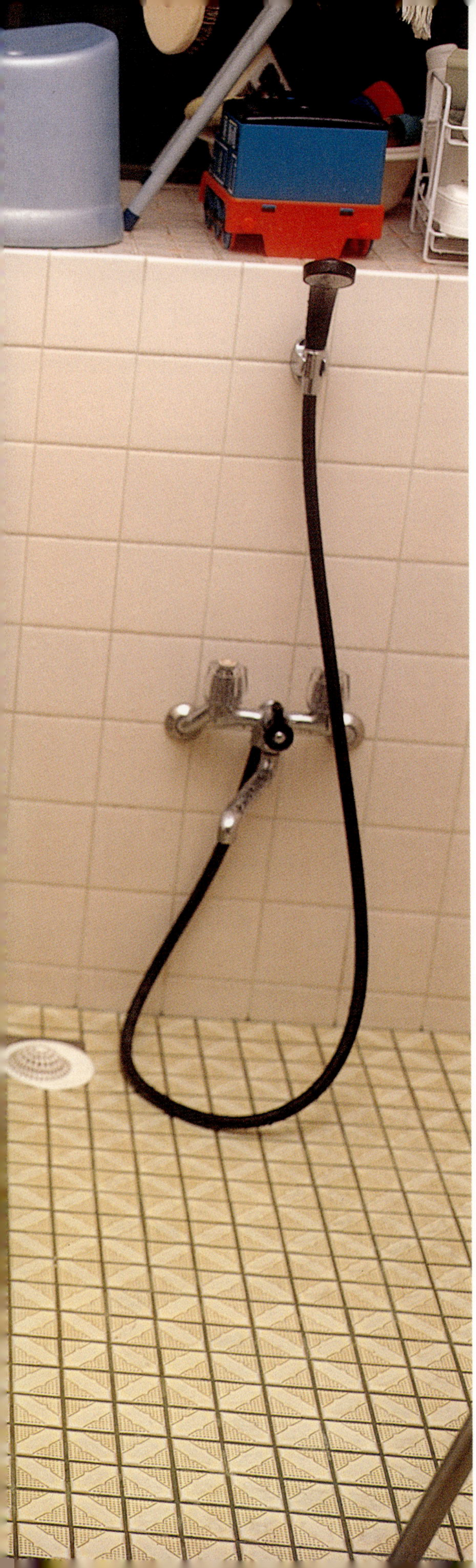

A typical family bath. For a father blessed with three children, this is one of life's most precious moments.

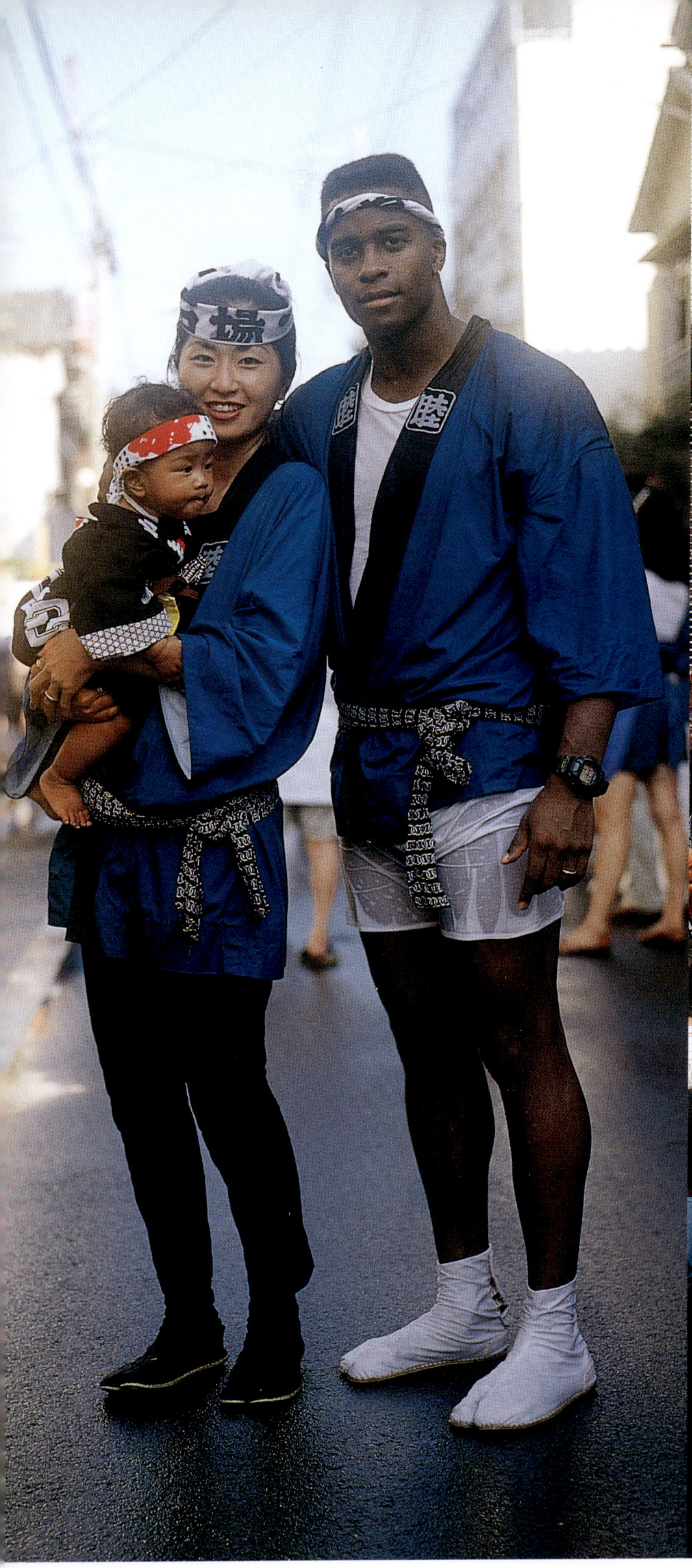

This couple and their baby are dressed in traditional festival attire. Though it's not the custom in his country, the man wears his *happi* coat well. He and his wife have been married for a year.

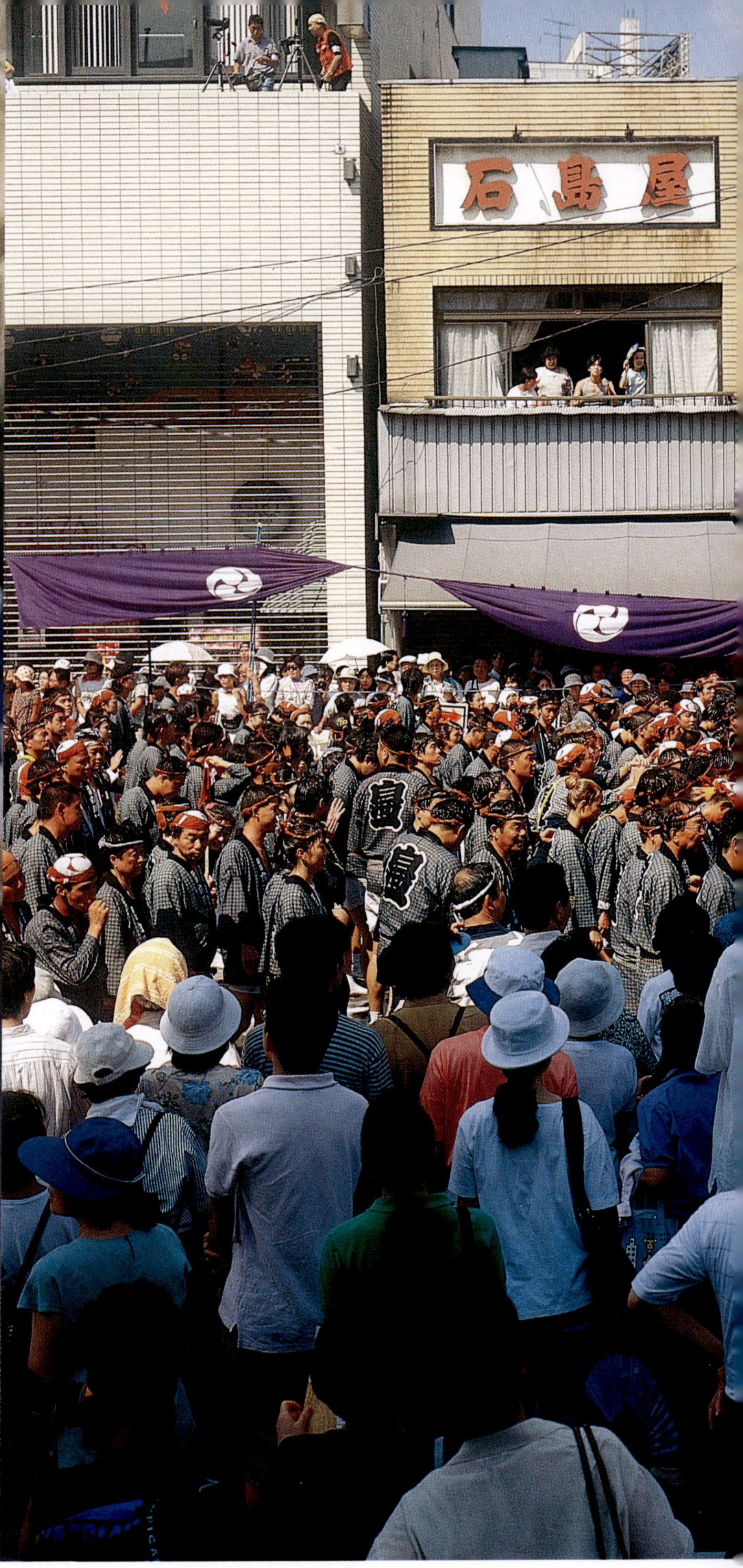


Participants in a festival hoist a portable shrine on their shoulders. Carrying the shrine, they will jostle their way through crowded streets, chanting boisterously as they go. One aspect of festivals that has remained constant throughout the ages is the rowdy atmosphere; both those who participate and those who merely come to watch are invigorated by the spectacle. This photo was taken at the Fukagawa Hachiman Shrine Procession, one of the three major Edo festivals.

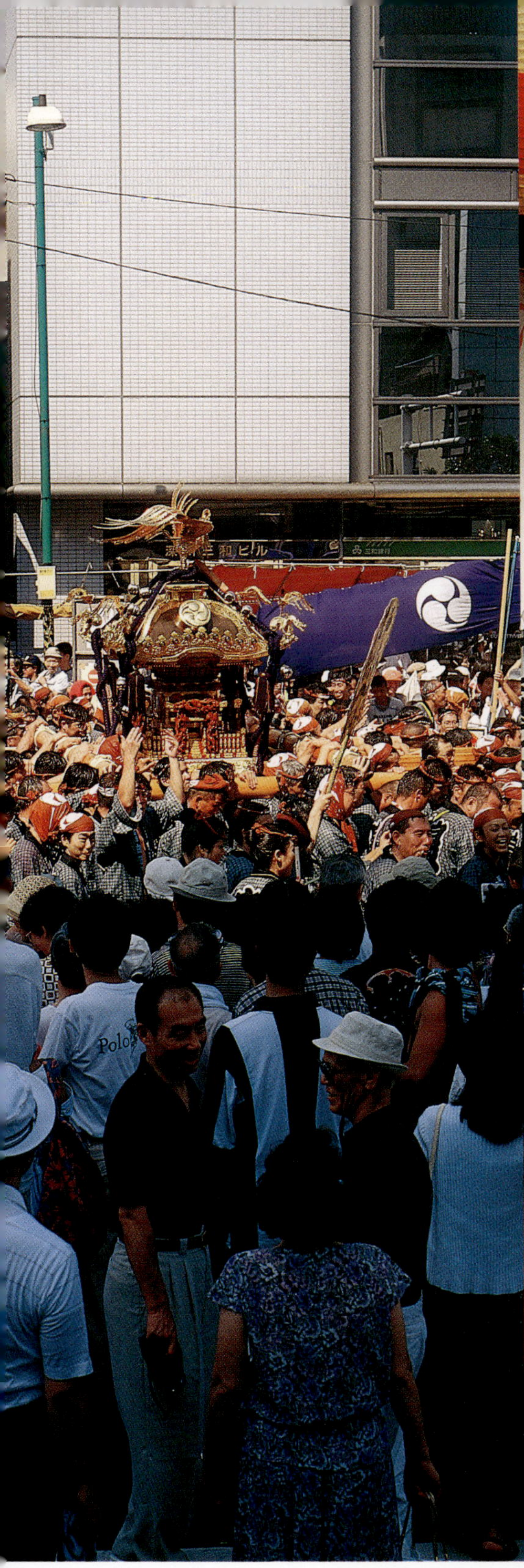

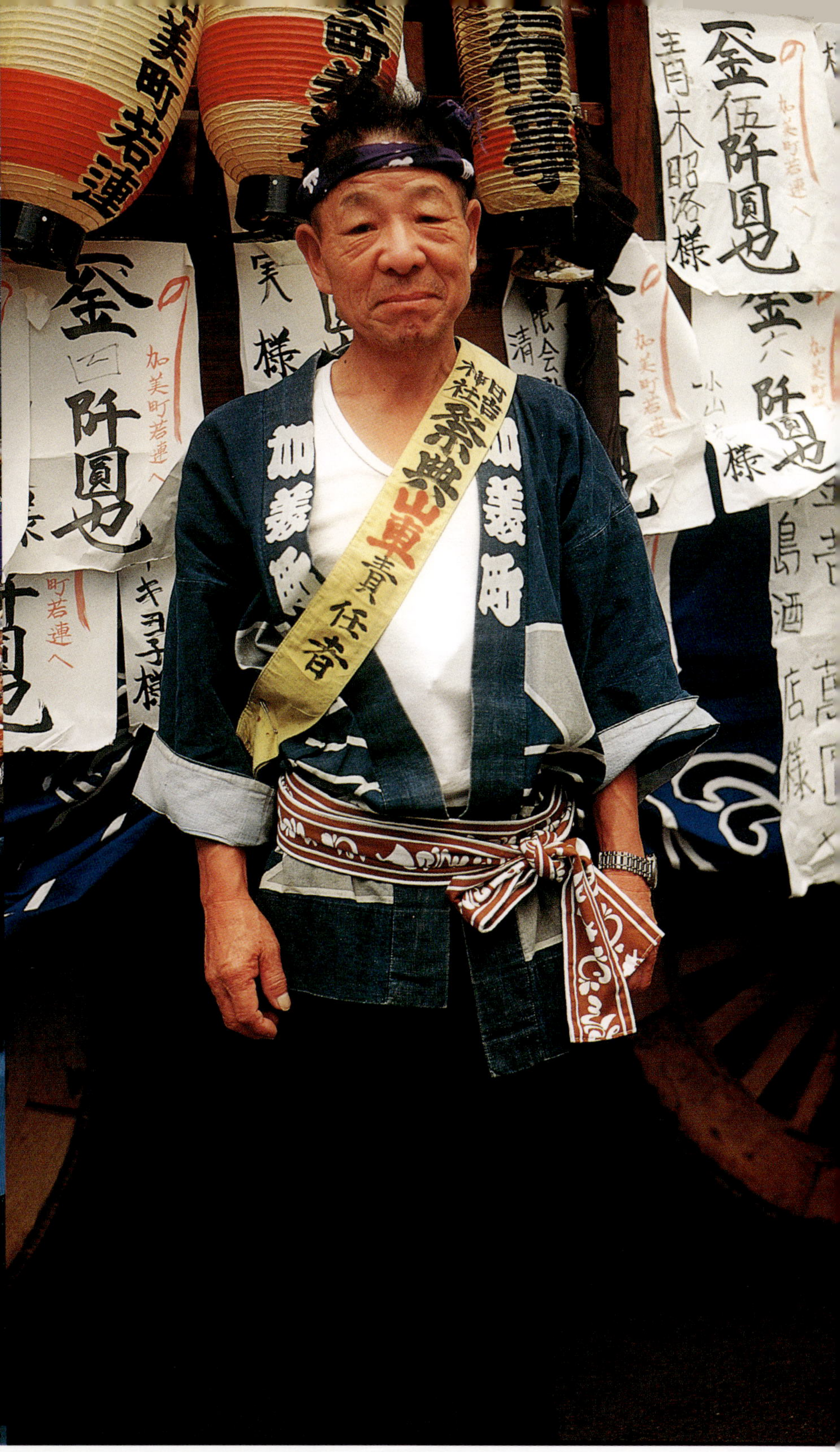


During autumn, many festivals are held to celebrate the harvest. The man in this picture is presiding over an autumn festival in a Tokyo suburb. Having enjoyed a cup of sake with friends, he is in high spirits.

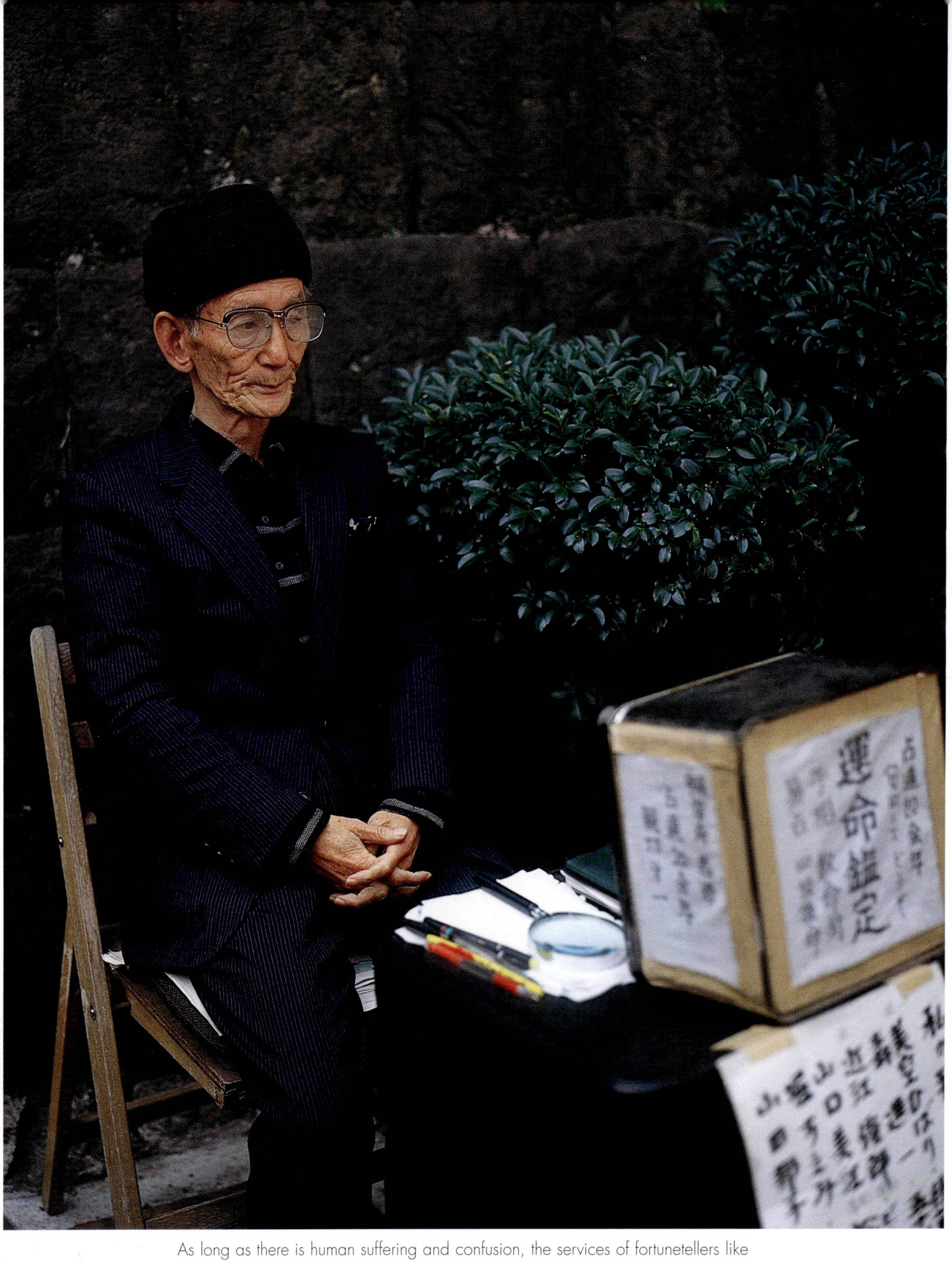


As long as there is human suffering and confusion, the services of fortunetellers like this palmist will always be in demand. Some fortunetellers build up such a following that people stand in line to hear their words of wisdom.

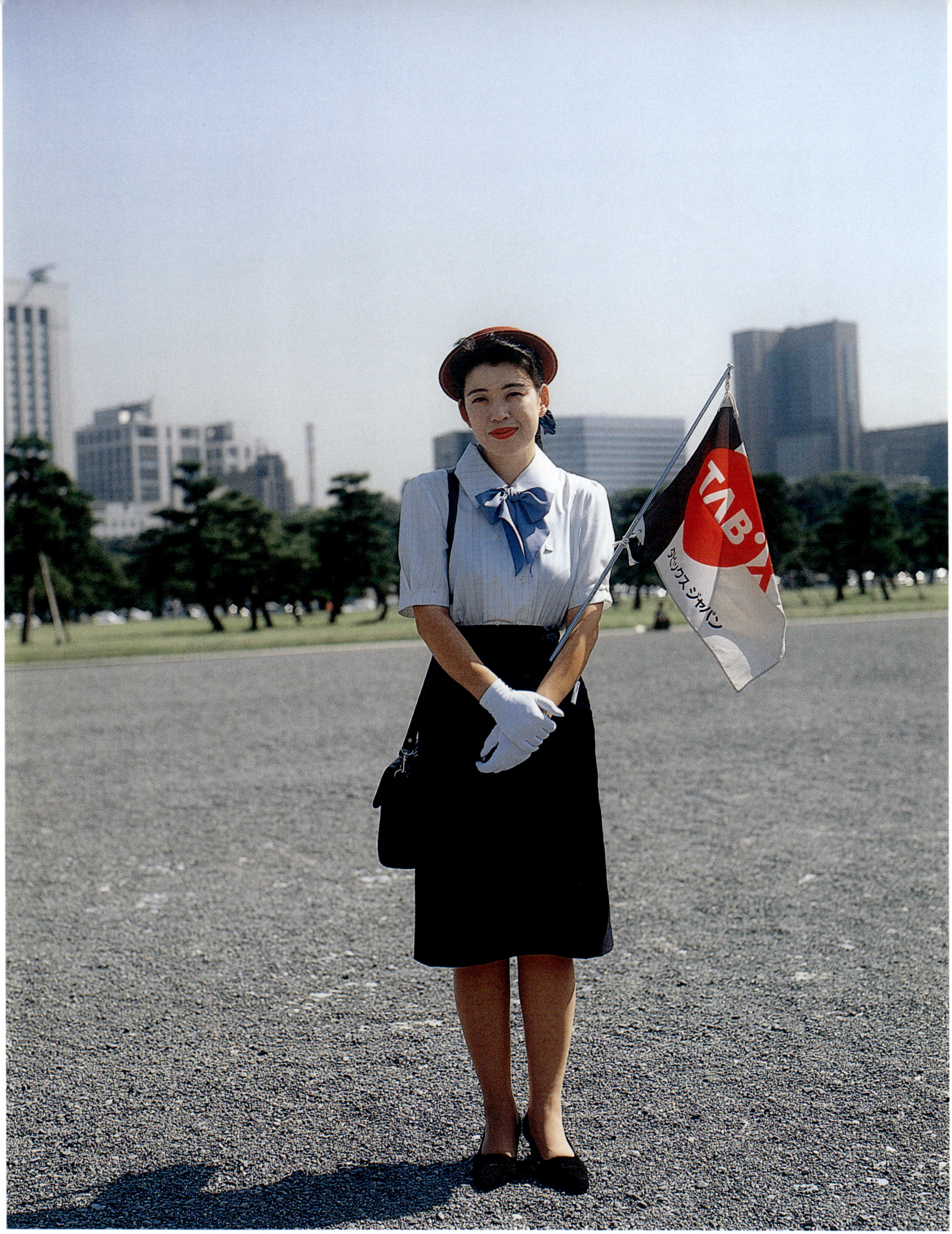


The Japanese love to travel in groups, and it's the job of this bus tour guide, flag in hand, to lead them. The guide is also a good singer and an adept conversationalist. After all, she has to keep her charges entertained.

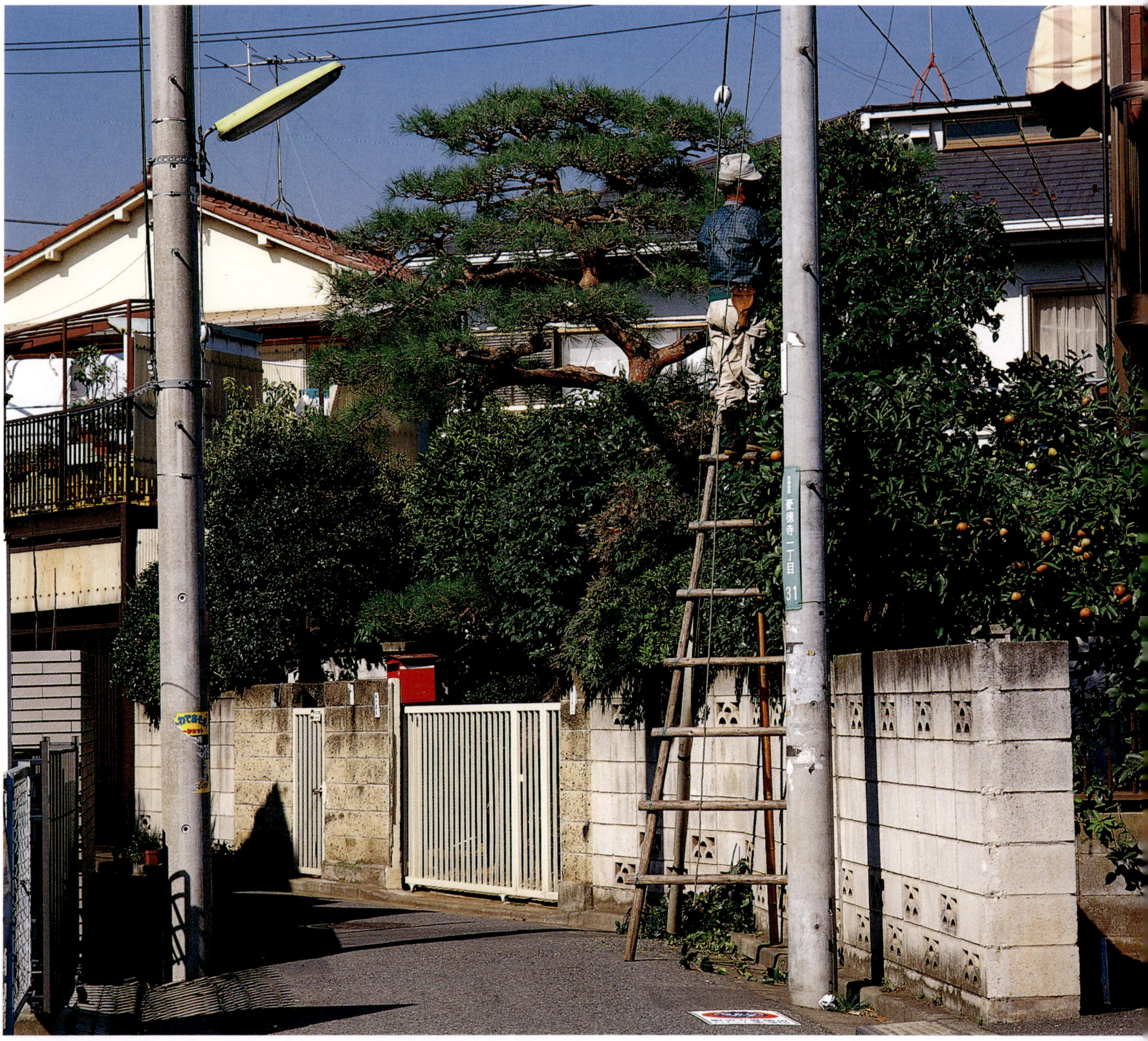


Residential streetscapes like this can be found just about anywhere in Tokyo.

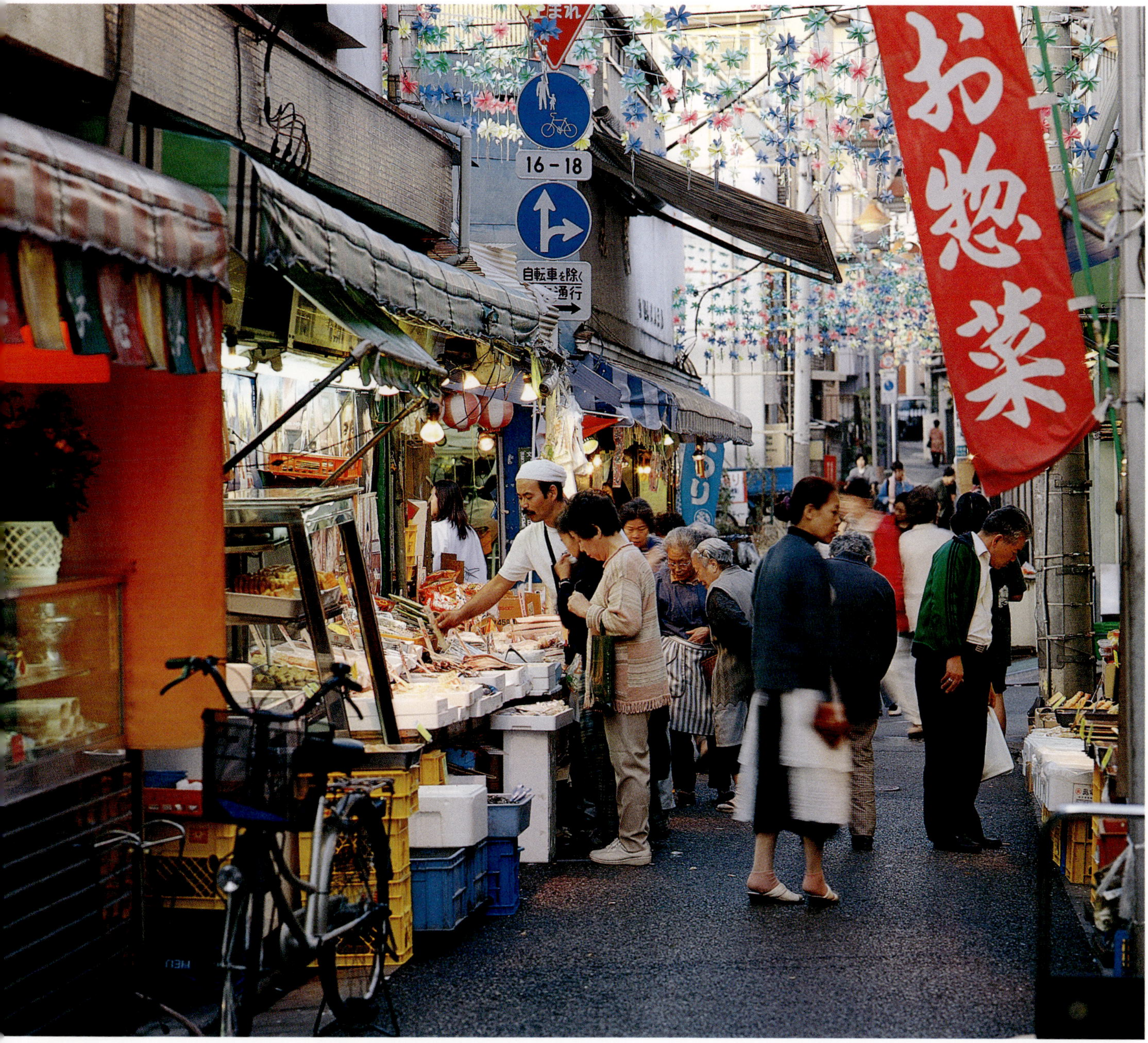


An old-style shopping street at dusk. This street, a holdover from bygone days, has a friendly, intimate quality about it.

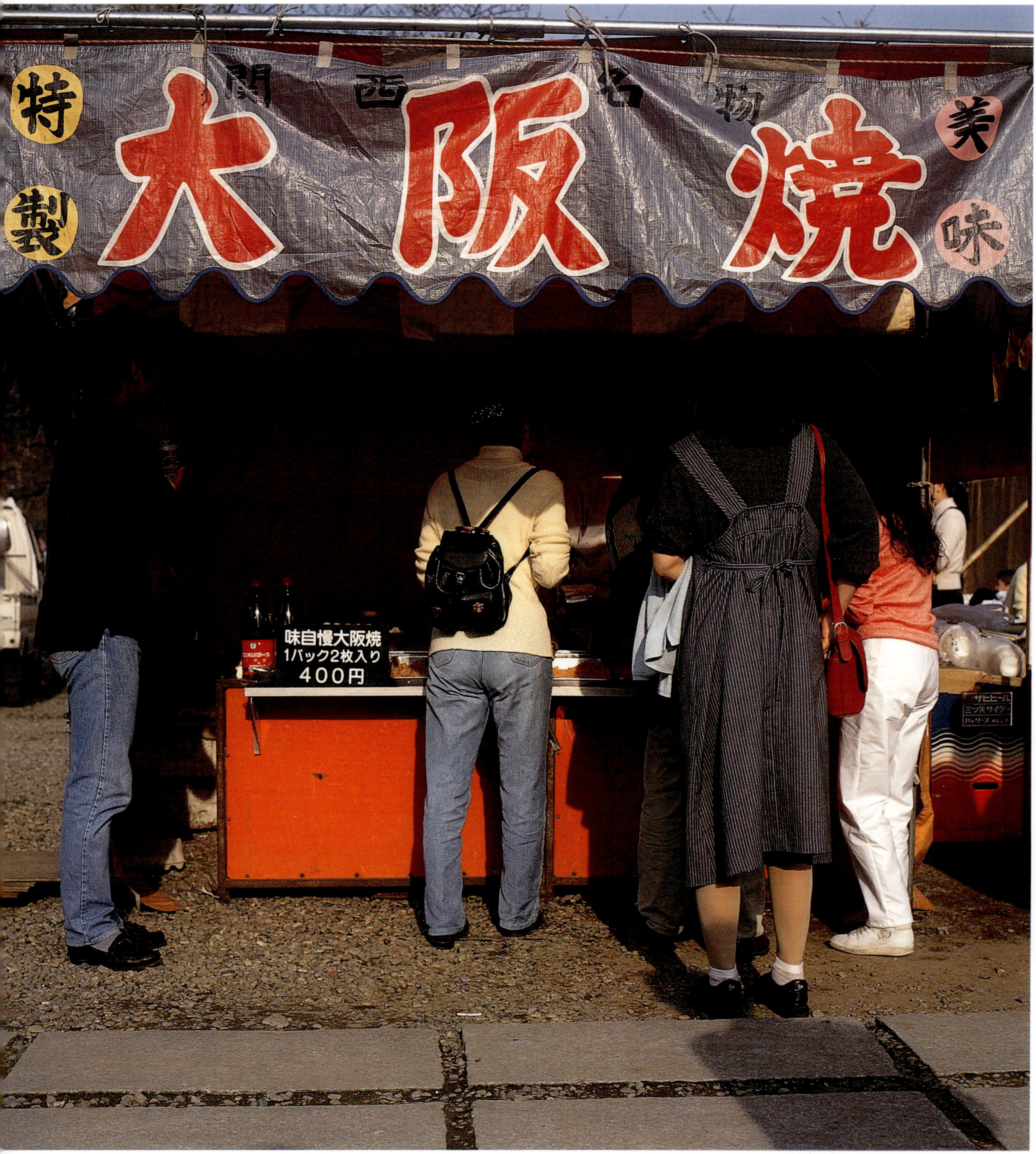


In the heart of Tokyo, this food vendor is offering *osakayaki*—Osaka-style savory pancakes. Traditional street stalls like this one typically appear at festivals or in other places where crowds of people gather.

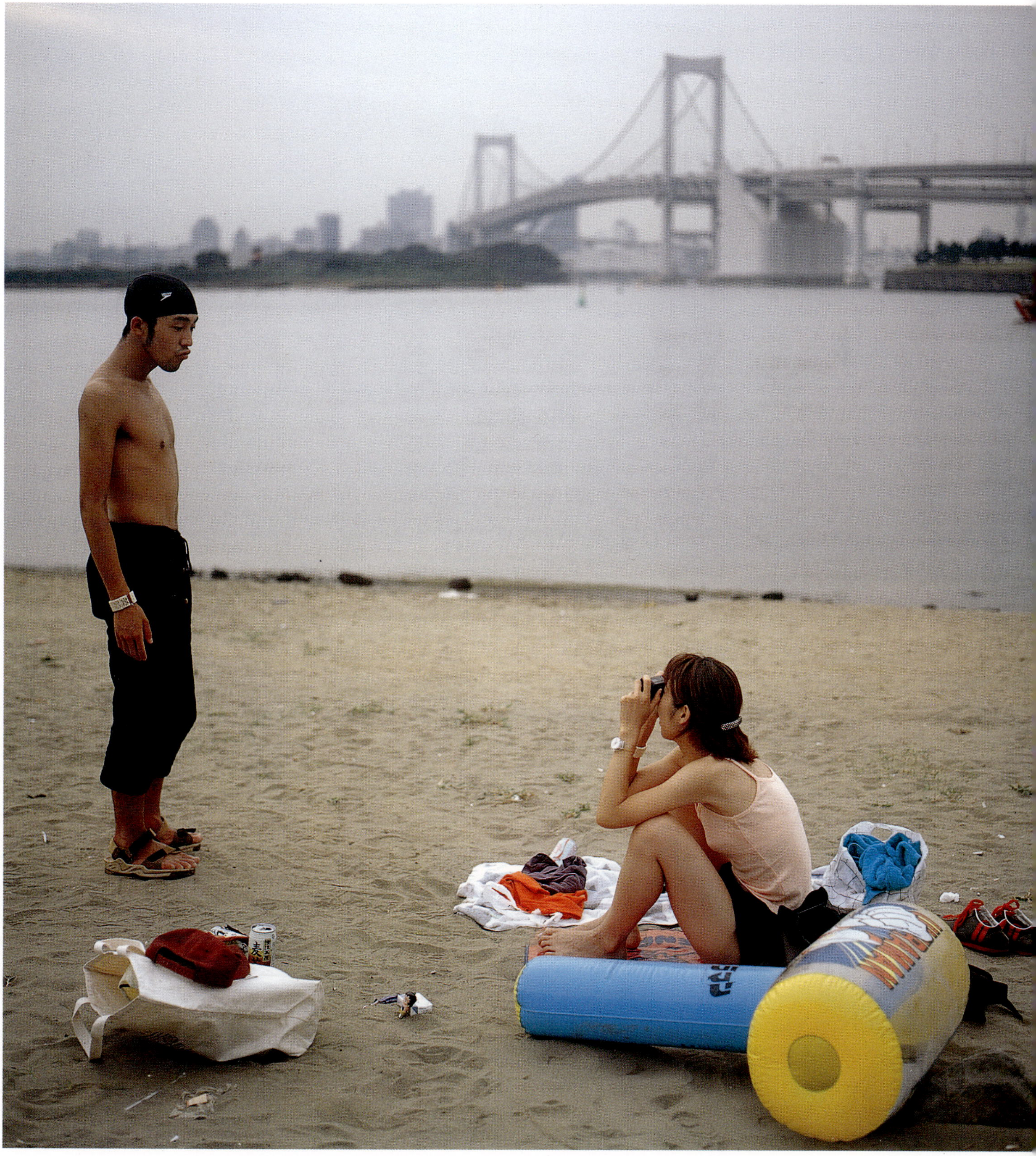

This manmade beach on Tokyo Bay is fine for sunbathing, but the quality of the water makes it unsuitable for swimming.

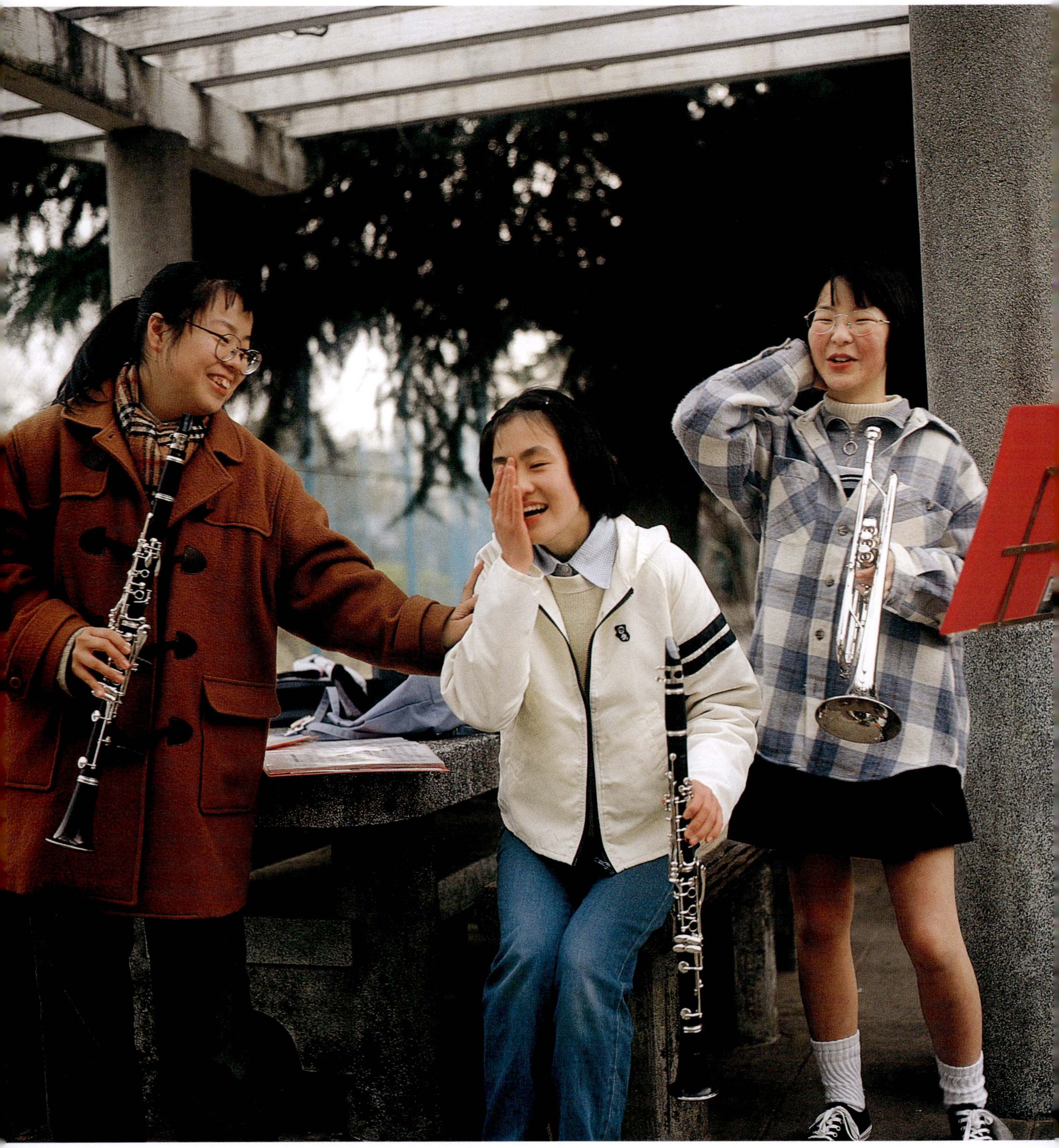

Music students from a junior high school practice in a park.

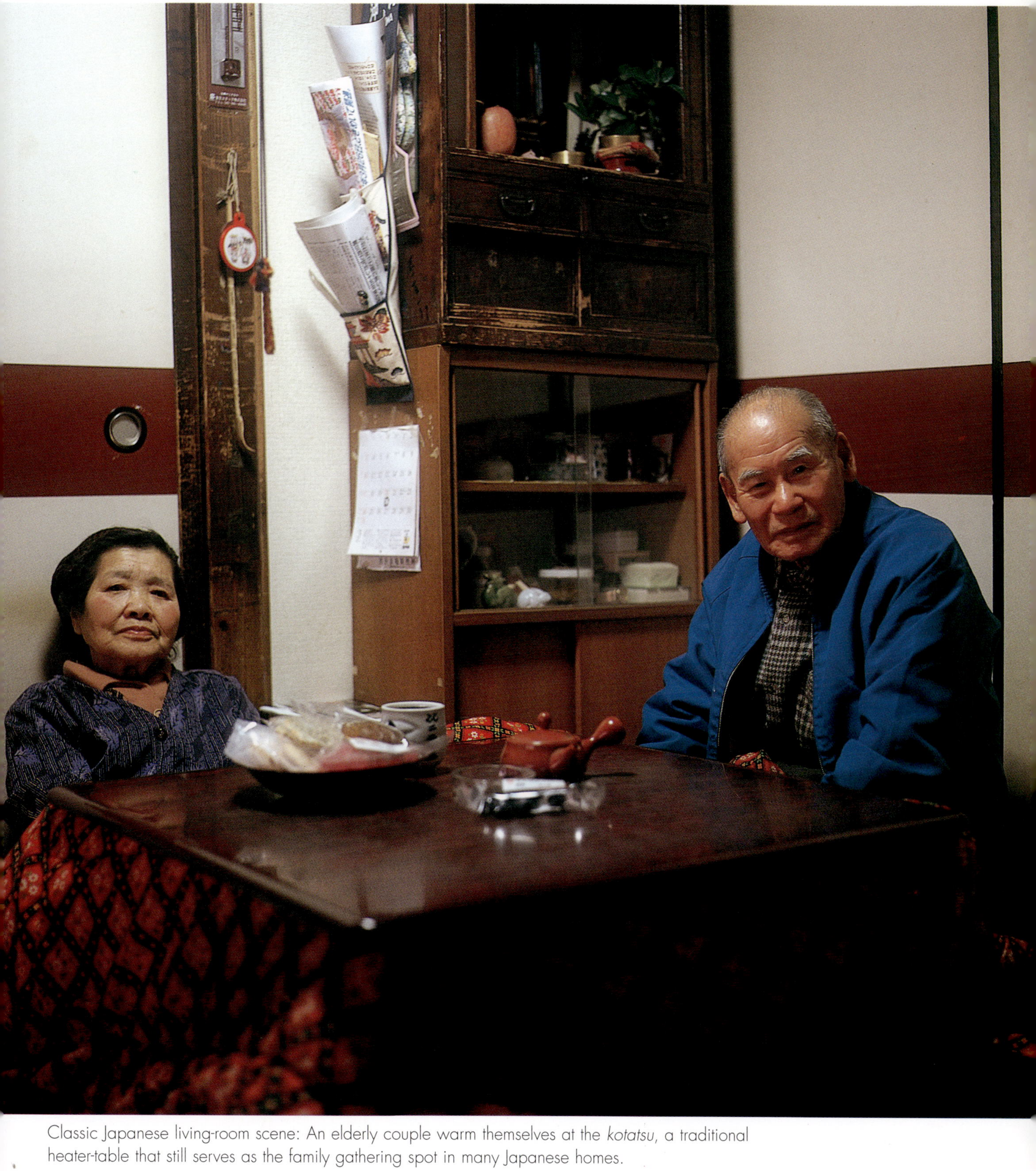

Classic Japanese living-room scene: An elderly couple warm themselves at the *kotatsu*, a traditional heater-table that still serves as the family gathering spot in many Japanese homes.

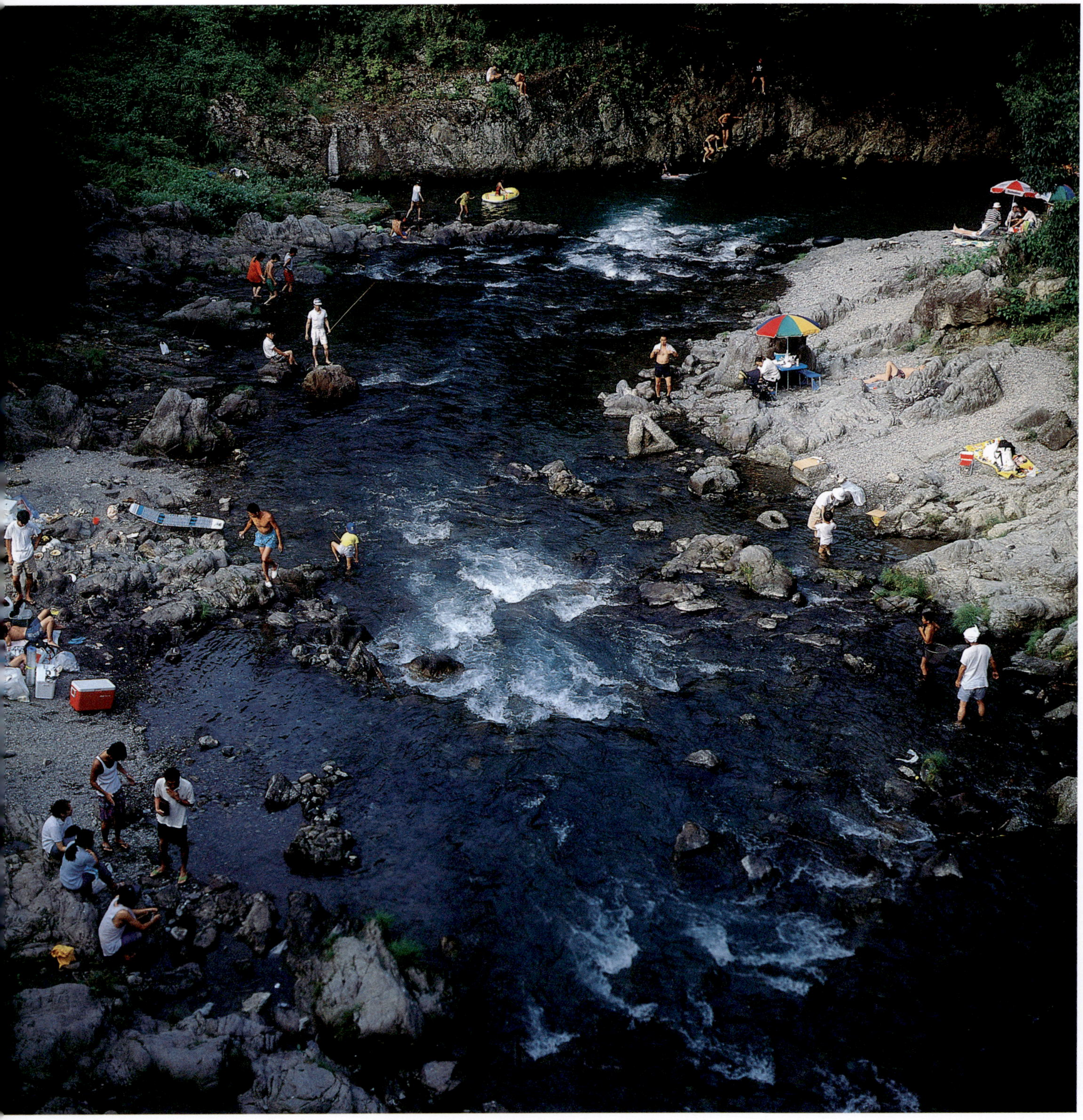

Even within Tokyo's borders, some areas of unspoiled natural beauty remain. The Akigawa river in northwestern Tokyo Prefecture is one example. On a summer day, the river is alive with people who have come to fish and play.

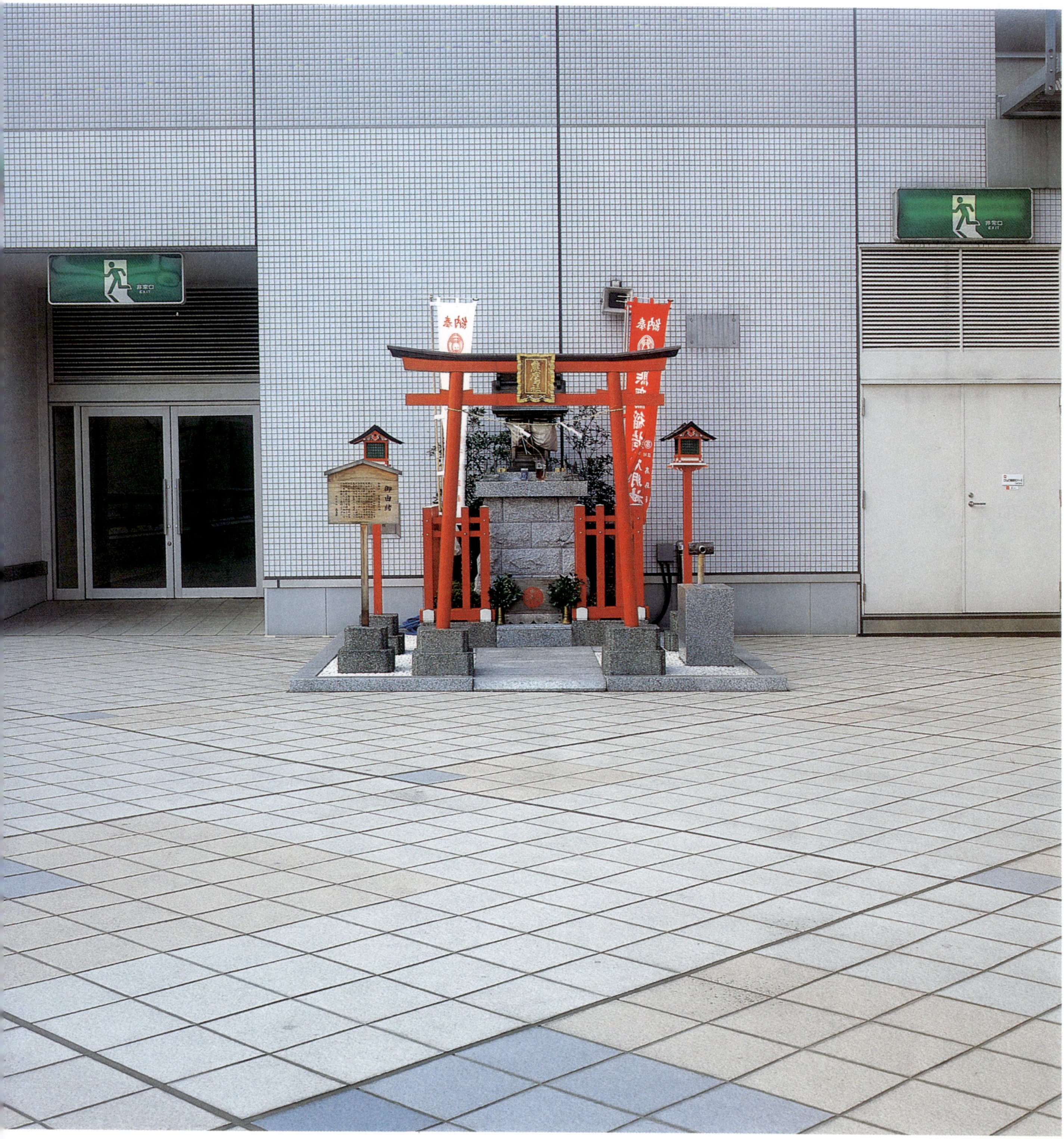

This shrine, which now sits atop the roof of a department store, probably occupied this piece of land long before the store was built.

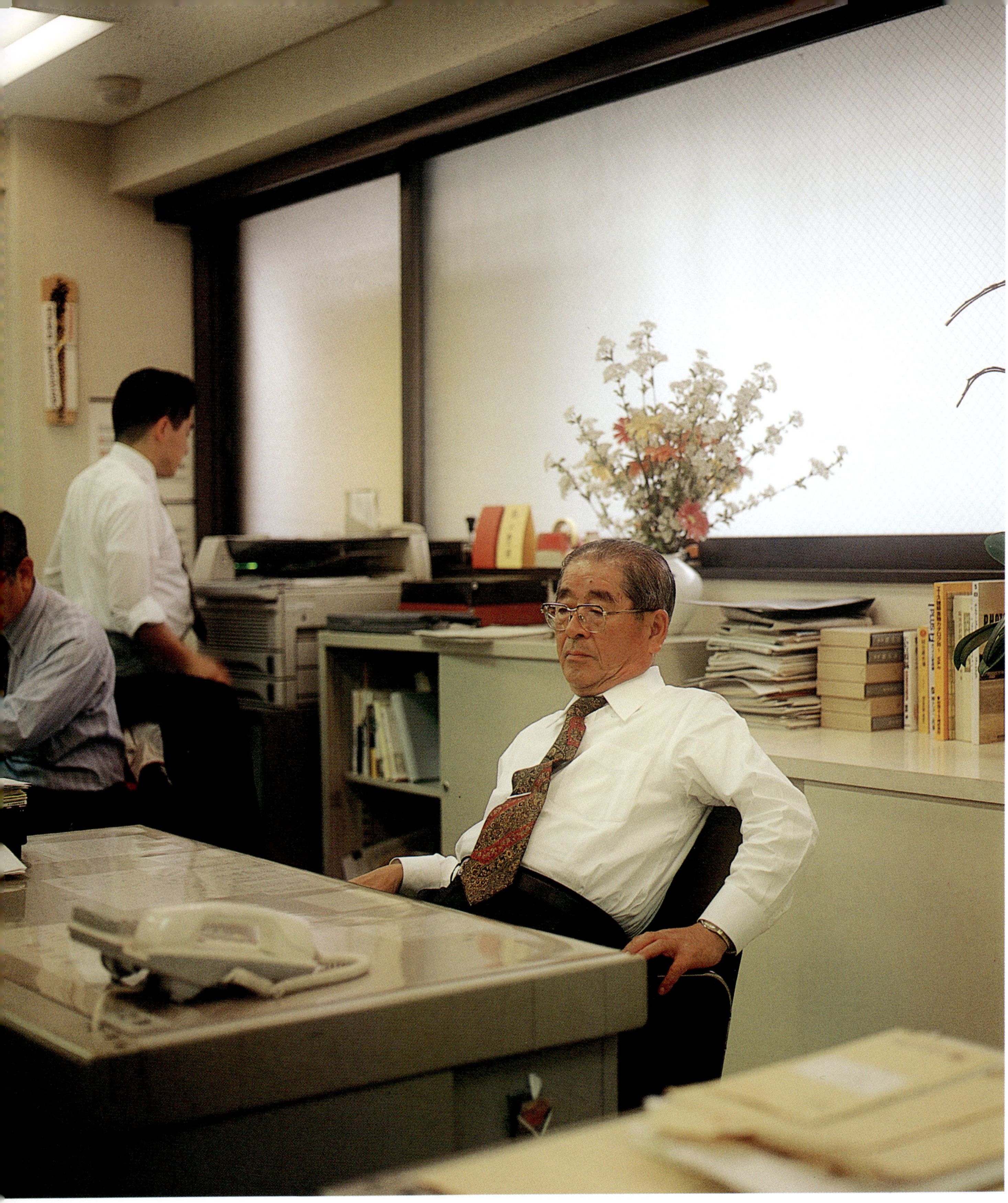

Until quite recently, Japan's corporate culture has been characterized by lifetime employment and seniority-based promotion, but these norms are currently in the process of breaking down.

This character, known as Peko-chan, is the mascot for a well-known manufacturer of baked goods. Her cheery presence has been gracing the streets for over 40 years now.

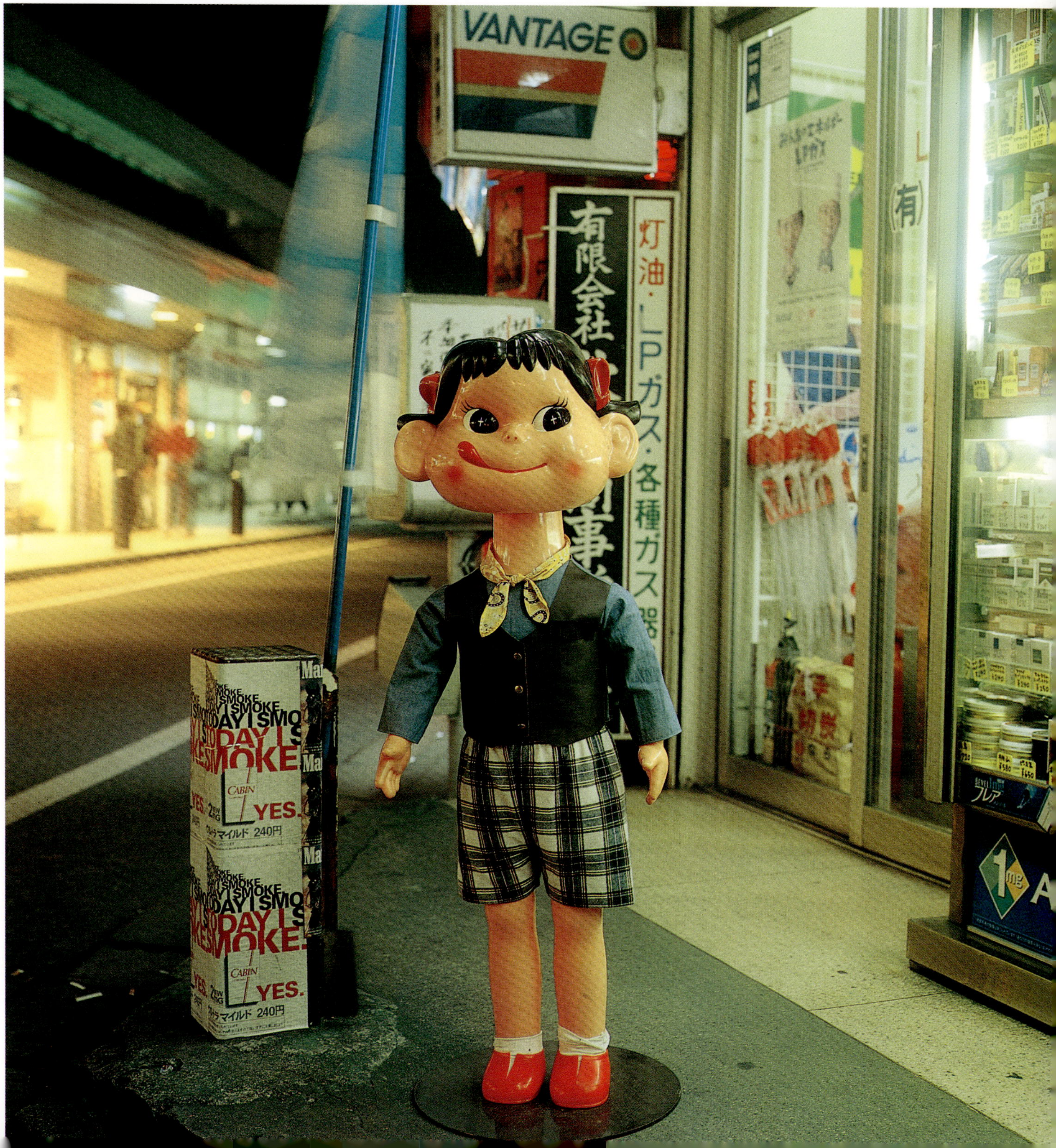

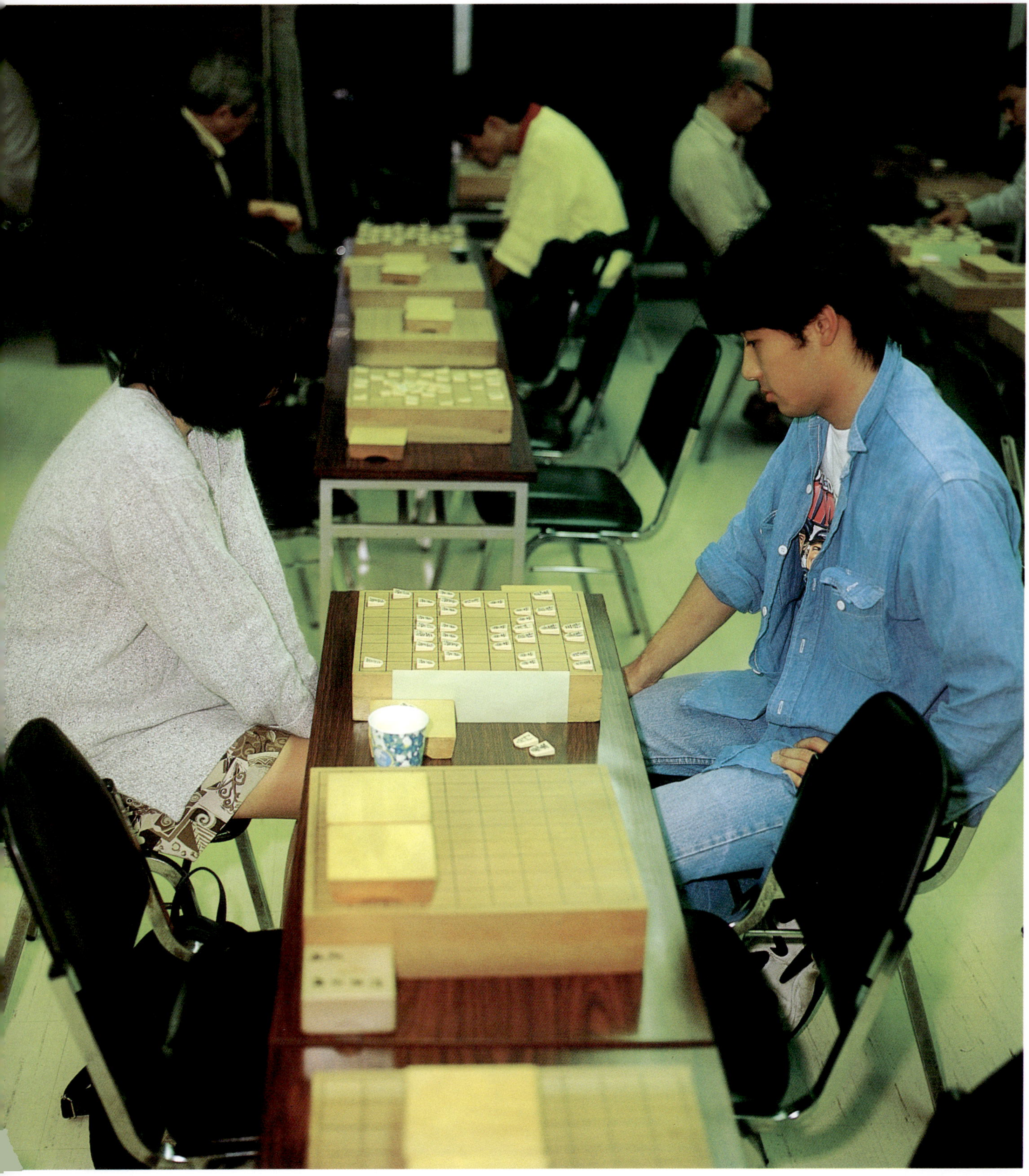

Amateur players at a *shōgi* club. *Shōgi* is a uniquely Japanese form of chess with a history dating back about 500 years. At the professional level, some *shōgi* tournaments offer cash prizes equivalent to several hundred thousand dollars.

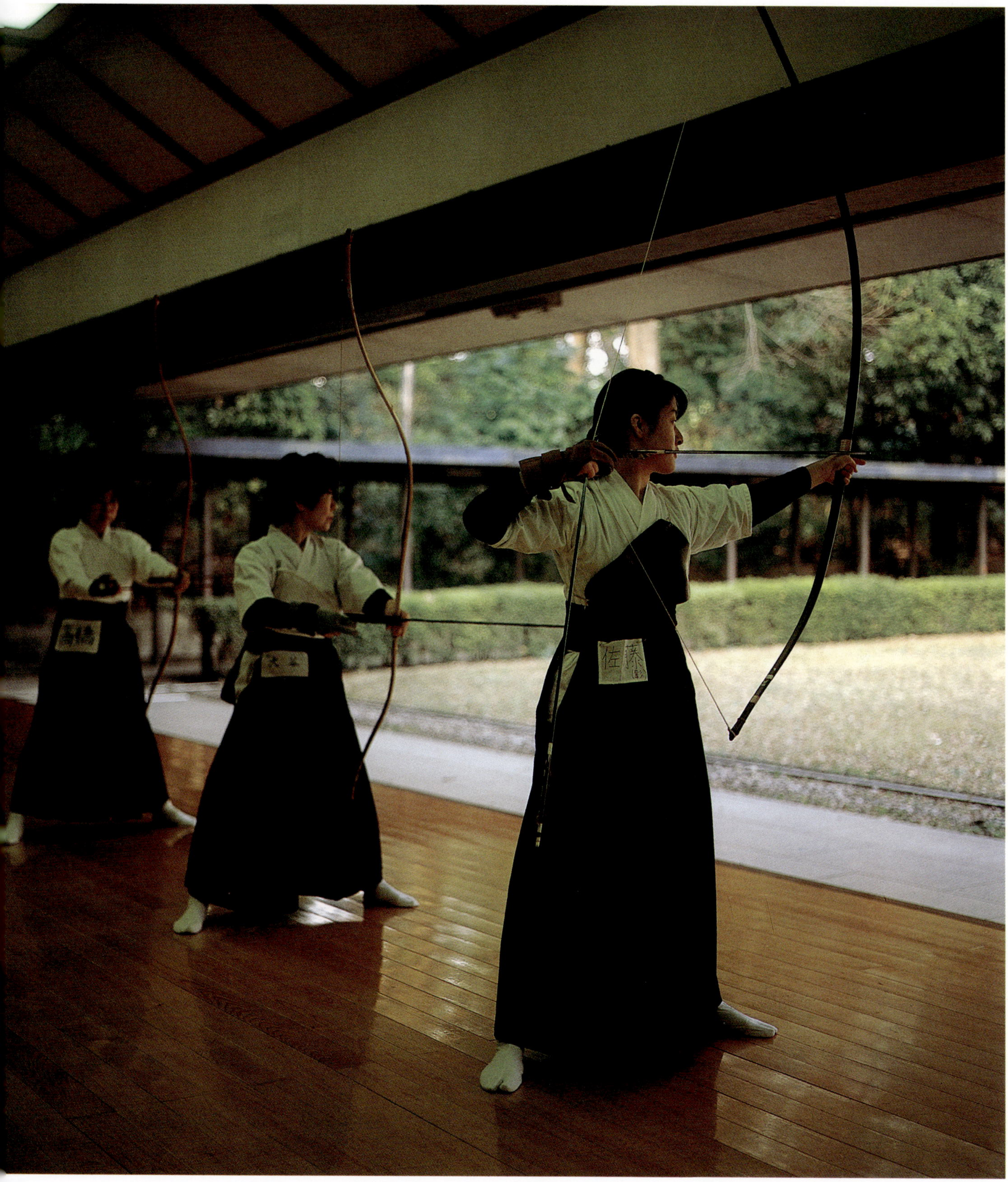


Japanese archery, or *kyūdo*, is one of the traditional Japanese martial arts. A solemn atmosphere fills the dojo, the practice arena. In *kyūdo*, as in other martial arts, great importance is placed not only on technique, but also on attitude, in the form of proper etiquette and peace of mind. Currently, about half of the competitors in this sport are women.

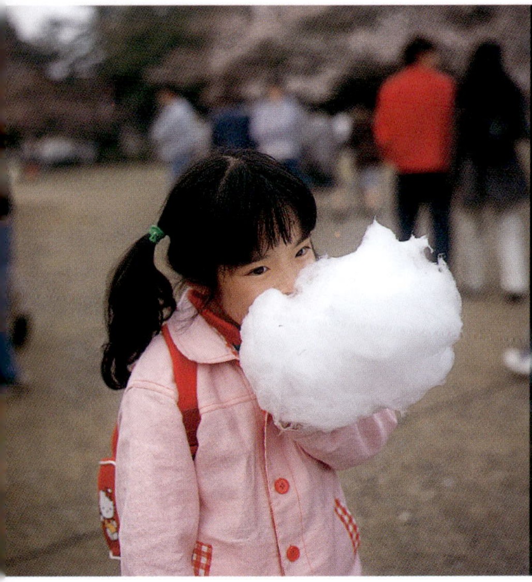

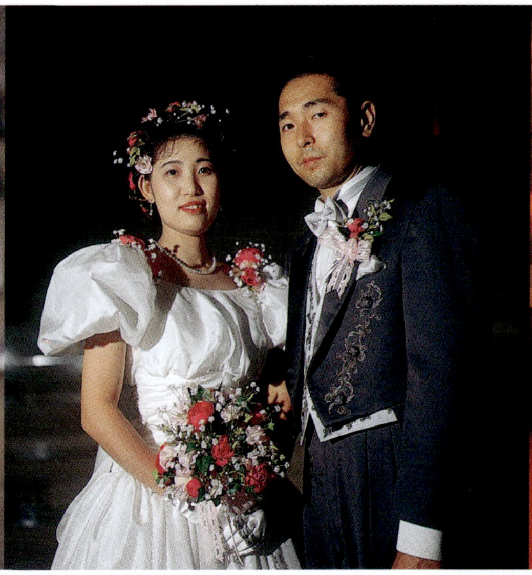

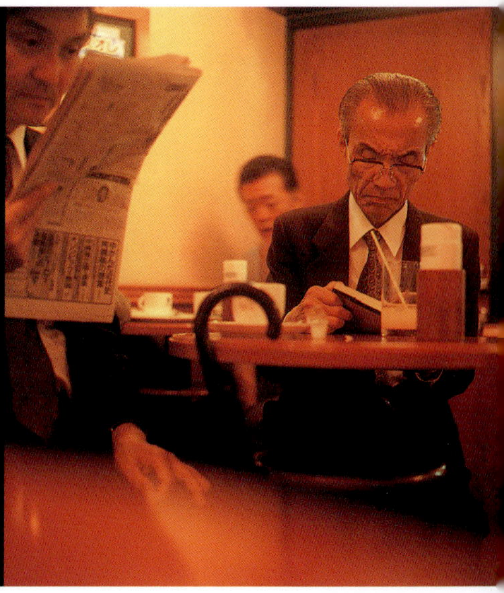

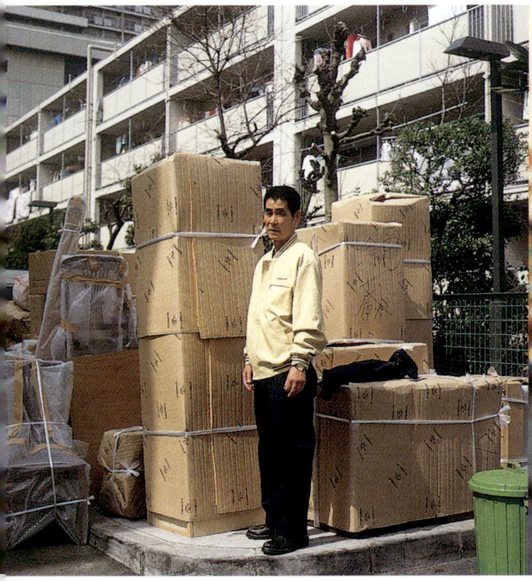

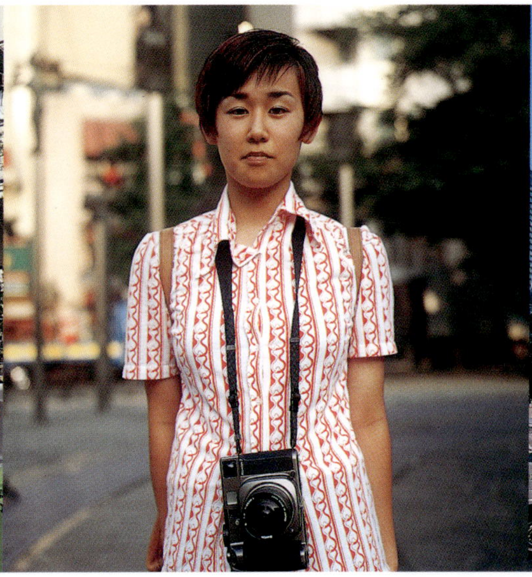

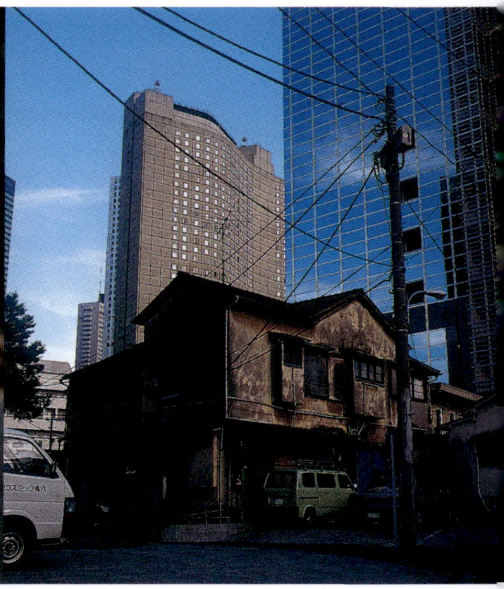

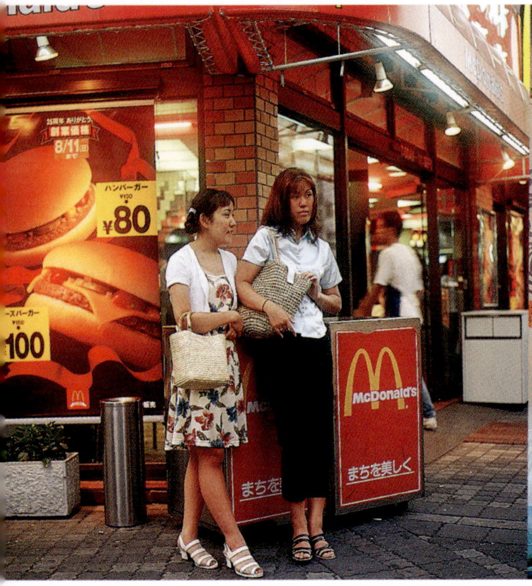
ハンバーガー
¥80
100
McDonald's
まちを美しく

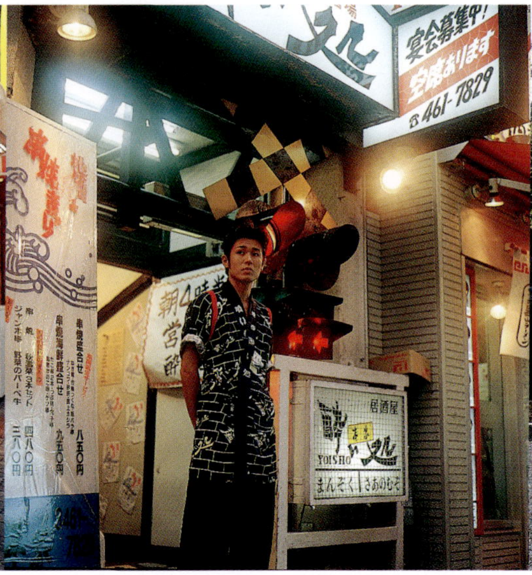
宴会募集中!
461-7829
居酒屋

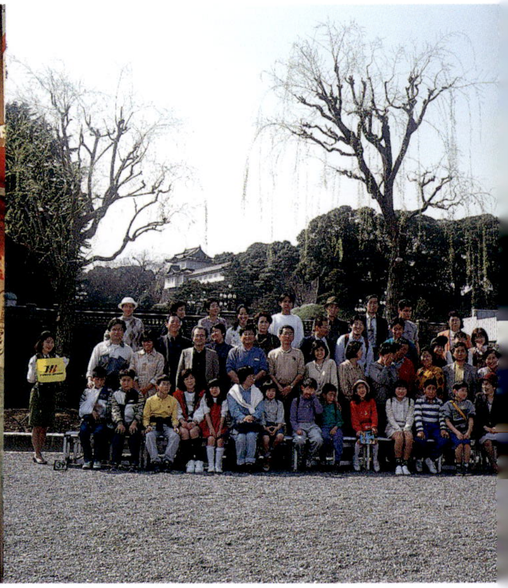

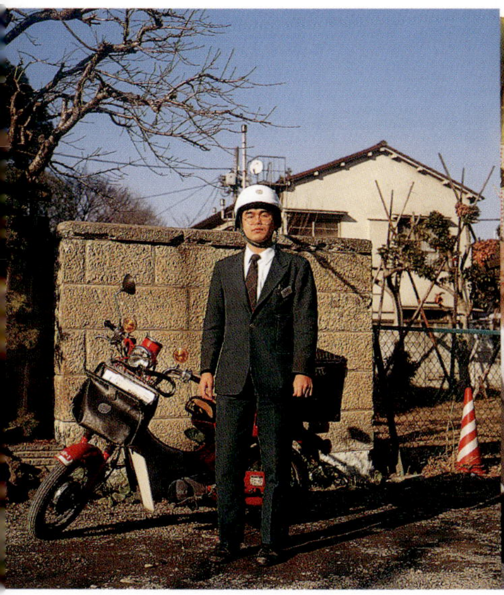

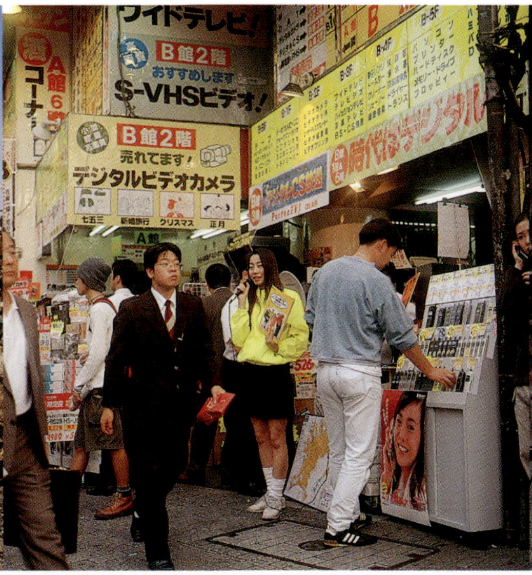
ワイドテレビ!
B館2階
おすすめします
S-VHSビデオ!
B館2階
売れてます!
デジタルビデオカメラ

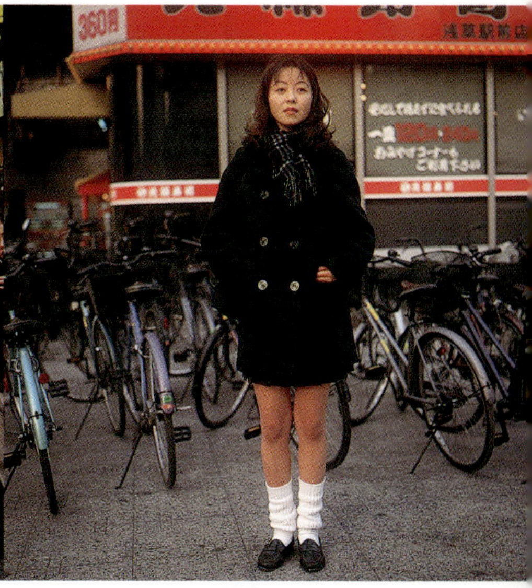
360円
浅草駅前店

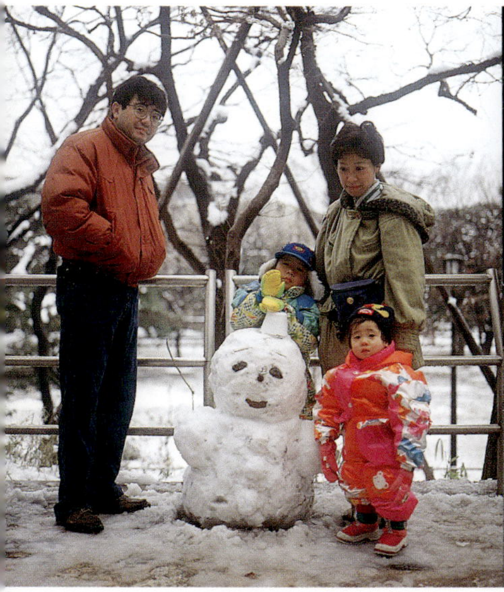

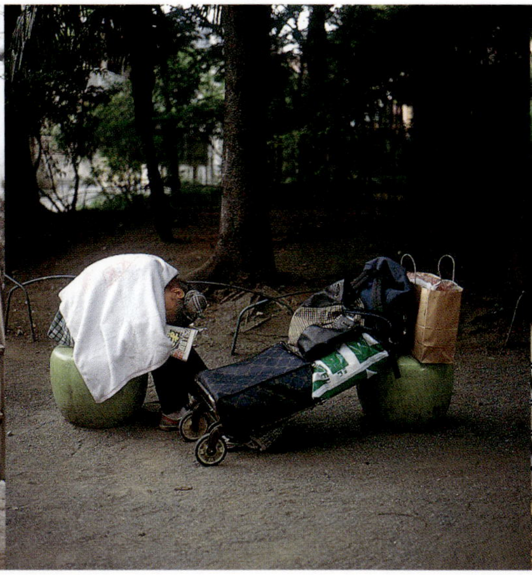

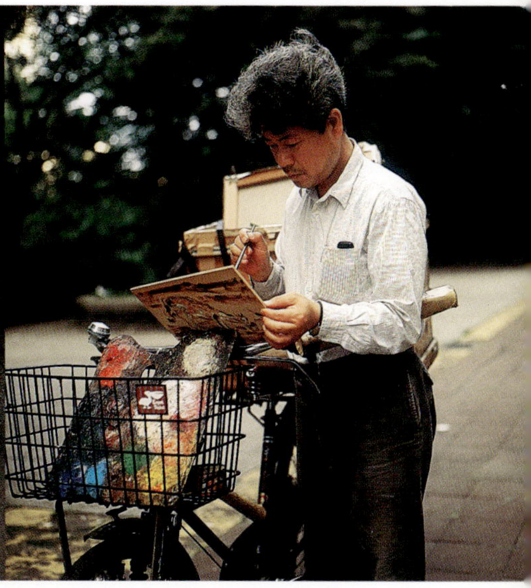

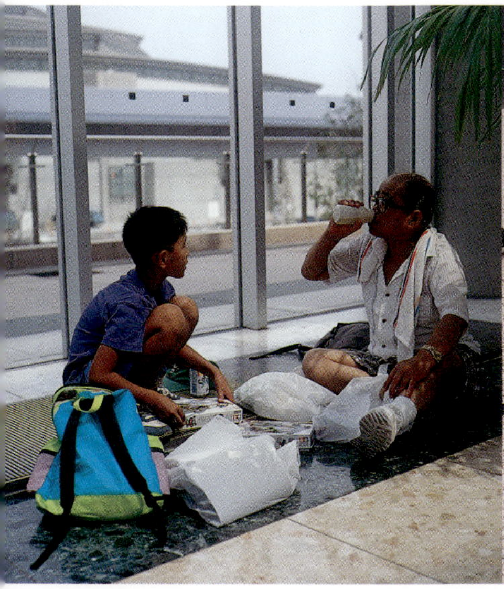

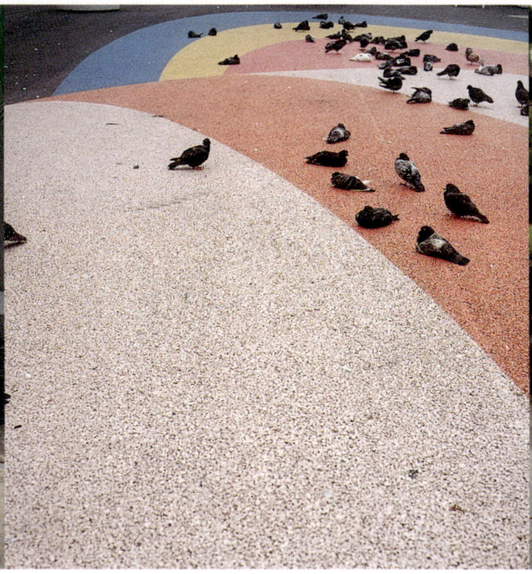

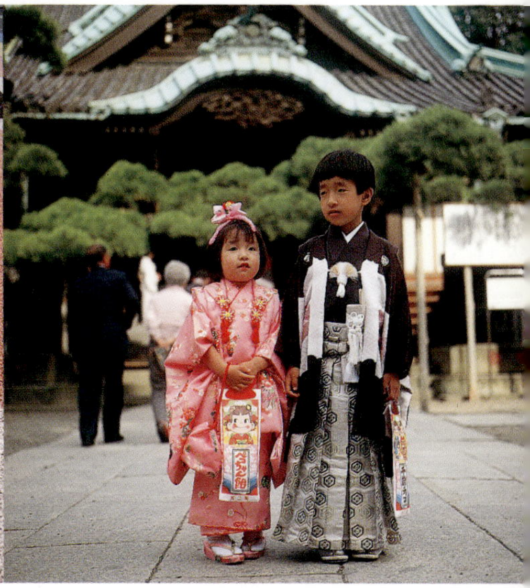

Open 24 hours a day, seven days a week, throughout the year, convenience stores are an essential fact of life for city dwellers.

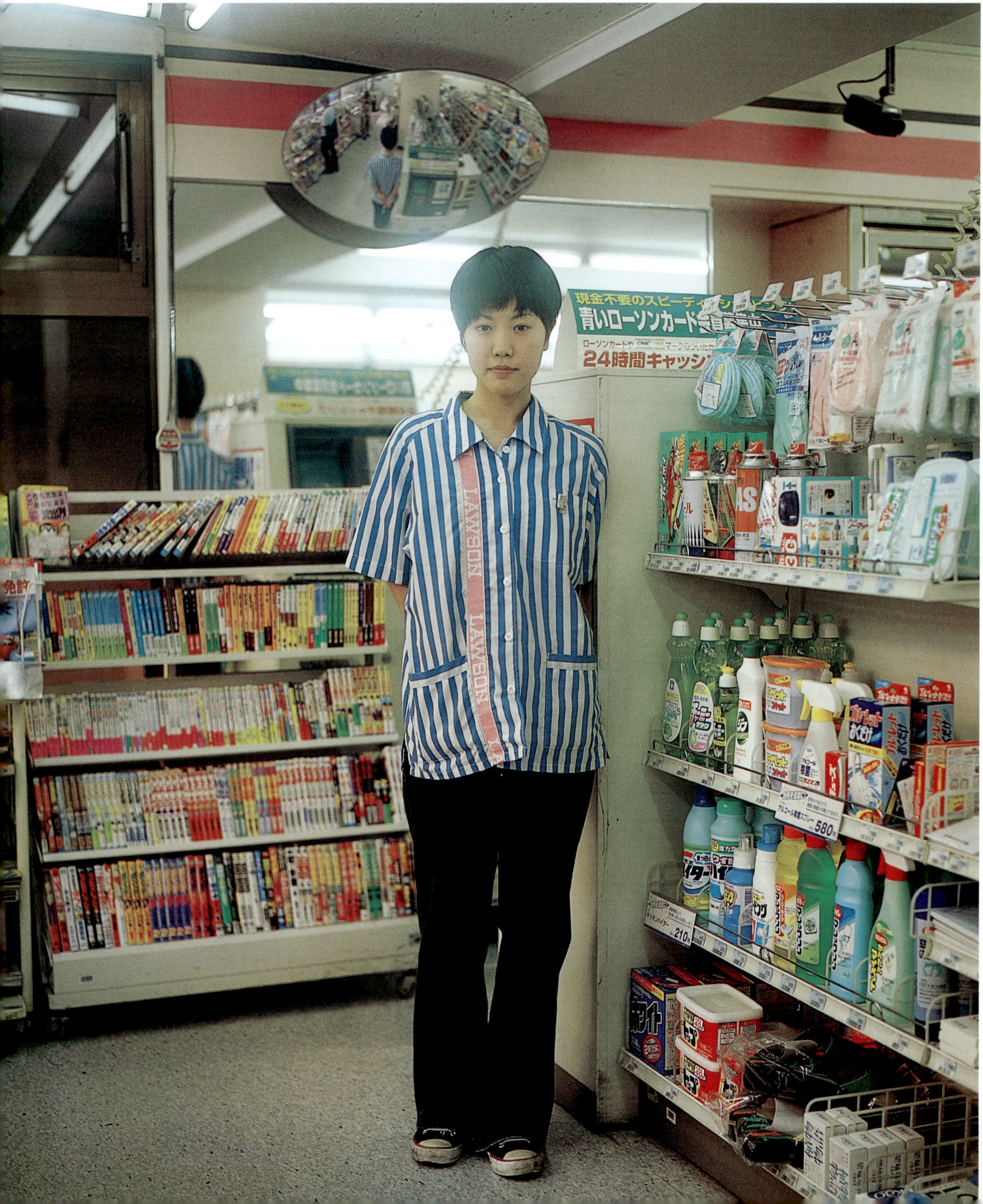

Youth fashions change at a dizzying rate. For young people, clothes are not only a vehicle for self-expression, but also a way to let off steam.

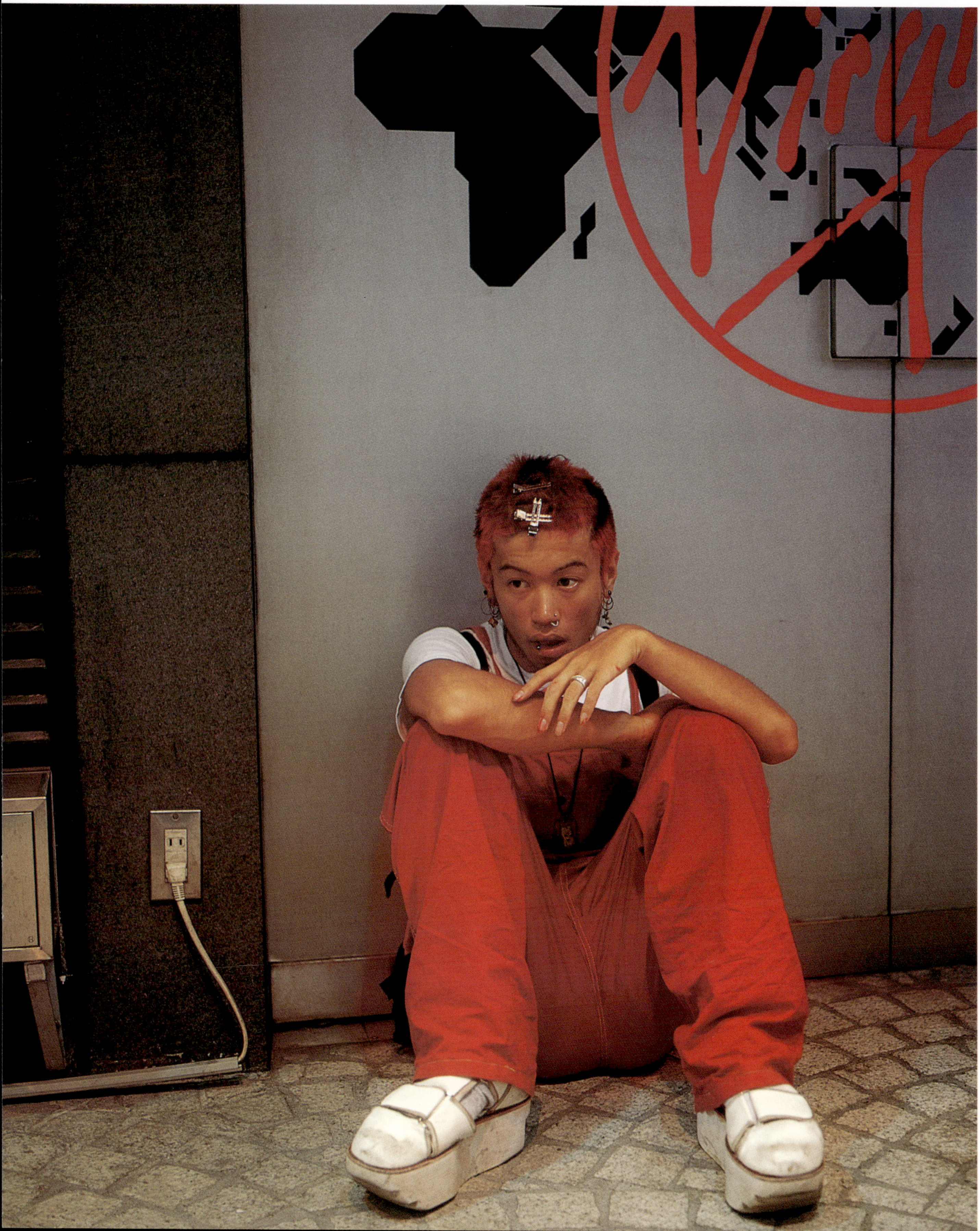

Tokyo's population of about 12 million is squeezed into an area of 2,186.61 square kilometers. In the underground plaza at Ikebukuro station, the human tide flows uninterrupted from early in the morning until late at night.

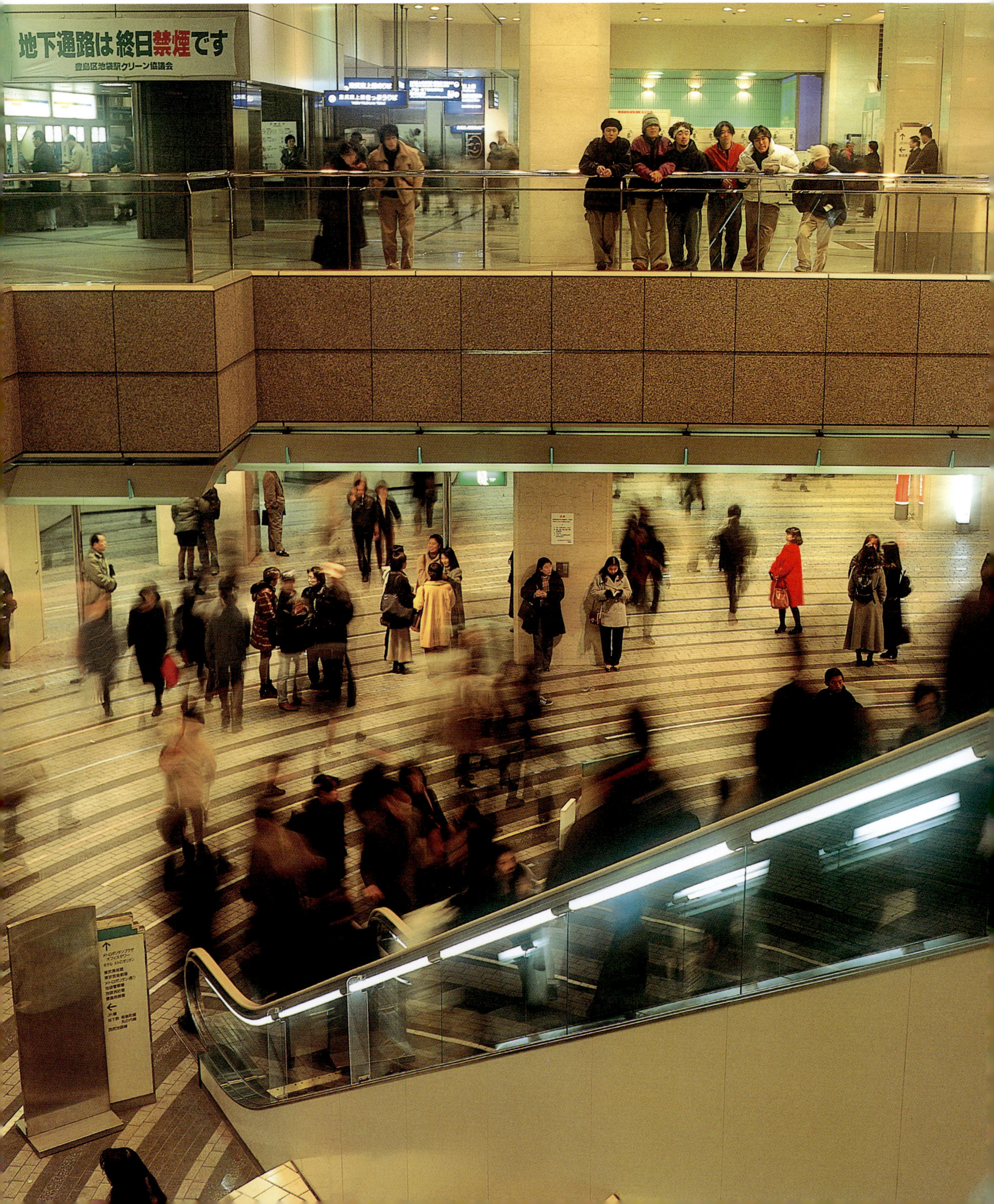

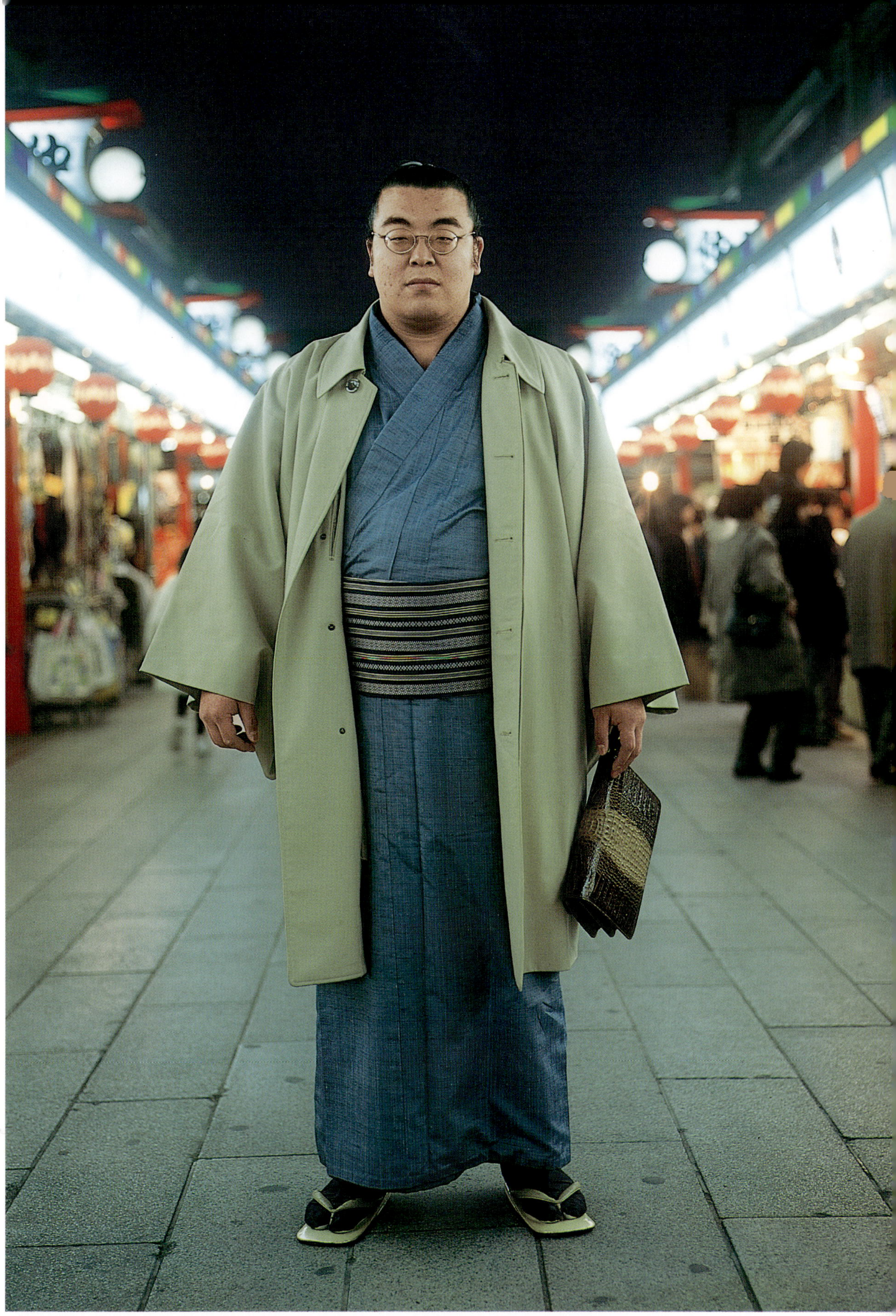

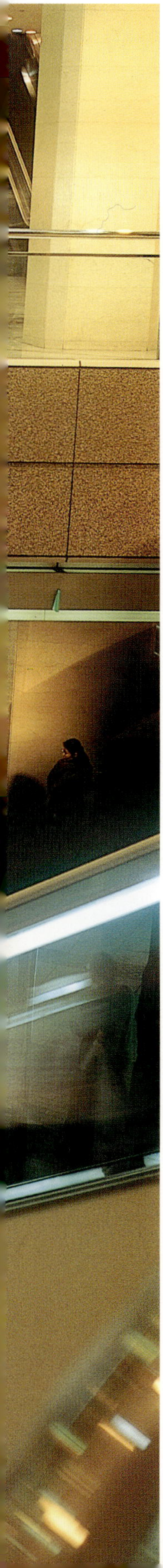

With his hulking stature and distinctive topknot, a sumo wrestler stands out wherever he goes—even here on Nakamise-dori, an arcade of 80 shops with the atmosphere of old Edo that hawk a variety of trinkets, confections, and souvenirs.

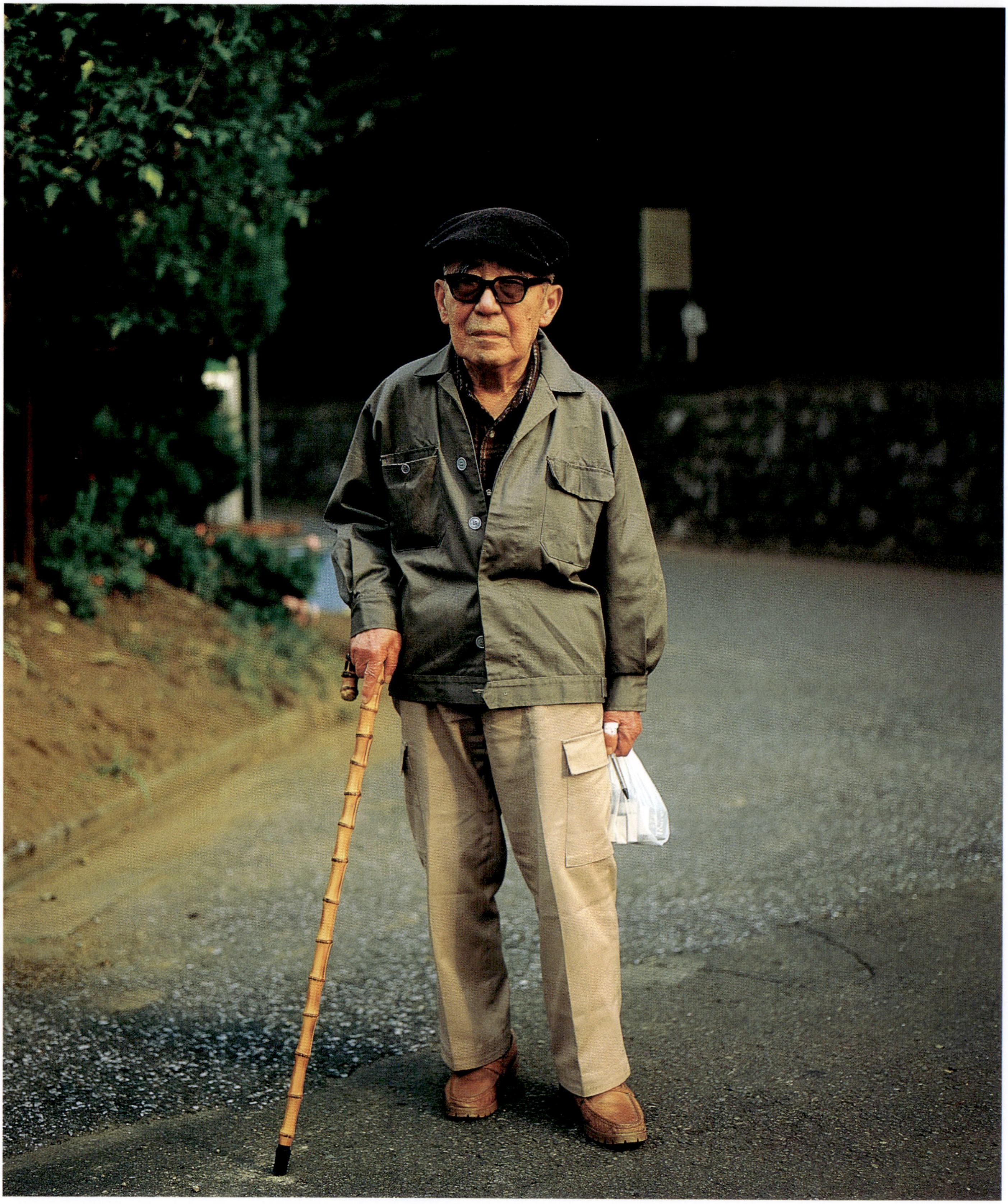

"Lately I get tired just going outside," says this elderly man out for a walk. "That's what happens when you get to be 95." Japan's elderly population is rising. According to current forecasts, by 2015, one in every four Japanese citizens will be aged 65 or over.

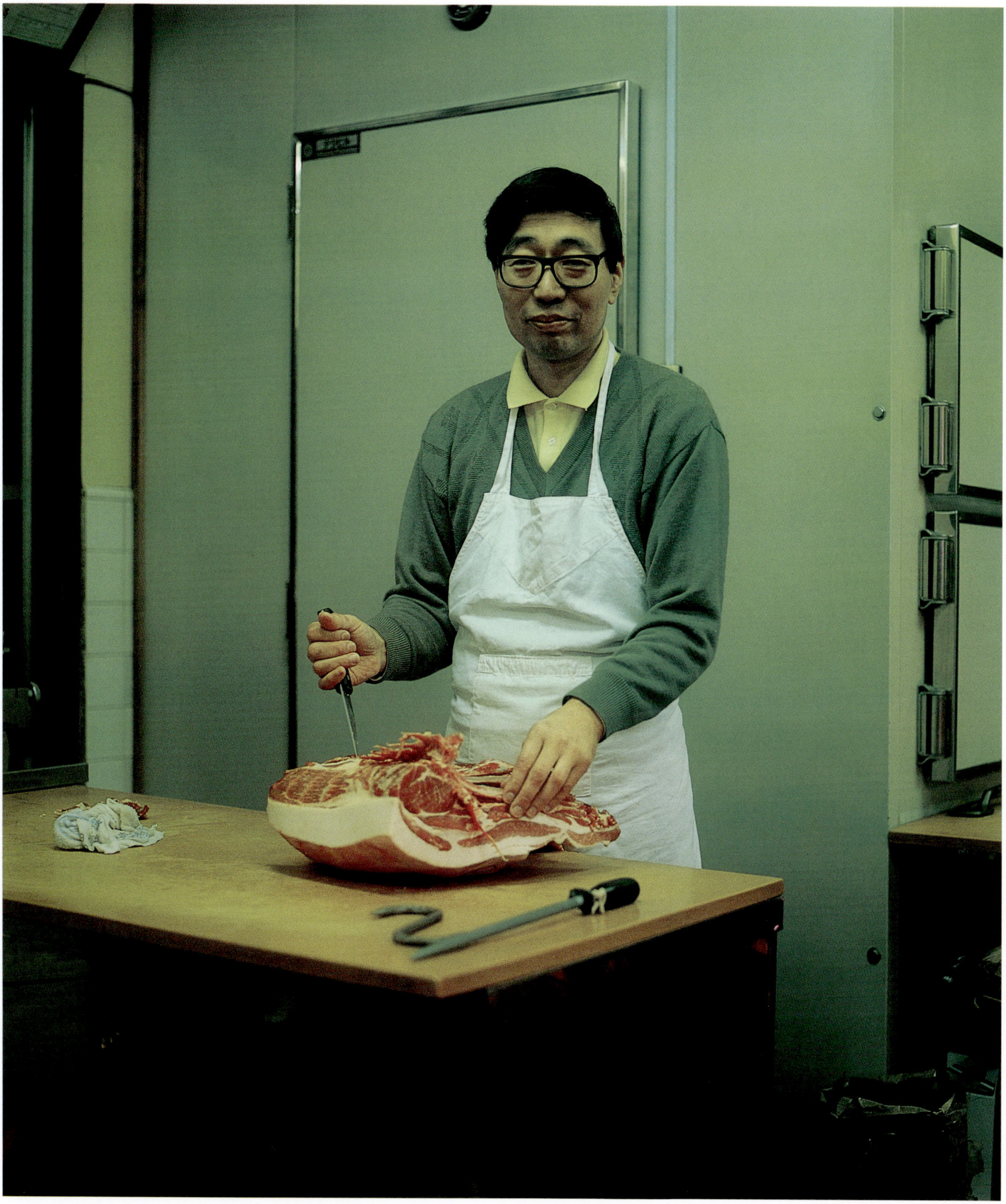

Supermarkets are making life difficult for family-run establishments like this butcher shop. Says the proprietor: "I'm a second-generation butcher. I take pride in bringing my customers good meat."

This university student, majoring in social welfare, is interested in creating a comfortable living environment for people with disabilities. He enjoys playing basketball and fishing. (Driving his car to the fishing hole is part of the fun.)

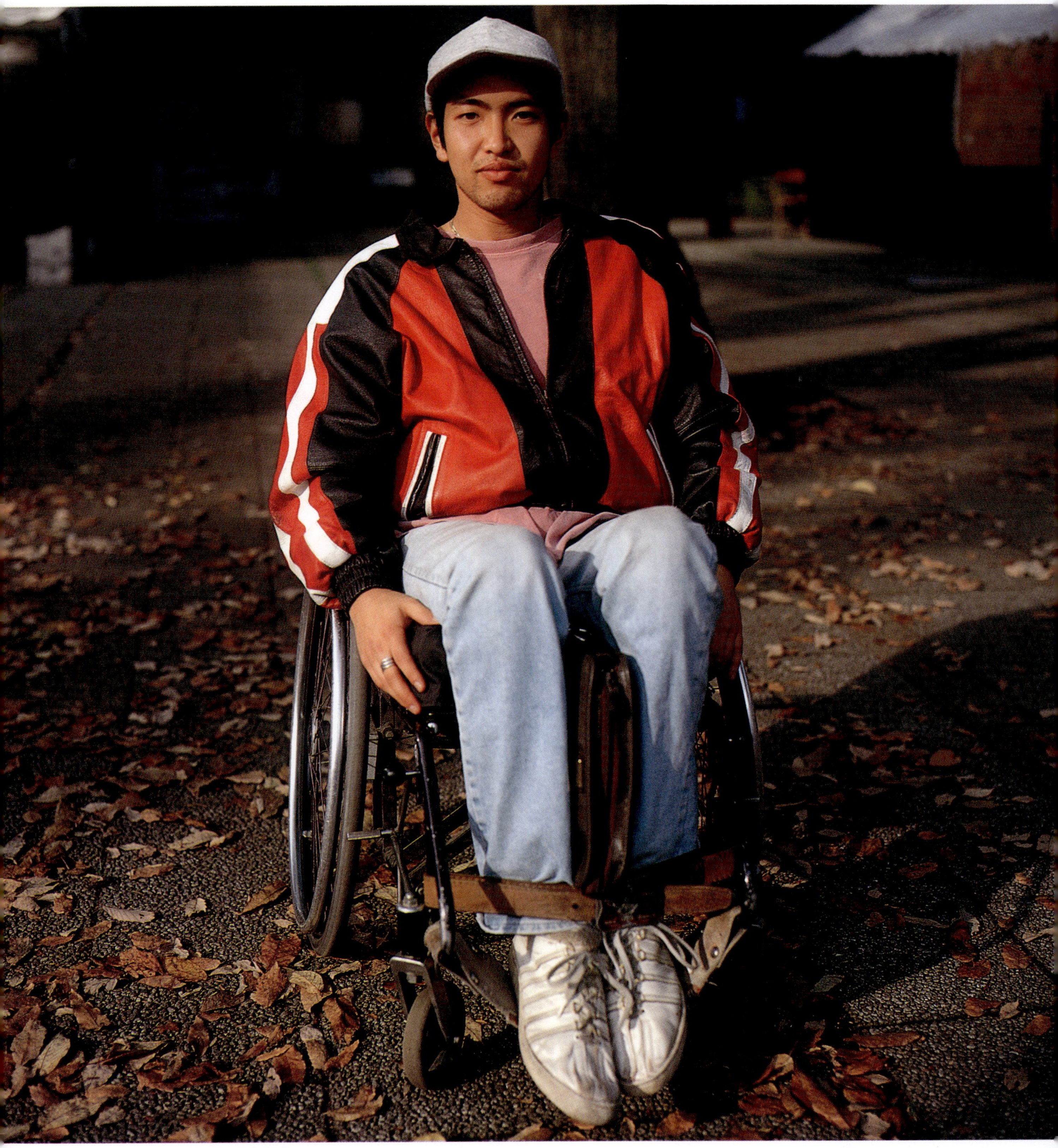

A young family out shopping. The building in the background was constructed on a landfill created using surplus soil from construction sites.

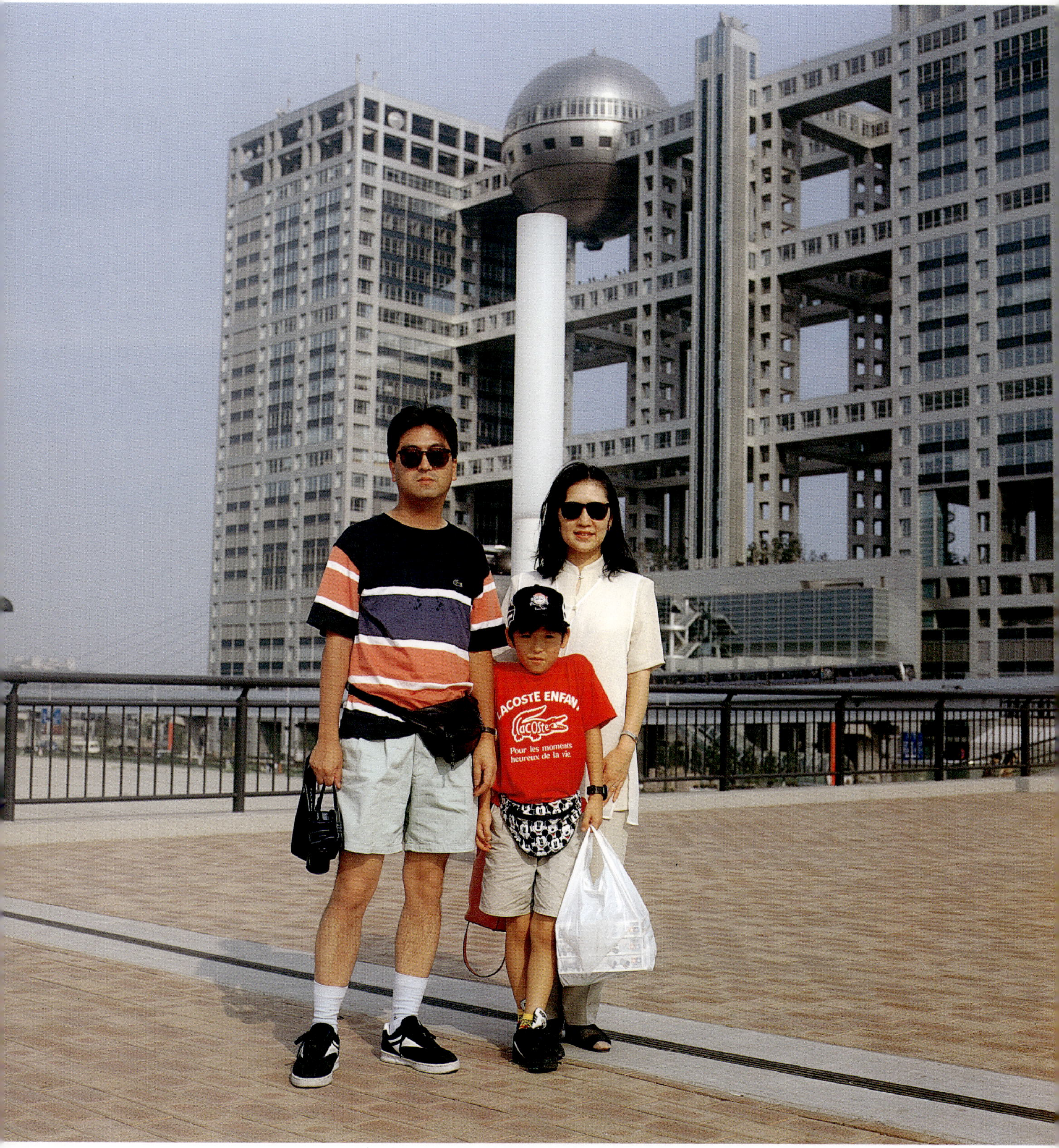

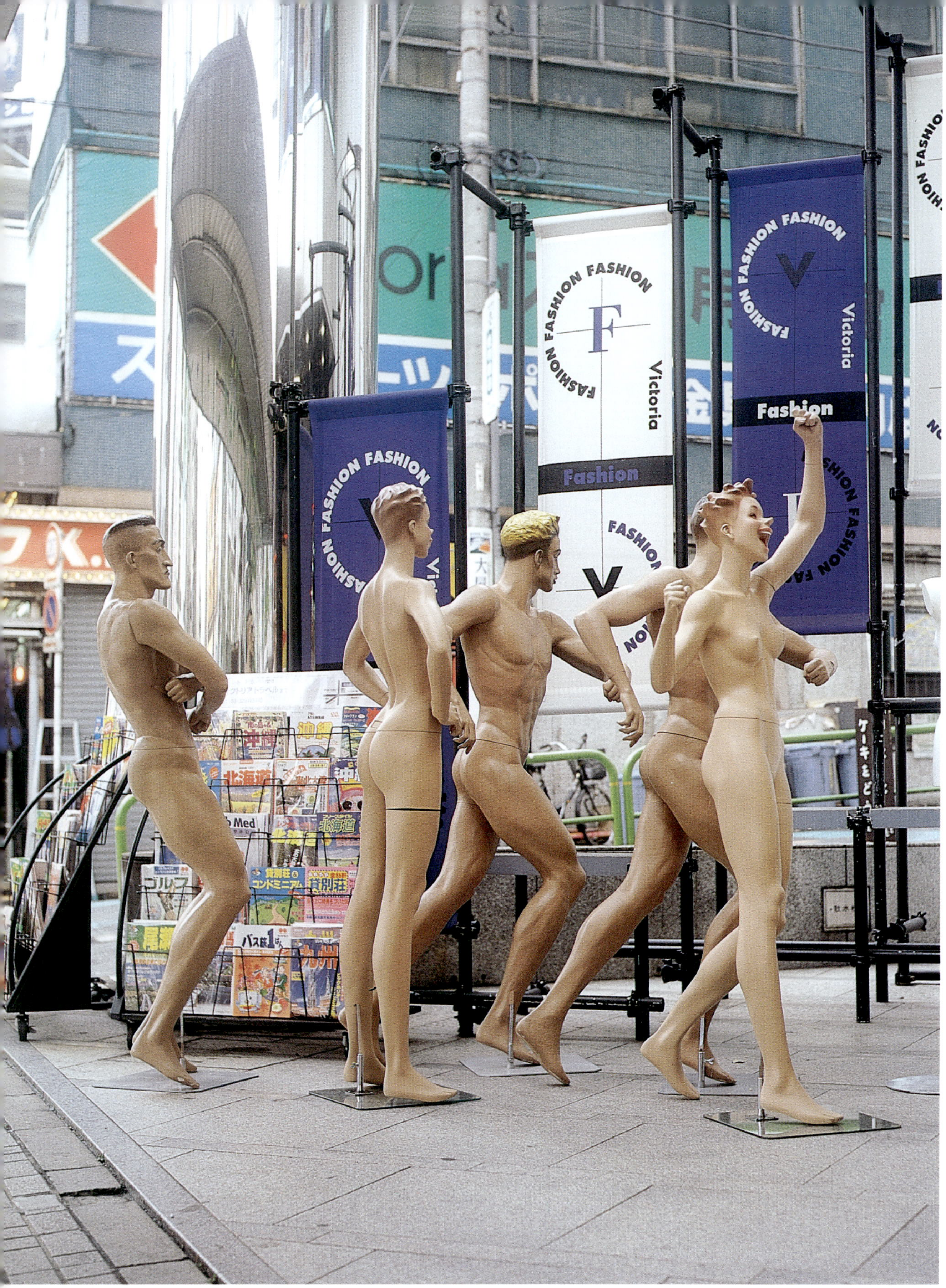


At a sporting-goods store: A bevy of bodies sculpted to perfection.

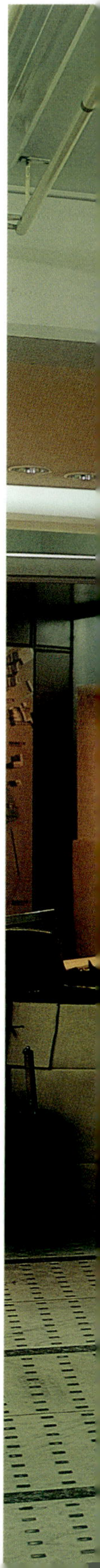

The underground plaza at Shinjuku station is occupied by many homeless people who have created rows of makeshift dwellings there. Murals painted on the cardboard walls by young artists add a splash of color. The Tokyo metropolitan government, with an annual budget of ¥7 trillion (about $66 billion), has made "a comfortable standard of living for citizens" its rallying cry.

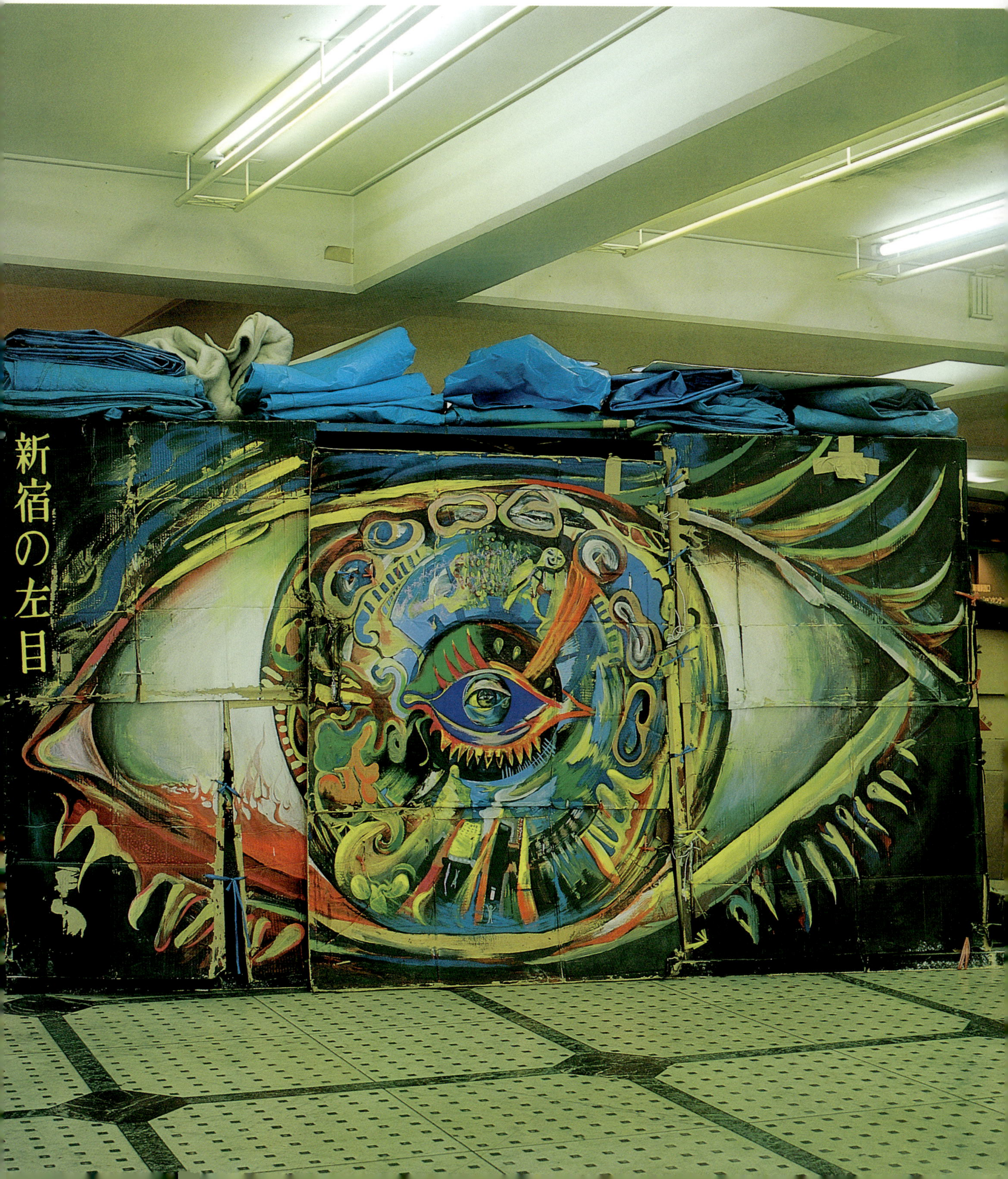

Vending machines like the ones shown here, which sell sacks of rice, have begun to appear in the suburbs. In Japan, you can get just about anything — juice, cigarettes, even a loan — from a vending machine.

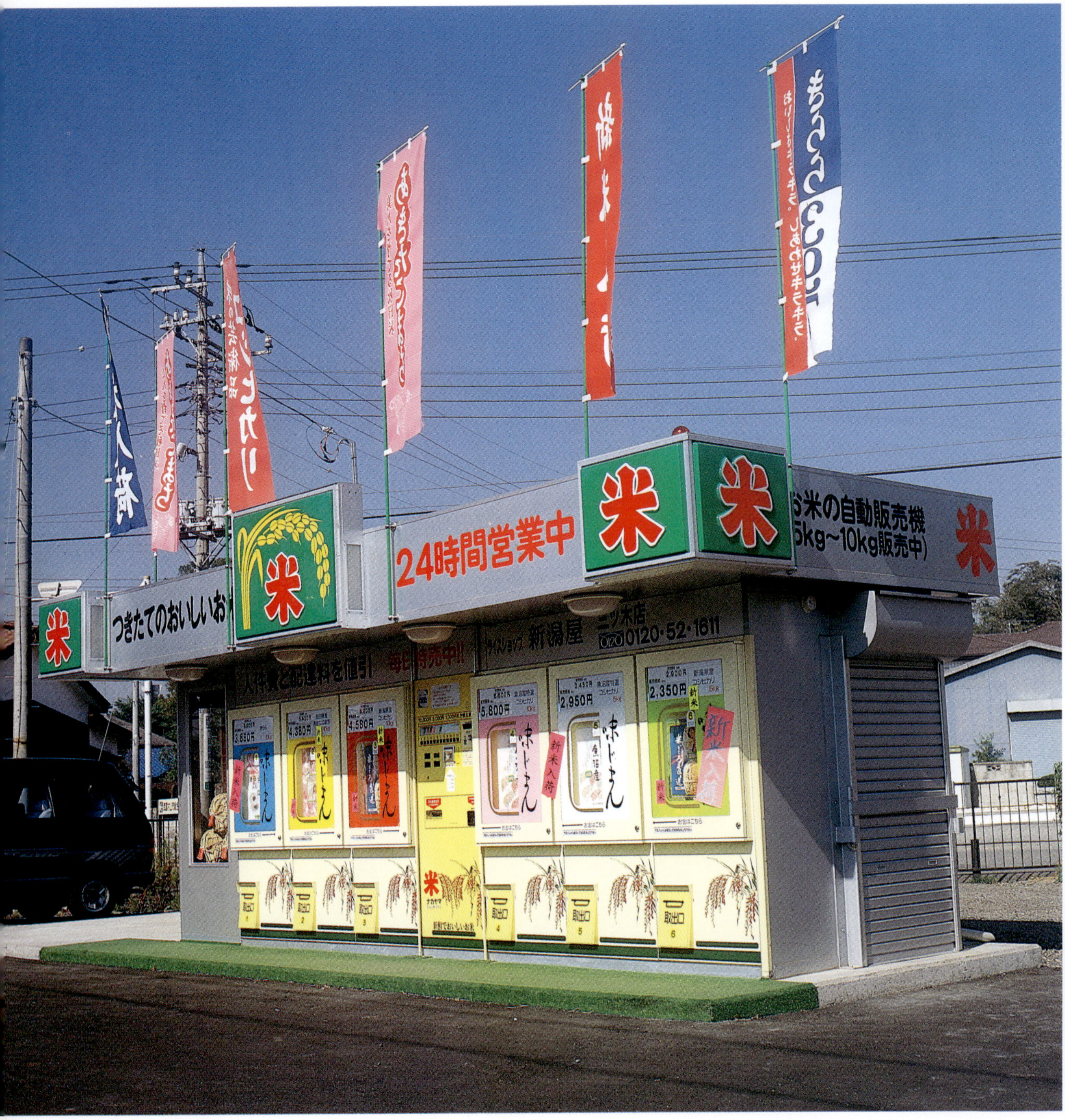


For most students, the after-school hours are filled with private tutoring, music lessons, or other structured activities. In Japan, adults aren't the only ones with busy schedules.

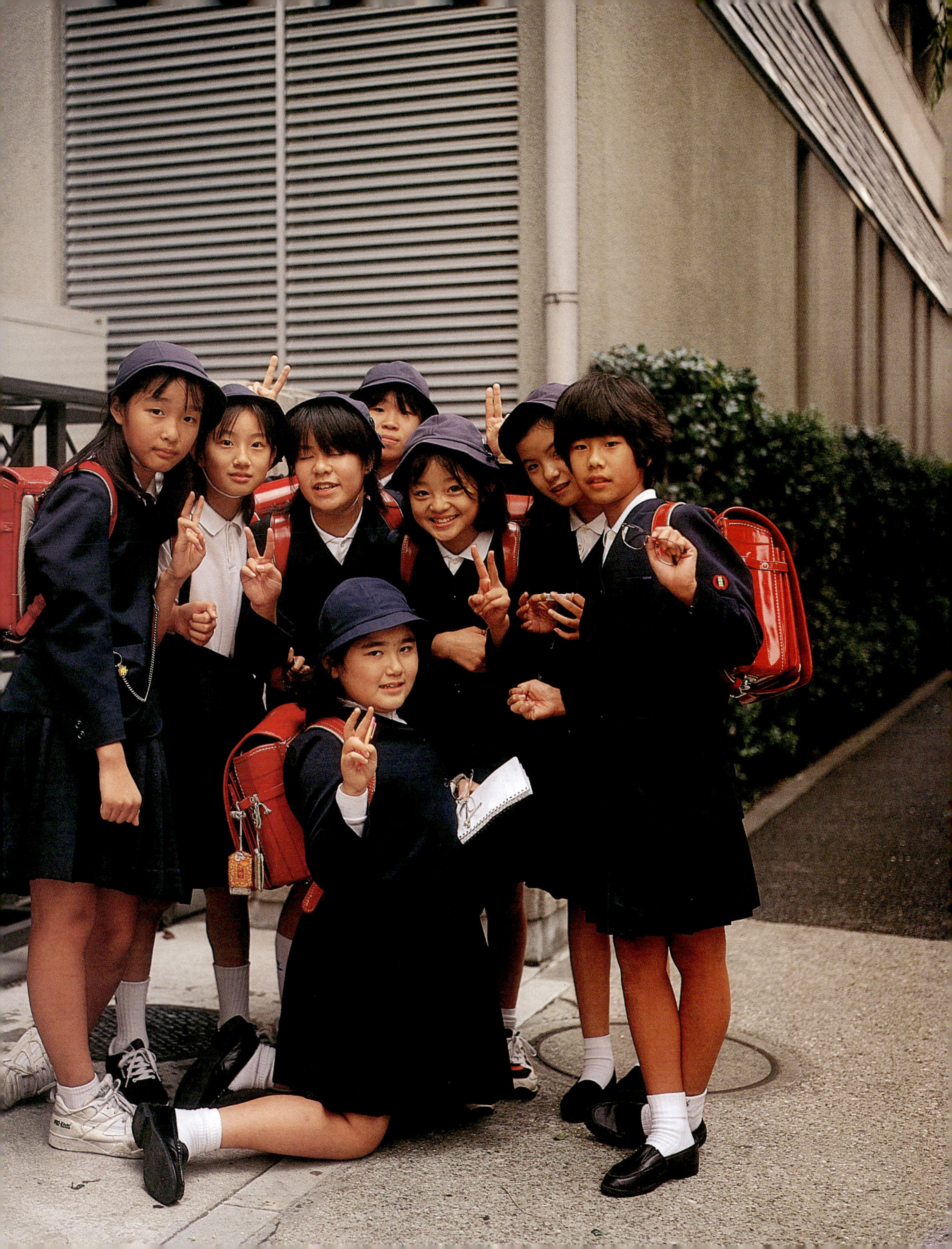

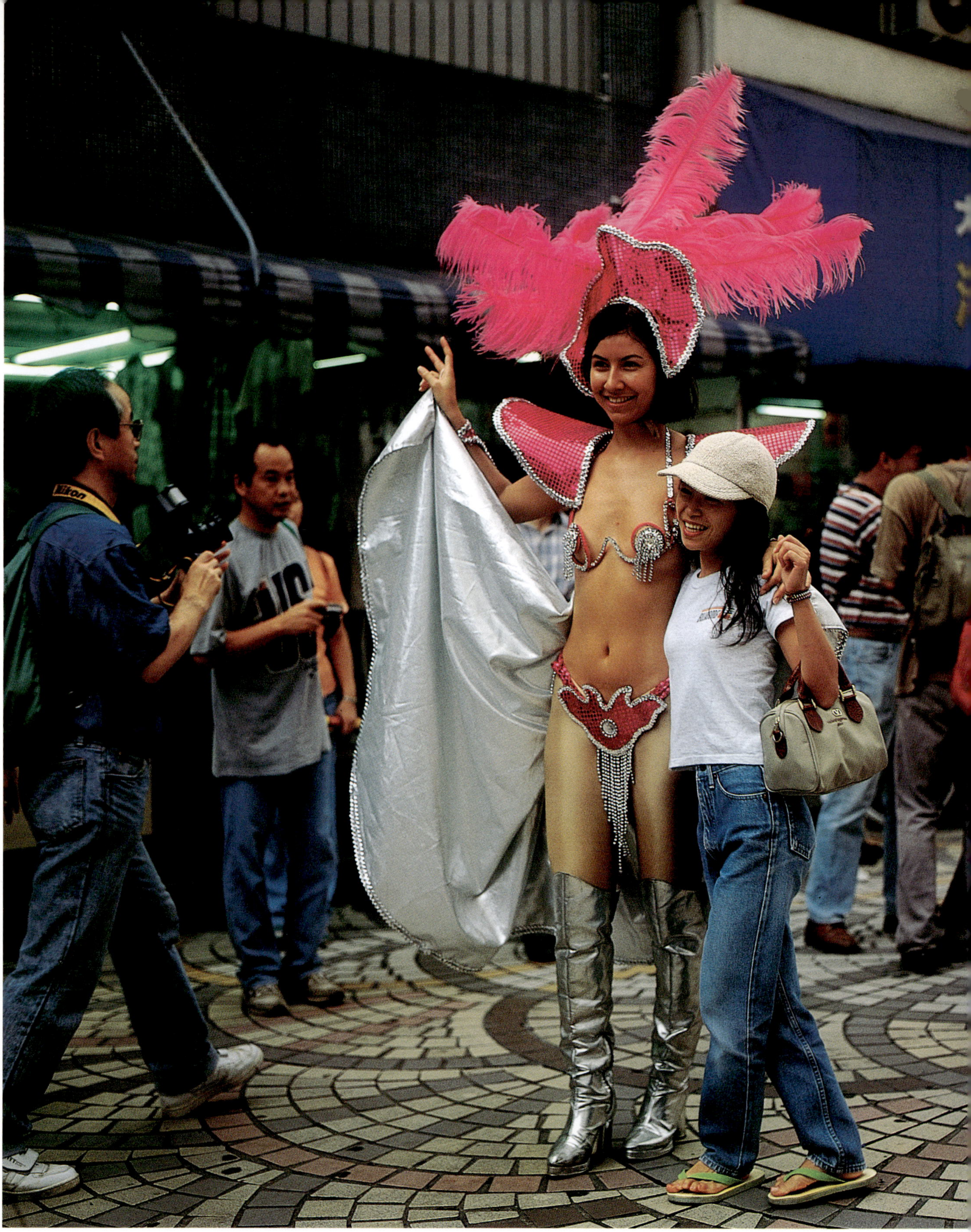

This photo was taken at the Samba Carnival, held every summer in Asakusa. The Japanese are highly adept at borrowing from other cultures.

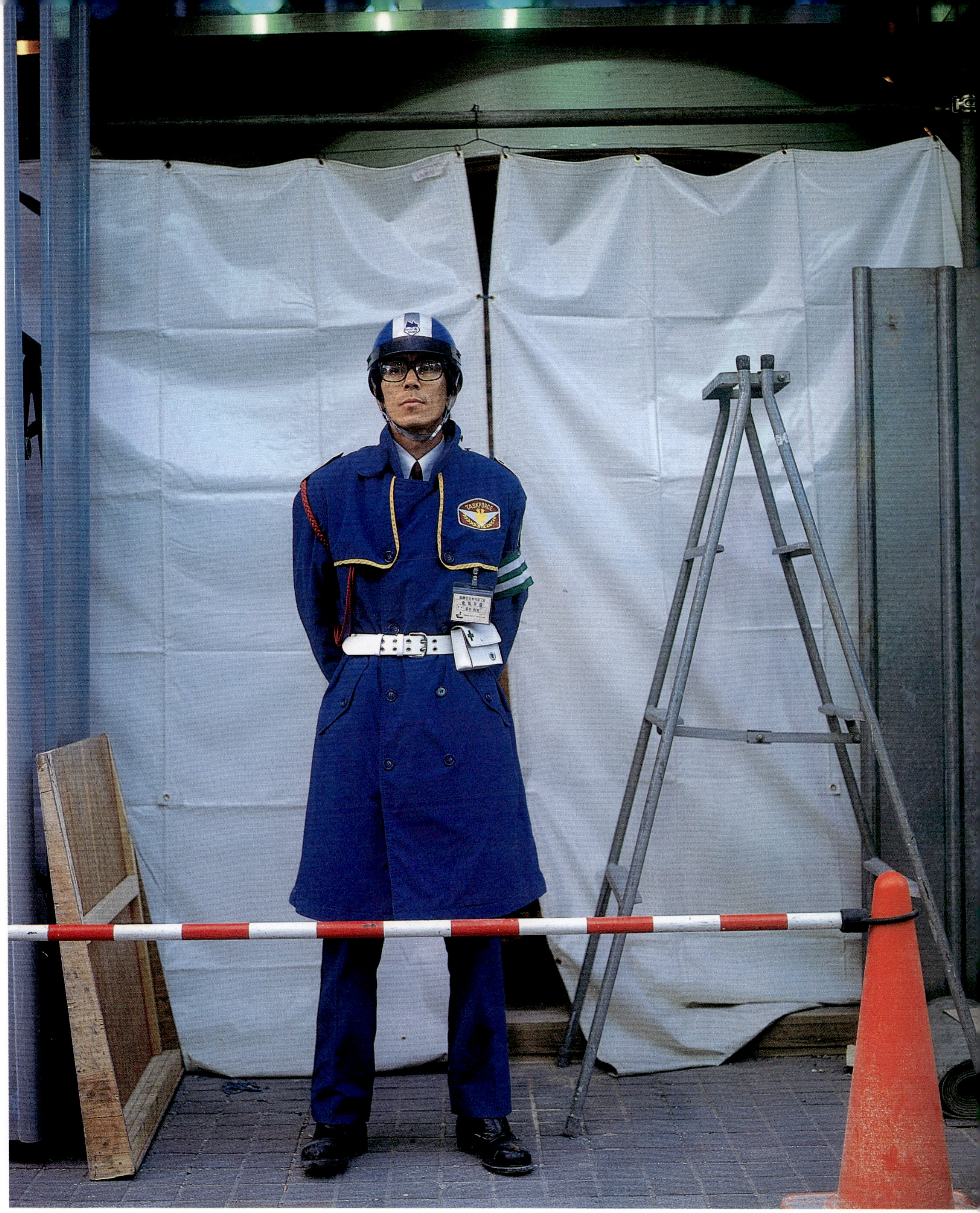


This guard at a construction site must remain constantly alert while staying on his feet for long periods of time—no easy task.

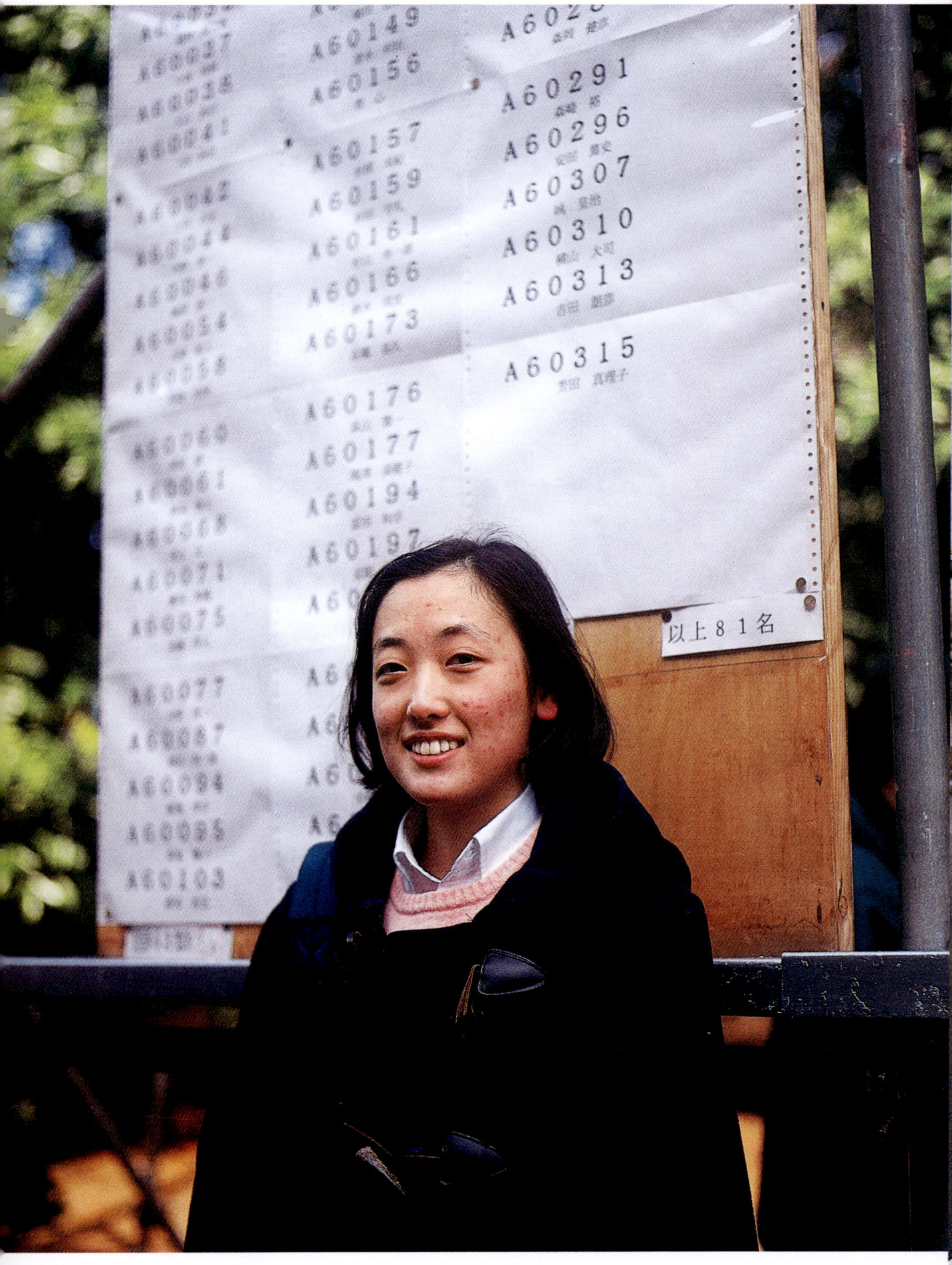

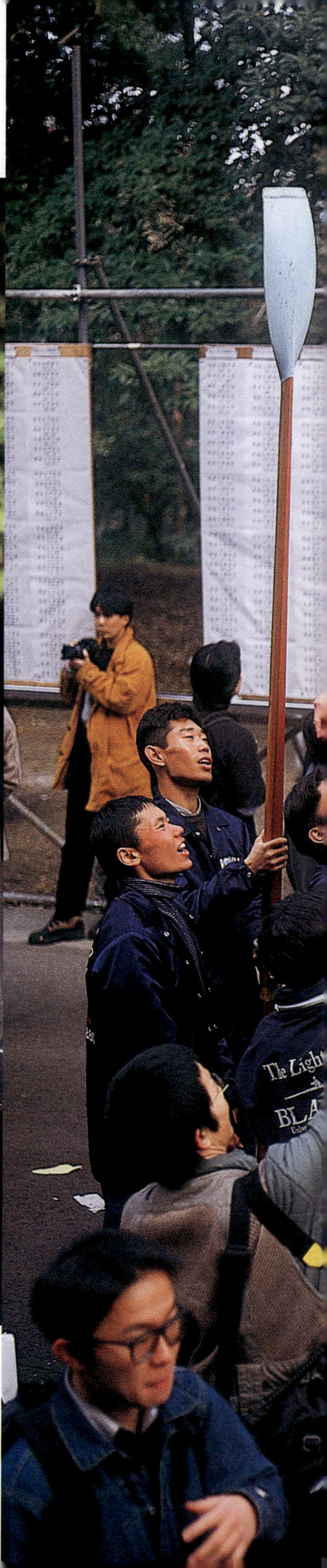

In a society that places great emphasis on academic records, the primary goal of every student is to get into a good university. These photographs were taken at Japan's most exclusive university, the University of Tokyo, on the day the school announced its admissions.

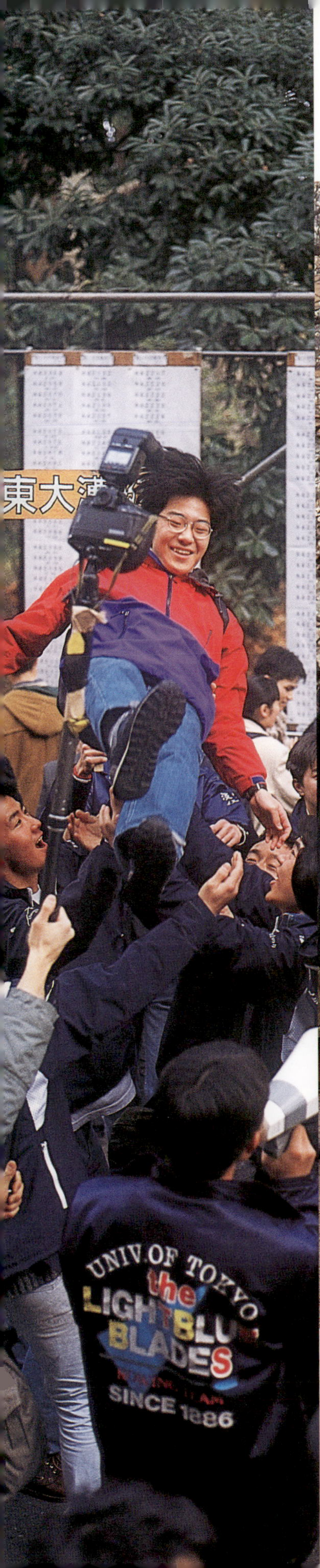


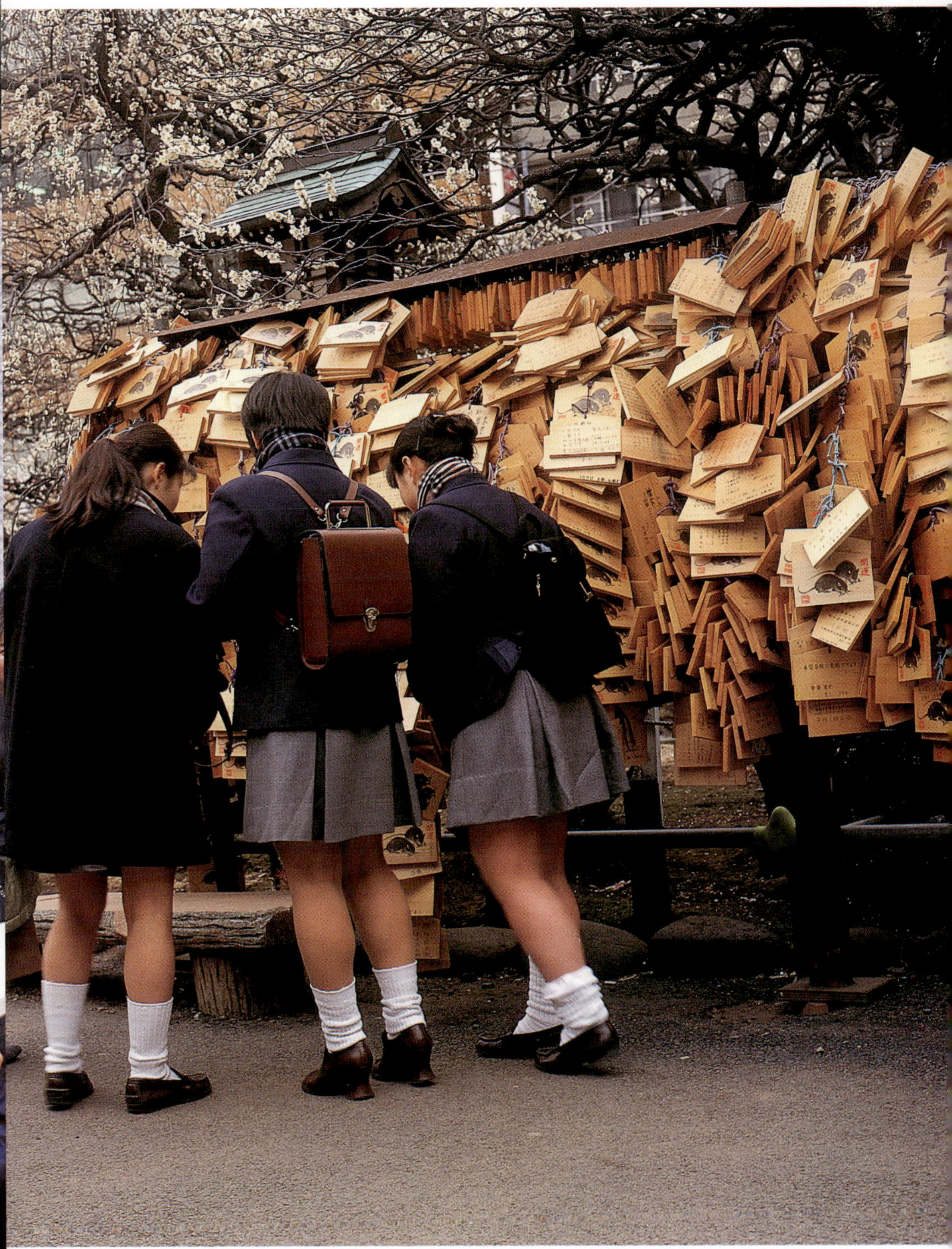

Students visiting Yushima Tenjin shrine. The wooden plaques are pictorial votive offerings, called *ema*, left by students who come to the shrine to pray for admittance to their university of choice. Human beings inevitably seek divine assistance in their hour of need.

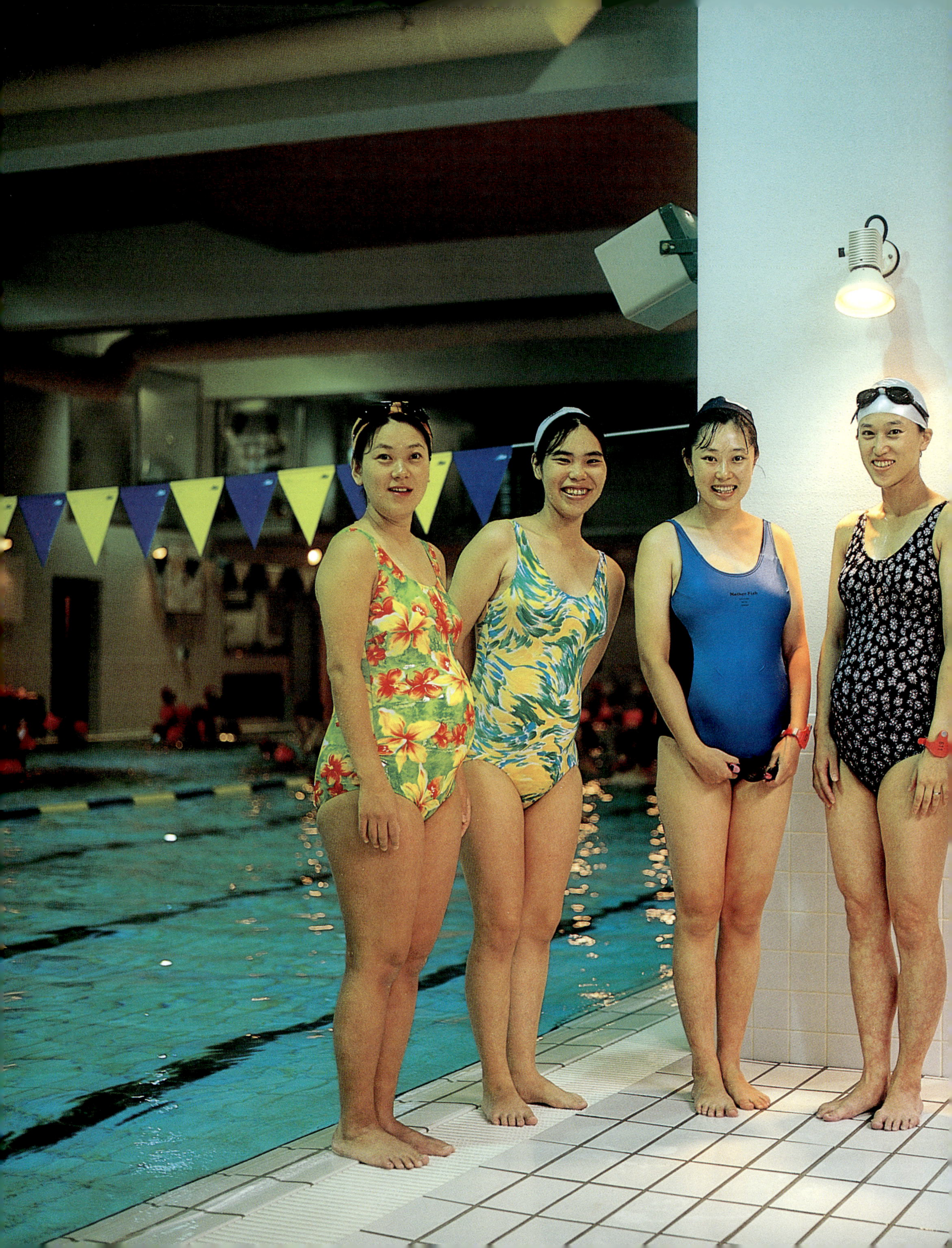
Mother Fish

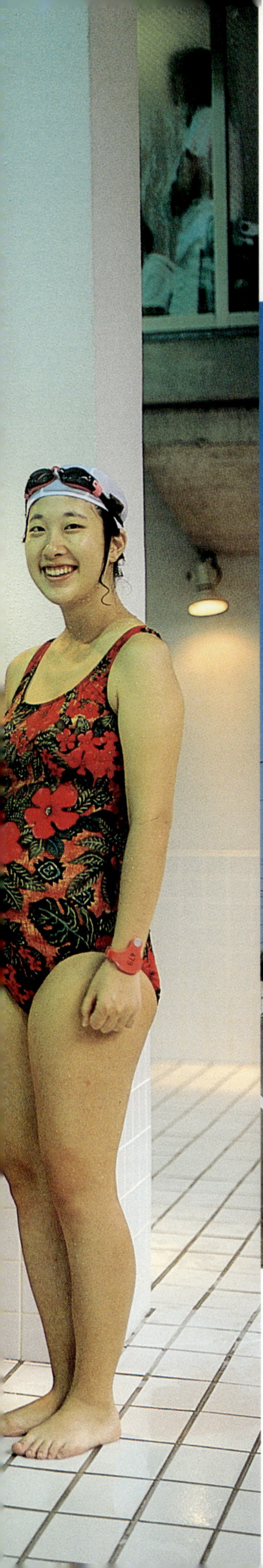

These women attending a swimming class are in the final stages of pregnancy. In Tokyo, the average number of children born to each woman is 1.11, the lowest in the country.

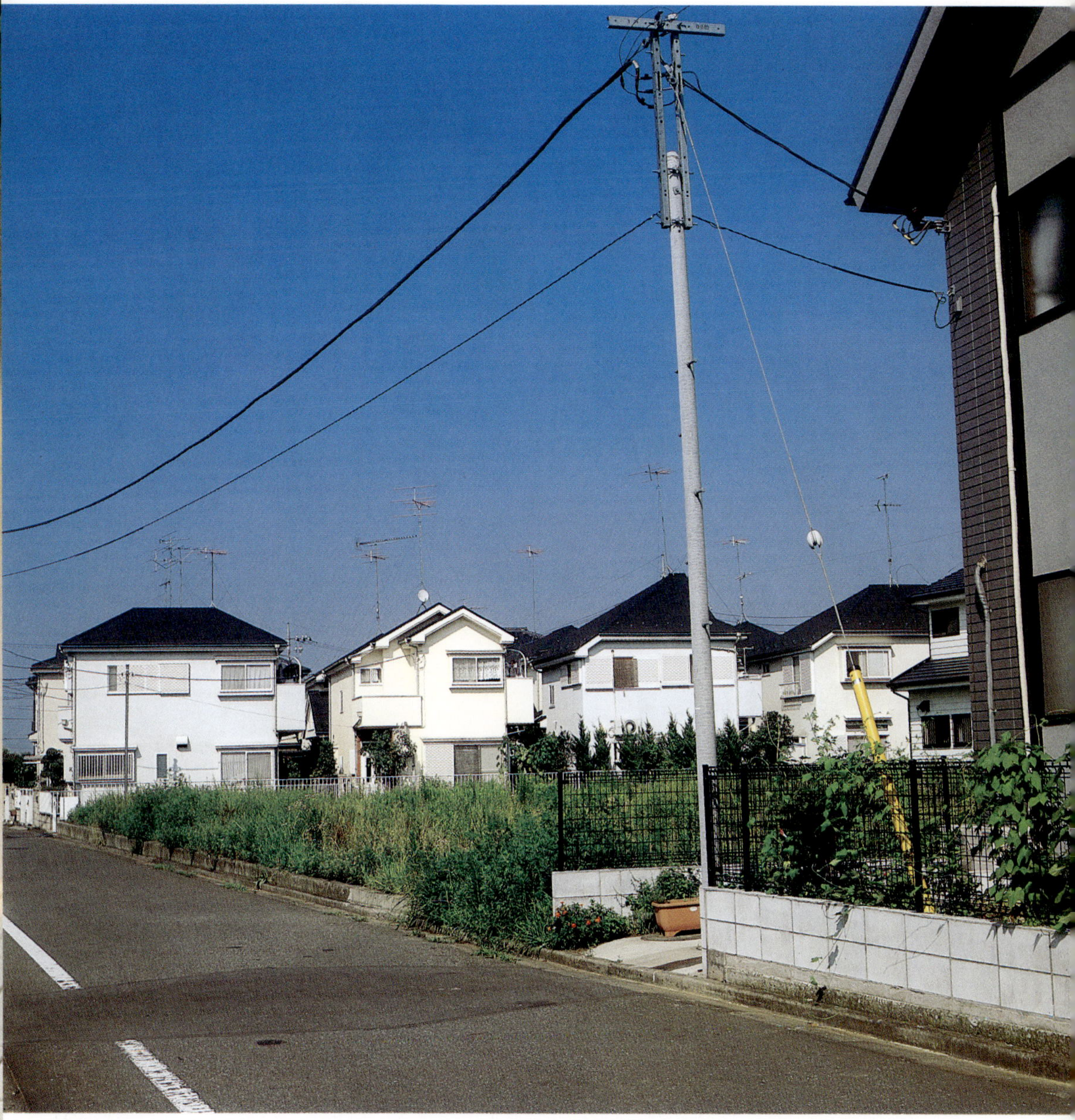

Some people can recall catching crayfish in this area, which once was covered by rice paddies. Now, just some 20 years later, its transformation into a residential district is complete. The empty lot in the foreground will also be packed with new houses before long.

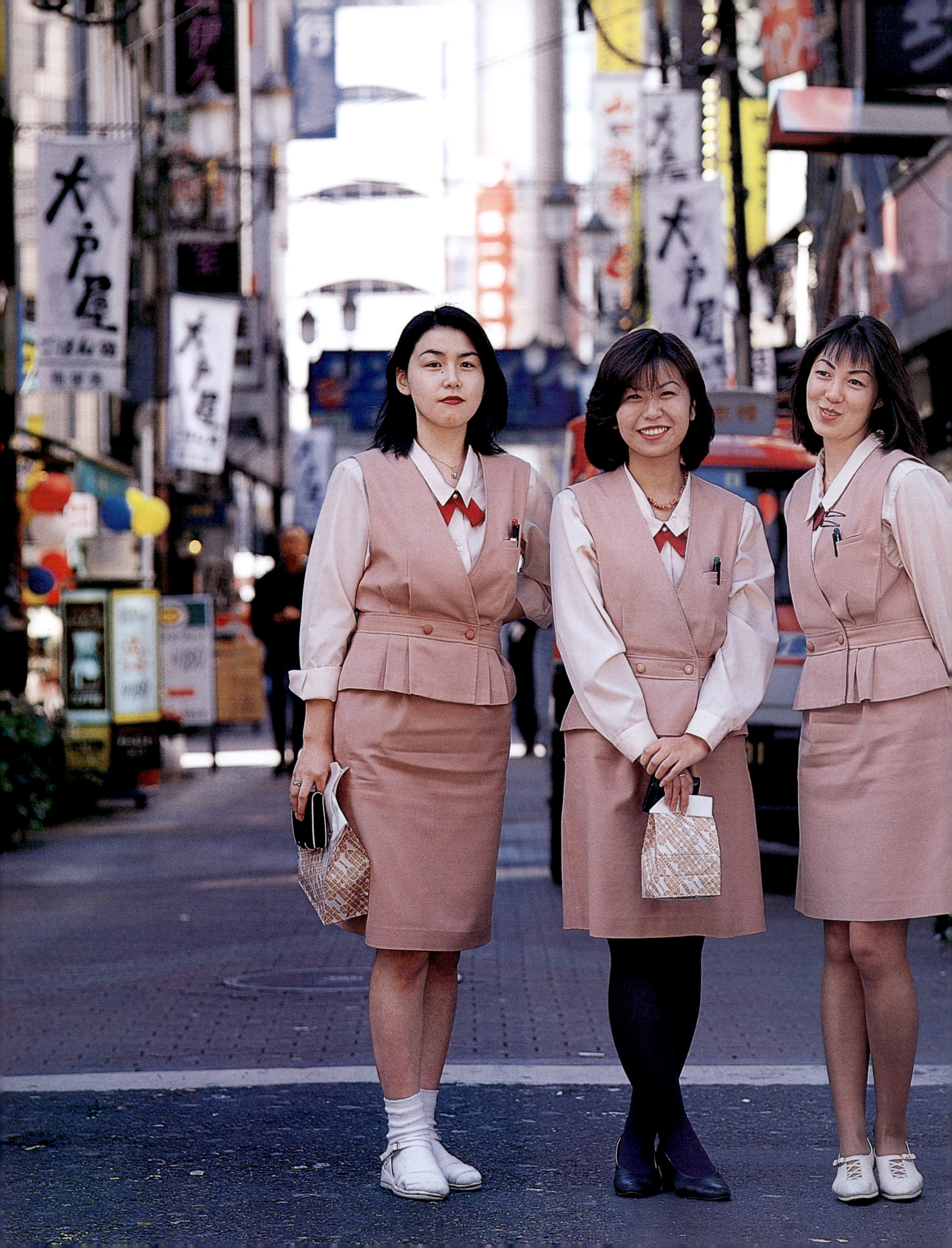
大戸屋
大戸屋
大戸屋

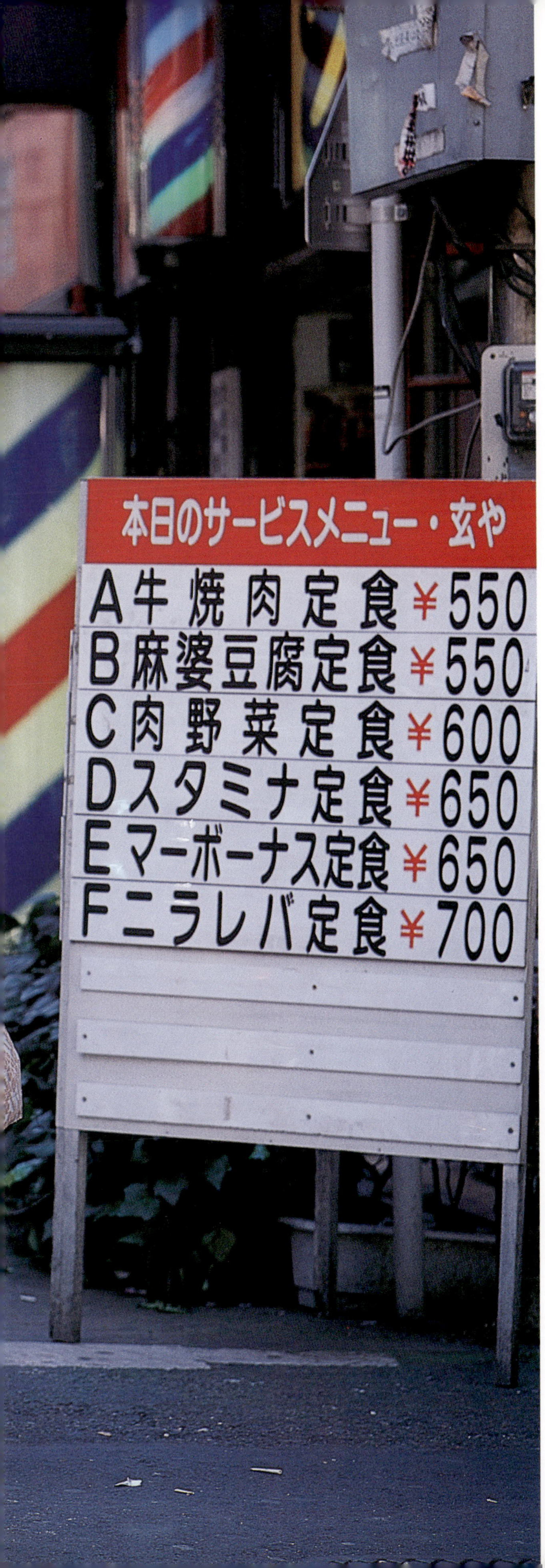


Office workers on their lunch break. The Japanese seem to have a fondness for uniforms; many companies in Japan require their female clerical employees to wear them.

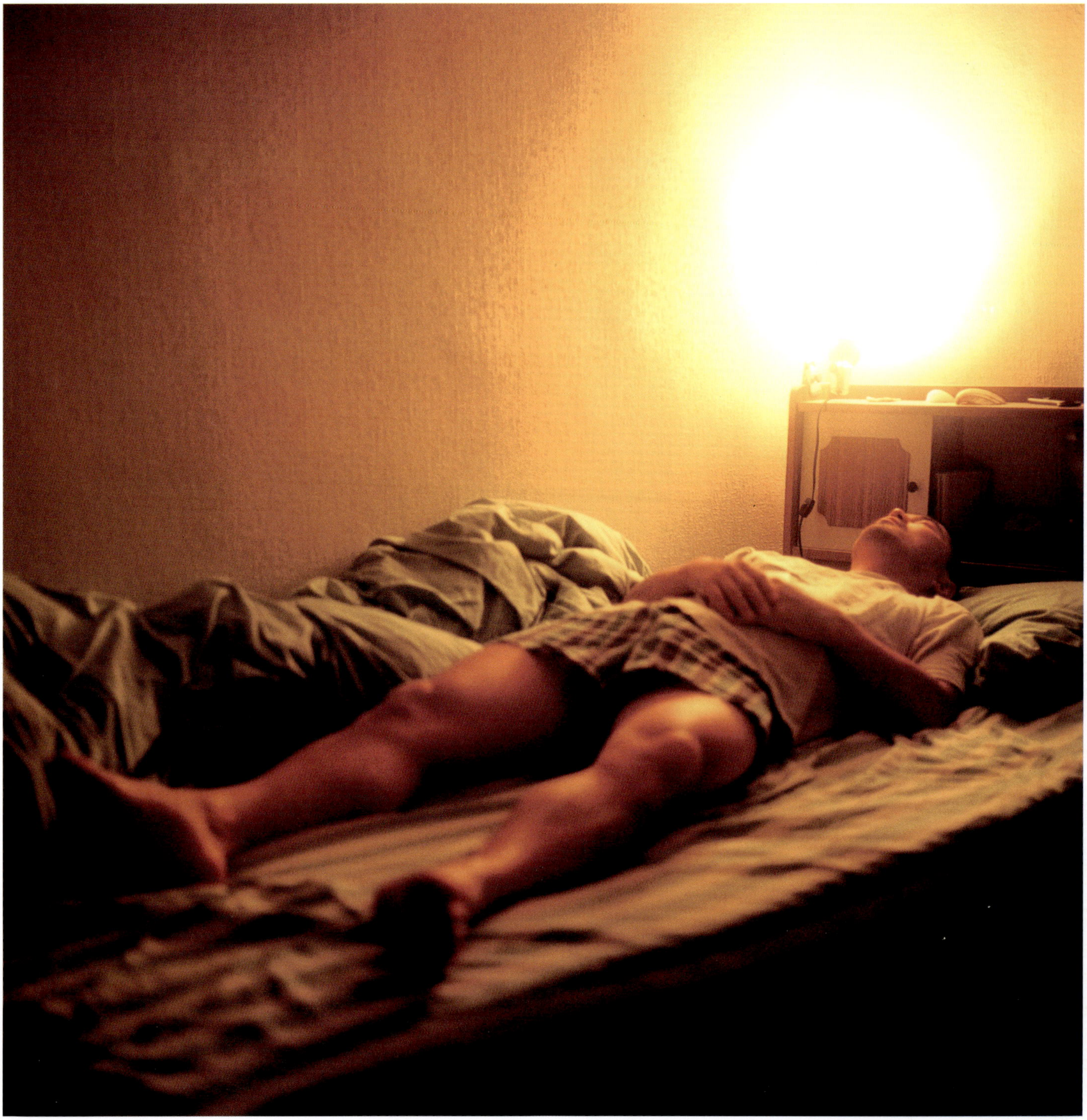

When the workday is over, this laborer collapses onto his bed and falls into a sound sleep.

These people are engaged in Zen meditation (*zazen*). They are among the many who come to this temple on Sundays to practice *zazen*. For them the time spent here is precious, affording as it does the opportunity to turn inward and find sanctuary from the frenetic pace of everyday life.

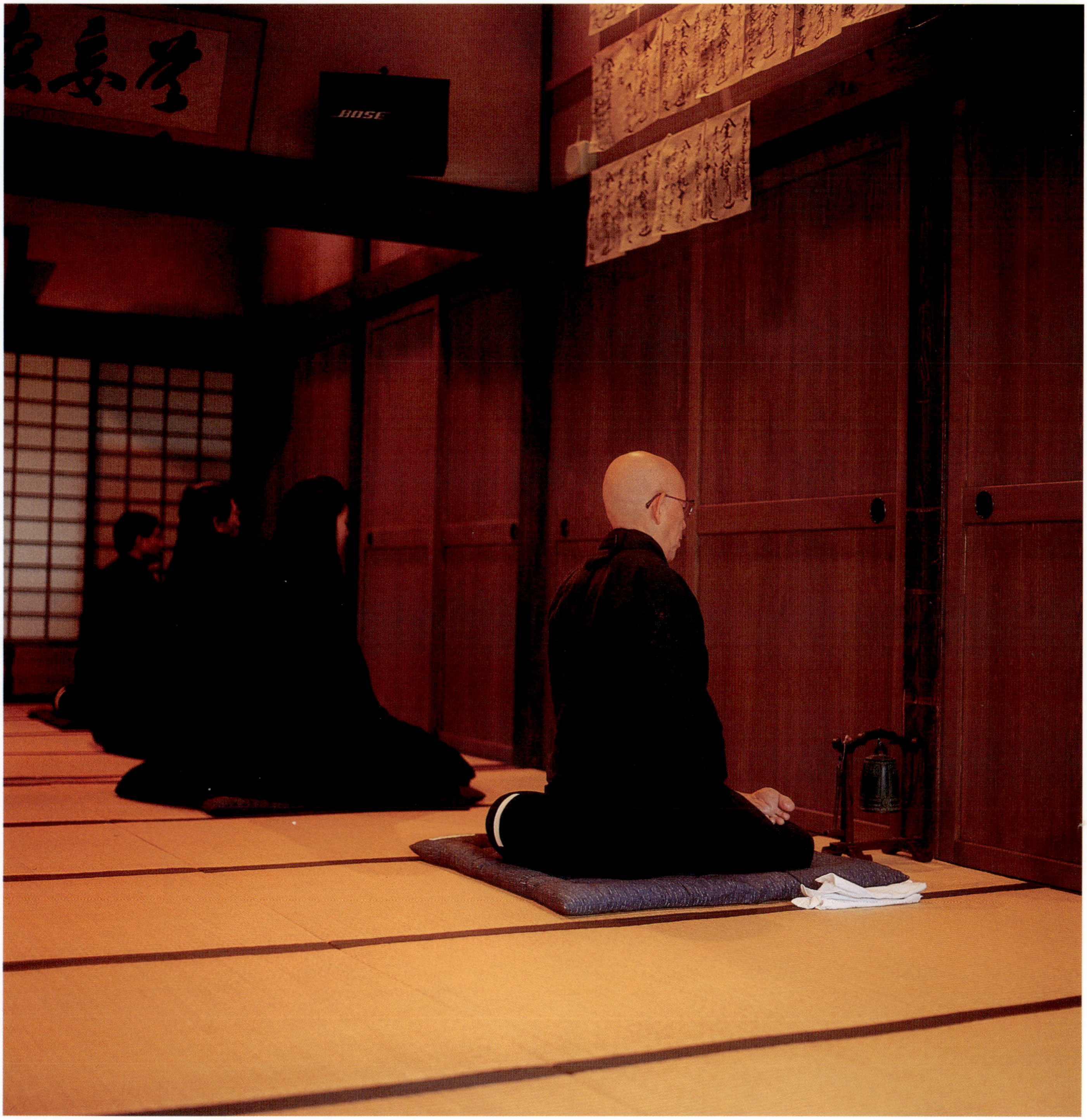

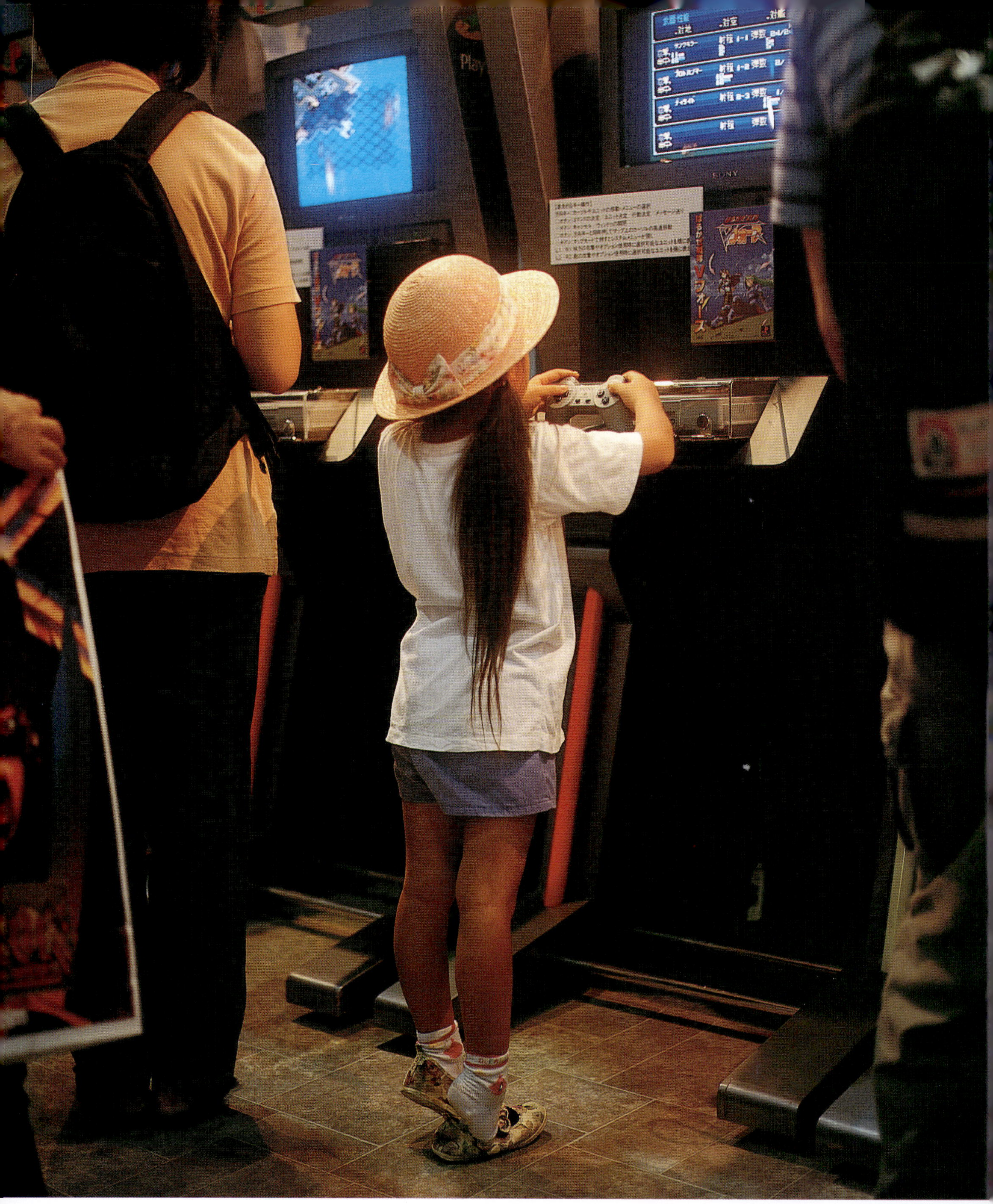


A child engrossed in a computer game. More and more these days, play revolves around virtual environments rather than real-world experiences; how this change will affect human beings remains to be seen.